"*The Great Disruption* is better understand and deal with geopolitical shifts and the unpredictable global business environment. By highlighting the importance of corporate nationality, geopolitical allies and rivals, and a structural perspective, this book helps managers to understand and navigate geopolitical tensions."

Heather Berry
Dean's Professor of Strategy and
International Business, Georgetown University

"A timely and erudite work, written by an expert scholar who has spent her career developing a unique and compelling understanding of the world of geopolitics as it connects to the world of management. Most work on geopolitics talks about tensions, primarily between the US and China, and aims to predict the future trajectory of such tensions and their effects on the macroeconomics of the world. Professor Jandhyala's ideas extend much beyond that context to provide unique insight into ways in which companies can manage the process. The management tactics include obfuscation, by disguising the ultimate national base of a company; to more critically discussing how geopolitics affects the ways in which the innovation process is managed. But, most captivatingly, Professor Jandhyala discusses and advises on how companies serious about geopolitics can internally build the corporate capabilities to organize the company and train people to be able to scan and detect, and ultimately manage, geopolitics as a source of company-specific advantage. Historically, most companies have eschewed geopolitics as being a corporate activity that is outsourced to consultancies and other external experts. But, much like the outsourcing debate for production, Professor Jandhyala builds a compelling case for why and how companies need to insource the political management function – to reshape their corporate organization, their capabilities, their approaches to AI, and the sourcing and training of their staff to better detect and manage geopolitical tensions, especially in frontier industries such as e-commerce and green energy. Overall, *The Great Disruption* is a gripping read, filled with rich anecdotes and the sharp thinking that has been a mainstay of Professor Jandhyala's scholarship and career."

Andrew Delios
Professor in the Department of Strategy & Policy,
NUS Business School, National University of Singapore

"Srividya Jandhyala's analysis of the new geopolitical realities and how companies can cope is pathbreaking and highly informative. The specific applications to the future of work, e-commerce, and green energy throw light into some of the most vexing issues affecting global competition. Her skillful use of examples and her insights concerning the interaction between business and government make this a unique book."

Mauro F. Guillén
William H. Wurster Professor of Multinational Management,
The Wharton School, The University of Pennsylvania

"A masterclass in weaving academic perspective together with headline news to offer insight into the resurgent role of geopolitics in global strategy. Jandhyala offers clear and cogent examples, updating the field of political risk management from its historical focus on infrastructure with applications spanning the new economy."

Witold Henisz
Vice Dean and Faculty Director, The Environmental,
Social and Governance (ESG) Initiative, The Wharton
School, The University of Pennsylvania

"Multinational corporations previously stood astride a borderless world, in search of maximum efficiencies. Jandhyala's book is a valuable guide to an emerging world, where companies must find their long-lost passports and navigate a new era where the economics of efficiency are joined by the economics of statecraft to determine commercial success."

James R. Sullivan, CFA
External Associate, Economic Conflict and Competition
Research Group, King's College London

The Great Disruption

In an era marked by new challenges – from trade wars and sanctions to supply chain disruptions and political instability – understanding the relationship between geopolitics and business is more crucial than ever. How are companies impacted, and why should they care? This book explores how geopolitical shifts, including the rise of China, the US–China tech competition, and regional conflicts, affect markets, industries, companies, managers, and employees. Uncovering the structural changes reshaping the global business environment, the business risks from an increasing national security focus, and the implications of trade wars and global conflicts on innovation, Srividya Jandhyala offers practical strategies and skills for managers and employees to manage these risks. With a focus on real-world case studies and actionable insights for businesses, *The Great Disruption* is as an essential resource, offering a roadmap for companies to navigate an evolving but unpredictable global business landscape.

SRIVIDYA JANDHYALA is associate professor of management at ESSEC Business School, specializing in global strategy, geopolitics, and international business. An award-winning researcher with a PhD from The Wharton School, she has published widely for academic and practitioner audiences. She also has extensive experience teaching executives and students in global business environments.

The Great Disruption
How Geopolitics Is Changing Companies, Managers, and Work

SRIVIDYA JANDHYALA
ESSEC Business School

CAMBRIDGE
UNIVERSITY PRESS

Shaftesbury Road, Cambridge CB2 8EA, United Kingdom

One Liberty Plaza, 20th Floor, New York, NY 10006, USA

477 Williamstown Road, Port Melbourne, VIC 3207, Australia

314–321, 3rd Floor, Plot 3, Splendor Forum, Jasola District Centre, New Delhi – 110025, India

103 Penang Road, #05–06/07, Visioncrest Commercial, Singapore 238467

Cambridge University Press is part of Cambridge University Press & Assessment, a department of the University of Cambridge.

We share the University's mission to contribute to society through the pursuit of education, learning and research at the highest international levels of excellence.

www.cambridge.org
Information on this title: www.cambridge.org/9781009499965

DOI: 10.1017/9781009499989

© Srividya Jandhyala 2025

This publication is in copyright. Subject to statutory exception and to the provisions of relevant collective licensing agreements, no reproduction of any part may take place without the written permission of Cambridge University Press & Assessment.

When citing this work, please include a reference to the DOI 10.1017/9781009499989

First published 2025

A catalogue record for this publication is available from the British Library

A Cataloging-in-Publication data record for this book is available from the Library of Congress

ISBN 978-1-009-49996-5 Hardback
ISBN 978-1-009-49999-6 Paperback

Cambridge University Press & Assessment has no responsibility for the persistence or accuracy of URLs for external or third-party internet websites referred to in this publication and does not guarantee that any content on such websites is, or will remain, accurate or appropriate.

श्री यागेश्वरगुरु चरण कमलेभ्यो नमः||
To Ira and Aadya

Contents

List of Figures	*page* xii
List of Tables	xiii
Acknowledgments	xiv

1	Changing Global Order	1
	Looking Back, and Looking Ahead	3
	Geopolitics Is about Economics	6
	Geopolitical Risk Depends on Corporate Nationality	9
	Impact of Geopolitical Tensions	12
	Corporate Diplomacy	27
	Unintended Consequences of Corporate Diplomacy	31
	Previewing the Path: Chapters Ahead	33
2	Corporate Nationality	35
	Rootless and Stateless Companies?	35
	Corporations Bound to a Nation	36
	Corporate Nationality Shapes Global Businesses	40
	What Is Corporate Nationality Anyway?	55
	Shaping Corporate Nationality	57
	Closing Reflections on Corporate Nationality	66
3	Geopolitics and Innovation	67
	The International Face of Innovation	68
	Innovation as the Battlefield of Geopolitical Tensions	74
	Consequences for Corporate Innovation	86
	Managing Innovation in the Shadow of Geopolitics	89
4	Corporate Strategies for Managing Geopolitics	91
	The Structural Approach	92

	Cognitive Frames for Strategic Decisions	93
	Strategies for Managing Geopolitical Risks	97
	Only for Strategic Sectors, Right?	115
	Only for Large Multinational Firms, Right?	118
	Navigating Complexity	120
5	**Managing Geopolitics: Whose Job Is It?**	**121**
	Skills for Managing Geopolitics	121
	Whose Job Is It?	131
	Focusing Attention	135
	Looking Ahead to Architectural Changes	137
6	**Geopolitics and the Future of Work**	**140**
	"Who" Works?	141
	"Where" Can Work Be Done?	150
	Reshaping "How" Work Is Done	156
	Leading Forward	166
7	**Computational Geopolitics**	**169**
	Why Now? The Relevance of a Computational Approach	169
	Methodological Approaches	171
	Tools and Techniques in Computational Geopolitics	172
	Challenges and Limitations of Computational Geopolitics	189
	Empowering Insights	192
	Some Data Sources	192
8	**Geopolitics and E-Commerce**	**197**
	Industry Features	199
	Geopolitics and the Global E-Commerce Market	205
	Strategies for Managing Corporate Nationality and Geopolitical Tensions	219
	Corporate Diplomacy	223

9	Geopolitics and Green Energy	225
	Industry Features	226
	Geopolitics of Green Energy	233
	Strategies for Managing Corporate Nationality and Geopolitical Tensions	246
	Corporate Diplomacy	251
10	Looking Ahead	253
	National Security and Economic Policy	253
	Government Control of the Commanding Heights	255
	Navigating the Choppy Waters of Geopolitical Tensions	258
	Index	261

Figures

1.1	A firm's geopolitical risk	*page* 14
5.1	Skills for managing geopolitics	122

Tables

2.1	US subsidies for foreign companies from selected locations	page 49
2.2	Foreign investment in the US, selected nationalities	50
4.1	Managing geopolitical challenges	114
7.1	Data sources for international trade and investment flows	192
7.2	Data sources for measuring geopolitical tensions	193
7.3	Data sources for government policy measures	195
7.4	Data sources for international enterprise and public opinion survey data	196

Acknowledgments

Several years ago, I sat in a book publishing workshop, paying scant attention to the details, certain that I was never going to attempt to write a book. To go from there to putting the finishing touches on this manuscript would not have been possible without several people who helped along the way.

I want to extend my heartfelt thanks to the many colleagues, collaborators, and coauthors who have helped to sharpen my thinking and shape my arguments. I am especially grateful to Daniel Blake, Quan Li, and Rob Weiner for the many, many long conversations and occasional debates. Your insights and perspectives not only challenged my thinking but also helped solidify concepts that might have otherwise remained fleeting thoughts. Thank you for your patience as I rambled on and for your unwavering support.

My appreciation goes to all the practitioners who have engaged in countless discussions about their work over the years. Each chat added layers of depth and richness to my understanding of the field. Thank you for sharing your experiences and insights so generously.

To my students who challenged me to demystify some of these ideas. Every class I prepared for helped to clarify and crystallize the message a bit more.

I would like to thank my editor, Valerie Appleby, for believing in the book from the very beginning and taking a chance on me. Your expertise and guidance were crucial throughout the process as was the encouragement you provided along the way. I am grateful to the publisher for supporting the book and helping navigate the complexities of publishing.

I first explored the ideas for the book during my sabbatical, for which I thank both ESSEC Business School, which gave me the time and space to work on it, and the National University of Singapore for hosting me. Thank you to my colleagues at both institutions for making this possible.

To each of my family and friends who read multiple drafts of the manuscript, provided constructive feedback, shared ideas, and brought a unique lens to the material. You also checked on me, made sure I kept writing even when it was hard, and helped me take a break when I needed it. The prodding certainly helped, and I have certainly exploited your goodwill. Thank you to Amma, Amy, Aswin, Krish, Nanna, Poornima, Ram, Rocio, and Shruthi. I am also grateful to my extended family around the world for their encouragement, inspiration, and support.

Thank you to Ira and Aadya for sharing inspiring writing ideas (including on descriptions and robots) and for listening to my endless descriptions of the book and the writing process. You put up with the hours and the early morning disappearances, while bringing tons of laughter and joy. Your good humor made the whole process a lot more fun.

Most of all, to Kumar. This book would never have been written without your constant support, encouragement, and effort. You saw the possibilities before I did and worked hard to convince me that I had a book in me. You provided wisdom and laughter. And you cheered me on even when self-doubt crept in. Thank you for being a part of this adventure!

1   Changing Global Order

How long does a direct flight from Helsinki to Tokyo take? When Finnair launched its daily flight schedule between the two cities in March 2020, the flight time was about nine and half hours.[1] But by 2023, flying time was over thirteen hours. The two cities hadn't drifted apart – certainly not over a few short years. But Finnair could no longer fly the same route. European airlines were banned from Russian airspace after war broke out between Ukraine and Russia, which meant that Finnair had to avoid the time and fuel saving great circle route over northern Russia. This was a big problem for Finnair because their revenues depended on flights to Asia. The company operated flights to twenty-one Asian destinations in 2019 and generated 44 percent of its revenue from those flights. No wonder then that the company's stock dropped 21 percent following the ban.[2] But importantly, Chinese carriers were still allowed to fly over Russia and take shorter routes to Europe. So, when Chinese tourists and business travelers returned to popular destinations in Europe, the airlines they chose to fly were determined not just by the comfort of the seats, quality of the meals, and price of the ticket but also the nationality of the airline. European airlines claimed geopolitical factors gave the Chinese an unfair advantage.[3] Whether

---

[1] Finnair to Add Daily Flights to Tokyo Haneda Airport. *Business Traveller*, October 8, 2019. Available at: www.businesstraveller.com/business-travel/2019/10/08/finnair-to-add-daily-flights-to-tokyo-haneda-airport/

[2] Finnair Shares Plummet as Airline Is Banned from Russia's Airspace. *Financial Times*, March 1, 2022. Available at: www.ft.com/content/e0dc3e5b-dd14-4051-9068-87f71aa5a895

[3] Airlines Say Chinese Have "Unfair Advantage" Flying over Russia. *Financial Times*, February 17, 2023. Available at: www.ft.com/content/21d7272a-af56-492d-ace1-57428c7219b5

unfair or not, Chinese carriers increased the number of flights to Europe within a couple of years while European airlines slashed flights to Asia.[4]

ChatGPT, the AI-powered chatbot developed by OpenAI, was released in late 2022 and drew so much attention from curious users that it crashed several times.[5] Its popularity shocked even executives at OpenAI[6] and led to another furious round of contemplation about the future of work. Microsoft's multiyear, multibillion dollar investment in OpenAI may change the way we interact over the internet, but the transformative impact of large language models will depend on so much more than machine learning algorithms. Where (the markets) it will be available, who (which users) can benefit from it, and how (applications) they use it will be subject to national and international political calculations.

When ChatGPT was released, it was not available in China. However, shares in the Chinese search engine and technology company Baidu soared about 15 percent when it announced the launch of its own AI chatbot "Wenxin Yiyan" (or "Ernie Bot" in English).[7] But while Baidu's Ernie drew on decades of data from running China's biggest search engine, they found themselves in a tough spot when processing those data. They couldn't easily access the AI chips they needed for data processing. Nvidia, the US company that made the fastest chips, and controlled about 80 percent of the world's AI chip market,[8] faced

---

[4] Western Airlines Slash Flights to China. *Financial Times*, August 19, 2024. Available at: www.ft.com/content/9156b23b-c74d-4daf-bfb2-c8ed61aebd7a

[5] ChatGPT Is Too Popular for Its Own Good. *Gizmodo*, December 13, 2022. Available at: https://news.yahoo.com/chatgpt-too-popular-own-good-213000757.html

[6] OpenAI Executives Say Releasing ChatGPT for Public Use Was a Last Resort after Running into Multiple Hurdles – and They're Shocked by Its Popularity. *Business Insider*, January 26, 2023. Available at: www.businessinsider.com/chatgpt-openai-executives-are-shocked-by-ai-chatbot-popularity-2023-1

[7] Baidu Stock Surges after Announcement of ChatGPT-Style AI Bot. *CNN*, February 7, 2023. Available at: https://edition.cnn.com/2023/02/06/tech/china-baidu-ai-bot-chatgpt-rival-intl-hnk/index.html

[8] Can a South Korean Startup Take on Nvidia in the AI Chips Market? *Tech Wire Asia*, January 11, 2023. Available at: https://techwireasia.com/2023/02/can-a-south-korean-startup-take-on-nvidia-in-the-ai-chips-mallarket/

export bans from its home government, preventing Baidu from buying the most advanced models.[9]

Finnair and ChatGPT are two examples, but they are hardly alone. Companies that came of age in the most recent era of globalization have taken for granted greater economic integration – with the associated global supply chains, international trade in goods and services, integrated financial markets, cross-border research and development, and increased foreign direct investment – as well as the institutional foundation that facilitates it. Individuals' choices related to jobs, careers, and lives have been built on this foundation. But this system is fraying. Shifts in the global balance of power, trade wars, US-China rivalry, the Ukraine war, technology decoupling, rising inflation, volatile politics, and nationalist and protectionist policies are reshaping the rules of the game, increasing uncertainty, and challenging the institutions that support international interactions. This will have profound implications for when, where, and how companies compete, the managerial talent needed to navigate these issues, and the nature of work available to employees in different parts of the world. And while boards and companies are increasingly concerned with geopolitical risks, not enough have the right expertise or confidence to manage the new environment.[10]

LOOKING BACK, AND LOOKING AHEAD

In 1989, a then staffer at the US State Department wrote an article titled "The End of History?." Francis Fukuyama's essay announced the triumph of liberal democracy. He argued that as history unfolded, it revealed an ideal form of political organization, one that emphasized

---

[9] See: Baidu/Chatbots: Heavy R&D Spend Means Talk May Be Cheap. *Financial Times*, February 8, 2023. Available at: www.ft.com/content/d46cc615-068b-4c87-b10f-278854676957. US Orders Nvidia and AMD to Stop Selling AI Chips to China. *CNN*, September 1, 2022. Available at: https://edition.cnn.com/2022/09/01/tech/us-nvidia-amd-chips-china-sales-block-intl-hnk/index.html

[10] Are You Making Political Risk a Strategic Priority? *EY Parthenon*, May 13, 2021. Available at: www.ey.com/en_gl/geostrategy/the-ceo-imperative-are-you-making-political-risk-a-strategic-priority

liberal democratic states linked to market economies. In the years that followed – even as this idea itself was debated widely – the Berlin wall collapsed, and the European Union project moved forward. At the end of the twentieth century, one could have assumed that the world was moving in a progressive, liberal, international direction. And the US, then the undisputed leader with its unparalleled advantages in military, economic, and technological capabilities, became the organizer and manager of the global system. The global system, in turn, was fashioned in its image, emphasizing open markets and free trade, international organizations, cooperative security, democratic solidarity, and liberal values such as political equality, human rights, and freedom of thought and expression.[11]

For companies considering international investments, long-standing challenges were rapidly being addressed. Thomas Friedman wrote in his book *The World Is Flat* that historical and geographic divisions were increasingly becoming irrelevant. Countries around the world opened their markets to foreign investors providing new opportunities. Liberalization and privatization, the buzzwords of the 1990s, allowed firms to compete in new industries and new geographies. Harmonized global rules on trade and investment allowed firms to access scarce or low-cost resources from other countries. International treaties on property rights protection and dispute resolution allowed firms to deal with foreign markets, customers, suppliers, and governments more confidently.[12] The result was an unprecedented exploitation of cross-border economic opportunities: Between 1990 and 2016, there was approximately a ten-fold increase

---

[11] For an overview of the US-led international liberal order, see: Acharya, A. (2018). *The end of American world order*. John Wiley & Sons and Ikenberry, G. J. (2010). The liberal international order and its discontents. *Millennium*, 38(3), 509–521.

[12] See, for example: Jandhyala, S., Henisz, W. J., & Mansfield, E. D. (2011). Three waves of BITs: The global diffusion of foreign investment policy. *Journal of Conflict Resolution*, 55(6), 1047–1073; Blake, D. J., & Moschieri, C. (2017). Policy risk, strategic decisions and contagion effects: Firm-specific considerations. *Strategic Management Journal*, 38(3), 732–750; and Jandhyala, S., & Weiner, R. J. (2014). Institutions sans frontières: International agreements and foreign investment. *Journal of International Business Studies*, 45, 649–669.

in worldwide inflows of foreign direct investment.[13] Multinational corporations invested in locations that made most economic sense, that is, minimizing costs and maximizing profits.[14]

As companies expanded their geographic reach during the early years of the twenty-first century, aspiring managers flocked to business schools to hone their skills in economics, reading financial statements, analyzing investments, selling to old and new customers, and managing a distributed and diverse workforce. They spent little-to-no time thinking about grand politics and its role in international business. Today, as business students of the 2000s come of age in the corporate and investment worlds, the landscape is vastly different, and unfamiliar. And they are discovering that global politics is fundamentally reshaping the business world. Mark Carney, a former leader of both the Bank of Canada and the Bank of England, noted that the world is at a "moment ... where the accepted forces and policies that have been in place virtually all my adult life are changing."[15] Even companies that had previously largely been insulated from geopolitics had to figure out how to respond.

A new world order taking shape, with economic power distributed between the US and China.[16] Considering purchasing power parity, China has already surpassed the US as the world's largest economy. It has become the number one trading partner for most countries and established itself as the most essential link in the world's critical global supply chains. It is also home to the largest

---

[13] World FDI inflows were approximately US 204 billion and 2.07 trillion in 1990 and 2016, respectively (UNCTADStat, https://unctadstat.unctad.org/wds/TableViewer/tableView.aspx?ReportId=96740).

[14] This is not to suggest that the liberal international order did not have its drawbacks or critics. Income stagnation, increased inequality, lower growth, heightened risk, and lost jobs have been widely documented.

[15] Could Mark Carney Lead Canada? *The Economist*, December 12, 2023. Available at: www.economist.com/the-americas/2023/12/12/could-mark-carney-lead-canada

[16] For more details on the comparison between China and the US, see Allison, G., Kiersznowski, N., & Fitzek, C. (2022). "The Great Economic Rivalry: China vs the U.S.," Harvard Kenndey School Belfer Center Science and International Affairs Paper, March 2022.

number of the most valuable global companies on Fortune's Global 500 list for the first time. China has rivaled the US in attracting foreign investment and investing in research and development. On the other hand, the US dollar remains the world's dominant reserve currency and currency of choice in cross-border transactions, US equity markets remain the world's largest, and the US retains a significant lead in venture capital investments. The US continues to attract the most talented innovators and entrepreneurs in the world.

As the world becomes multipolar, it is likely to see greater frictions among great powers as traditional values of Western liberal democracy clash with the Chinese ideology. In their work, Jessica Chen Weiss and Jeremy Wallace argue that the major features of the Chinese Communist Party rule include "a prioritization of the state over the individual, rule by law rather than rule of law, and a renewed emphasis on ethnic rather than civil nationalism."[17] These features are inherently inconsistent with the tenets of the liberal international order such as individual freedom, rule of law, and free markets. One report argued that Chinese leadership rejects the concepts of independent judiciary and checks and balances as "erroneous Western thoughts."[18] It is no surprise that some consider the rise of China to be "a death knell for the liberal international order."[19]

GEOPOLITICS IS ABOUT ECONOMICS

A manager may ask herself, should my company expand abroad? Should we sell our products to customers in foreign markets? Should we operate new factories, offices, or subsidiaries in another country? In most cases, these are hard-nosed business decisions. How attractive is the foreign opportunity? What is the net present value of the

---

[17] Weiss, J. C., & Wallace, J. L. (2021). Domestic politics, China's rise, and the future of the liberal international order. *International Organization*, 75(2), 635–664.

[18] Written testimony of Dr. Moritz Rudolf before the US–China Economic and Security Commission, May 4, 2023. Available at: www.uscc.gov/sites/default/files/2023-05/Moritz_Rudolf_Testimony.pdf

[19] Mearsheimer, J. J. (2019). Bound to fail: The rise and fall of the liberal international order. *International Security*, 43(4), 7–50.

project? Can the firm manage risks associated with the investment? Is the cost of capital reasonable? What will the opportunity cost be? Does the company have sufficient human capital to manage this? At the end of the day, the company chooses to invest (or not) based on the direct costs and benefits that accrue to it.

But the company's corporate investment decision may also create indirect costs or benefits to other parties not involved in this transaction; what economists refer to as externalities. In particular, a business decision (invest or not) can have implications for a nation's security. It is a negative externality if it harms the country's security but a positive externality if it strengthens it. If what might be a smart business decision for a company is not considered to be so good for the country's economic and military security, governments will try to incentivize and restrain the actions of private companies in ways that strengthen their geopolitical position.

Take the case of the semiconductor chips. China was a huge and lucrative market for US chip exports. American companies supplied chips that were crucial for smartphones, laptops, coffee makers, cars, and a range of other products that Chinese firms produced for domestic and export markets. Nvidia, an American technology company, for instance, generated about $400 million in quarterly revenue in 2022 by selling its most advanced chips to China.[20] Beyond rewarding shareholders, the additional revenue was invested in research and development, which resulted in this company (and the US semiconductor industry more broadly) retaining a competitive edge in the global industry – a positive externality for the US. At the same time, the US government was concerned that if advanced chips were available in China, it could give the country's military, intelligence, and security services an edge – a negative externality. To counter this, the US adopted sweeping restrictions on the sale of

---

[20] US Restricts Sale of Sophisticated Chips to China and Russia. *New York Times*, August 31, 2022. Available at: www.nytimes.com/2022/08/31/technology/gpu-chips-china-russia.html

advanced computing and semiconductor technology that was essential to China's military and economic ambitions.[21] Discussing the US approach, the Deputy Secretary of Commerce explicitly noted that the government's focus was "in key areas ... where private industry, on its own, had not factored in our national and economic security interests."[22] On the other hand, while many Chinese firms benefited economically from accessing American technology, the Chinese government worried about foreign control of important industries. What would happen to Chinese firms, military, and industry if the US could turn on and off the supply of crucial semiconductor chips whenever it chose to? In a bid to become self-sufficient and spur domestic development, China gave local chip firms US$1.75 billion in subsidies in 2022.[23]

As this example shows, economic statecraft is a key element of geopolitics. Governments directly control and influence the actions of private enterprises with an explicit purpose of weakening opponents and strengthening their geopolitical positions. Although it is most evident in the case of the US and China, the two great powers of today, other countries also leverage their economic sectors to position themselves favorably in a global system in flux. Countries that control critical networks in the global supply chain actively exploit them for geopolitical advantage.[24] French President, Emmanuel Macron, announced a €30 billion investment plan in 2021 to pour public money into nuclear power, electric

---

[21] Biden Administration Clamps Down on China's Access to Chip Technology. *New York Times*, October 7, 2022. Available at: www.nytimes.com/2022/10/07/business/economy/biden-chip-technology.html

[22] Remarks by Deputy Secretary of Commerce Don Graves at the Georgetown Business School Forum: Modern Industrial Strategy for U.S. Competitiveness, Equity, and Resilience. November 29, 2022.

[23] China Gave 190 Chip Firms US$1.75 Billion in Subsidies in 2022 as It Seeks Semiconductor Self-Sufficiency. *South China Morning Post*, May 7, 2023. Available at: www.scmp.com/tech/tech-war/article/3219697/china-gave-190-chip-firms-us175-billion-subsidies-2022-it-seeks-semiconductor-self-sufficiency

[24] Farrell, H., & Newman, A. L. (2020). Choke points. *Harvard Business Review*, 98(1), 124–131.

cars, agriculture, space, biotechnology, and other sectors to make the country less reliant on foreign imports and reclaim its independence.[25] Others altered their domestic markets to signal belonging to a geopolitical camp or intensify preexisting interstate relations. For example, in the face of active US pressure, Italy announced its intention to exit the China backed Belt and Road Initiative by the end of 2023.[26] The Dutch government similarly faced pressure from the United States to restrict the sale of cutting-edge lithography systems developed by the Dutch company ASML to China. While sale to Chinese customers may be economically profitable to the company, Dutch politicians also worried that the technology could promote Chinese "self-sufficiency in its military-technical development" and that Dutch ASML tools would go into "high-value weapons systems and weapons of mass destruction."[27]

GEOPOLITICAL RISK DEPENDS ON CORPORATE NATIONALITY

Geopolitical risk is the threat, realization, and escalation of adverse events associated with interstate tensions.[28] It is the likelihood that when states prioritize national security and work to minimize the negative externalities of foreign investment, companies' ability to leverage their assets toward economic rents will be challenged. This can occur through actions by the company's own government, for instance, when a country limits a company's foreign sales through export bans of a product or technology. It can also occur through

---

[25] Macron Pushes Nuclear, Hydrogen Power in €30 Billion Plan to Reverse Industrial Decline. *France 24*, October 12, 2021. Available at: www.france24.com/en/france/20211012-macron-unveils-%E2%82%AC30-billion-investment-plan-to-re-industralise-france

[26] Italy Intends to Exit China Belt and Road Pact as Relations Sour. *Bloomberg*, May 9, 2023. Available at: www.bloomberg.com/news/articles/2023-05-09/italy-intends-to-exit-china-belt-and-road-pact-as-relations-sour

[27] Dutch Government Says China Seeks Military Advantage from ASML Tools. *Reuters*, February 20, 2024. Available at: www.reuters.com/technology/dutch-government-says-china-seeks-military-advantage-asml-tools-2024-02-19/

[28] Caldara, D., & Iacoviello, M. (2022). Measuring geopolitical risk. *American Economic Review, 112*(4), 1194–1225.

the actions of a foreign government. For example, a company is not allowed to acquire a foreign competitor because the other country's government prevents the transaction.

As discussed in recent work with my collaborators, underlying geopolitical risk is the idea that when a foreign firm – especially from an adversarial nation – operates in a country, it creates vulnerabilities in the nation's security.[29] There are at least three potential reasons for this concern. First, the foreign firm's commercial operations generate important revenues that can be converted to security advantages for its home country. For instance, by selling products to a rising middle class in Asia, Western multinational firms can repatriate profits to their home countries. Repatriated resources could then be used to create jobs at home, acquire companies domestically, build plants locally, and strengthen the economy in their home country rather than the country where profits were generated. Second, when a foreign firm plays an important role in the local economy, domestic industry could falter as local governments have limited means to encourage foreign firms to act in the "national interest." There are plenty of examples where domestic control of a company was deemed important by the local government. It was for this reason that the United States blocked the attempted acquisition of the American company Fairchild Semiconductor Corporation by Japan's Fujitsu Ltd in 1987. Similarly, the acquisition of US energy firm Unocal by the Chinese company COONC was blocked in 2005. The operation of US ports by the UAE-owned Dubai Ports World was also sidelined in 2006. The third reason is that the prevalence of foreign firms in a country can generate political leverage for the foreign government. Foreign firms can potentially act on behalf of their governments to collect information and/or spread propaganda in the country. Researchers in one study found that when people across nineteen countries in six

---

[29] See Blake, D., Jandhyala, S., Beazer, Q., & Cunha, R. (2024). Geopolitical Liability of Foreignness and Global Strategy. Working Paper; Wang, D., Weiner, R. J., Li, Q., & Jandhyala, S. (2021). Leviathan as foreign investor: Geopolitics and sovereign wealth funds. *Journal of International Business Studies, 52*(7), 1238–1255.

continents were exposed to a representative set of Chinese messages, their perception that the Chinese Communist Party delivers growth, stability, and competent leadership increased.[30] It also moved the average respondent from slightly preferring the American model to slightly preferring the Chinese model.

While these concerns exist with regard to all foreign firms, they are especially heightened when the foreign firm in question is from an adversarial rather than a friendly country. This is because security externalities are more likely to be exploited by rivals than friends. That is, rival countries have greater incentives to leverage "their country" multinational corporations to gain a political advantage. The distinction between foreign friends and rivals is seen in many domains. Across the world, trade occurs more intensively between geopolitical allies than rivals.[31] Countries prefer to engage with "like-minded" partners in international organizations.[32] American politicians were worried about the Japanese acquiring a flagship US semiconductor company because they could "end up with no US semiconductor industry," and they would "lose the technology race by default."[33] But the firm in question (Fairchild) had already been purchased unopposed by the French-controlled Schlumberger in 1979.[34] In other words, it was not that foreign ownership itself was problematic, but foreign ownership by a company that was from a perceived rival was the real challenge. Similarly, while the

---

[30] Mattingly, D., Incerti, T., Ju, C., Moreshead, C., Tanaka, S., & Yamagishi, H. (2024). Chinese state media persuades a global audience that the "China model" is superior: Evidence from a 19-country experiment. *American Journal of Political Science 00*, 1–18. https://doi.org/10.1111/ajps.12887.

[31] Gowa, J. (1995). *Allies, adversaries, and international trade*. Princeton University Press.

[32] Davis, C. L., & Wilf, M. (2017). Joining the club: Accession to the GATT/WTO. *The Journal of Politics*, 79(3), 964–978.

[33] The Fairchild Deal: Trade War: When Chips Were Down. *Los Angeles Times*, November 30, 1987. Available at: www.latimes.com/archives/la-xpm-1987-11-30-mn-16900-story.html

[34] One Defense Department consultant questioned: "This Japanese company could infuse a lot of technology into a failing Fairchild. Why was Fujitsu ownership bad when it was OK for a French company, that couldn't give it technology, to buy it?"

UAE-based company Dubai Ports World had to eventually sell off its US operations to an American company, the ports in question had already been operated by the British-owned Peninsular and Oriental Steam Navigation Company (P&O). Again, to the Americans, control by a British entity was not particularly concerning, but control of an American port by a middle eastern company might have been.

Taken together, geopolitical risk depends on where the firm is from, or its corporate nationality. If two companies – say "Alpha" and "Beta" – want to expand to another country, the company that comes from a geopolitical rival will face greater risk. Alpha and Beta might be comparable in their technology, competitiveness, cost, and other factors, but if Alpha's home country is a geopolitical rival to the host country, but Beta's is more friendly, then Alpha will face greater geopolitical risk. Simply being from a country that is viewed as a geopolitical adversary may be enough to engender government mistrust, lower customers' willingness to buy, and increase regulatory restrictions.

Thus, a core theme that I will return to several times in the book is this. *The geopolitical risk that a company faces depends on its corporate nationality.* Whether the company has an advantage or disadvantage in global competition will depend on its nationality. Simply put, companies from rival countries face greater geopolitical risk than companies from friendly countries.

IMPACT OF GEOPOLITICAL TENSIONS

How can companies, managers, and employees of global businesses make sense of rapidly evolving geopolitical tensions? How can they assess whether their risk is increasing or decreasing? What impact will it have on their companies, roles, and jobs?

Most analyses of geopolitical risk are centered around specific events, such as wars, trade disputes, or global pandemics. They emphasize the presence or absence of either cooperative or conflictual events between countries. A global company will expect geopolitical risk to be high if war breaks out between two countries and the risk to be low when the two countries establish a military alliance. A more sophisticated metric of geopolitical risk could classify the relevance and sentiment of each event into an index. This approach is helpful in generating a broad picture of whether a particular geopolitical event receives outsize attention in markets, the media, or among pundits.

But focusing only on specific events has two disadvantages. First, it does not account for structural changes that occur even when the attention to the specific event itself dies down. Consider, for instance, the events-based geopolitical risk indicator developed by BlackRock, an American investment company. In April 2023, the company argued in its note, distilling the insights of its specialist analysts, that deteriorating US–China relations posed high geopolitical risks. However, their geopolitical risk indicator did not seem to back this conclusion; it sat close to the historical average. This must mean one of two things: Either markets were underappreciating the potential impact of geopolitical risk or that some element of the risk was not being captured by the index.[35] The second issue with an events-based approach is that it fails to help companies determine *how* geopolitical events will affect their businesses. If US–China strategic competition is an important geopolitical event, what implications does it have for a company's strategy and operations? How should multinational companies across industries evaluate the risk? On what dimensions will a company's operations and profitability be impacted?

A structural perspective offers an alternate approach to evaluating geopolitical risk. The starting assumption is that during periods of heightened geopolitical tensions – when two or more countries contest for power in the international arena – economic statecraft becomes a key policy tool for great powers as well as other countries. Governments focus on specific policies to limit the influence

---

[35] Geopolitical Risks – May Update. Blackrock Geopolitical Risk Dashboard, April 28, 2023. Available at: www.blackrock.com/corporate/literature/whitepaper/geopolitical-risk-dashboard-april-2023.pdf

of foreign firms from adversarial countries. The tools are many, but they are all designed to give domestic companies and those from friendly countries an advantage over adversarial foreign rivals. Despite their varied forms, policy tools tend to cluster around four levers that reshape the basic market structure for global companies: *market access*, *level playing field*, *investment security*, and *institutional alignment*. These dimensions critically influence whether companies can operate internationally and sustain global strategies. In other words, policies chosen by national governments along these dimensions can be more (or less) enabling for foreign companies to operate. Further, these dimensions vary significantly across firms and industries, signifying that risk varies by actor. Together, these dimensions offer one path for systematic analysis of the impact of geopolitics on different firms, industries, and employees (Figure 1.1).

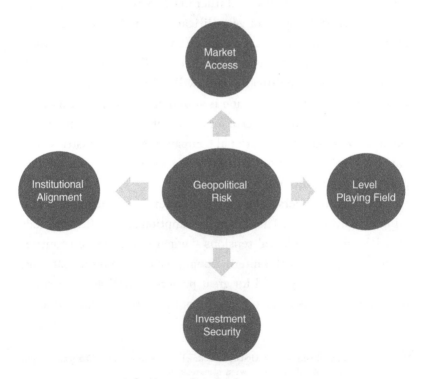

FIGURE 1.1 A firm's geopolitical risk

Market Access

In international transactions, market access refers to the ability of a company to enter a foreign market and operate or sell its goods and services there. However, governments can impose specific conditions and requirements for firms to access their domestic markets. Indeed, every country has some restrictions on cross-border trade and foreign direct investment. Common instruments to control market access include tariffs or customs duties, subsidies, import quotas, local content requirements, administrative policies, and technical requirements.

The restrictions on foreign transactions vary by jurisdiction and industry, but in the immediate post-Cold War era, they were rapidly dismantled. Across the developing world, policymakers' beliefs that attracting more foreign direct investment was in the best interest of their country led to widespread liberalization of laws and regulations affecting inflows of foreign direct investment: About 95 percent of FDI policies between 1992 and 2001 were liberalizing rather than restrictive.[36] With increased market access, foreign companies began to invest in new markets and industries.[37]

That trend changed. In 2021, the ratio of FDI policy measures that were less favorable to investment over those more favorable was the highest on record at 42 percent.[38] An increasing number of countries, predominantly developed economies, adopted additional screening of foreign investment in strategic sectors due to security concerns.[39]

---

[36] Kobrin, S. J. (2005). The determinants of liberalization of FDI policy in developing countries: A cross-sectional analysis, 1992–2001. *Transnational Corporations*, 14(1), 67–104.

[37] Mistura, F., & Roulet, C. (2019). The determinants of Foreign Direct Investment: Do statutory restrictions matter? OECD Working Papers on International Investment 2019/01. Available at: https://dx.doi.org/10.1787/641507ce-en

[38] UNCTAD World Investment Report, 2022. Available at: https://unctad.org/system/files/official-document/wir2022_en.pdf

[39] UNCTAD Investment Policy Monitor Issue 25, February 2023. "The Evolution of FDI Screening Mechanisms." Available at: https://unctad.org/system/files/official-document/diaepcbinf2023d2_en.pdf

These changes serve as a powerful reminder that geopolitical competition can close markets and limit market opportunities for firms.

The US–China trade war was, in essence, about market access. The Trump Administration in the US argued that making imported goods more expensive by imposing tariffs (or additional taxes) on them would encourage consumers to buy American products. It was supposed to protect domestic industry, especially those considered vital for national security, and incentivize foreign countries to change their practices. Over four rounds of tariffs between 2018 and 2019, Chinese imports worth more than $360 billion ranging from meat to musical instruments were hit with tariffs.[40] The Chinese government retaliated with additional tariffs on more than $100 billion of US imports. This changed the extent to which companies from either country could sell their products in the other country.

There are other types of measures, including ones that focused on particular companies and their continued access to specific markets. In late 2022, Canada ordered three Chinese companies to divest their stakes from Canadian mineral companies after concluding that the investments threatened national security. Tellingly, the Canadian Industry Minister was reported to have noted that the country welcomed foreign direct investment from companies that "share our interests and values" but would "act decisively when investments threaten our national security and our critical minerals supply chains."[41] China, on the other hand, launched a review into US chip manufacturer Micron Technology on "national security" grounds, as the country retaliates against increasing US curbs on Chinese access to semiconductor technology.[42] China is an important market for the

---

[40] A Quick Guide to the US-China Trade War. *BBC*, January 16, 2020. Available at: www.bbc.com/news/business-45899310

[41] Canada Orders Chinese Companies to Divest Stakes in Lithium Mines. *Financial Times*, November 3, 2022. Available at: www.ft.com/content/6ca9a470-59ee-4809-8a5b-35f6073c9907

[42] China Escalates Tech Battle with Review of US Chipmaker Micron. *Financial Times*, April 1, 2023. Available at: www.ft.com/content/79ddb4bb-cbfc-4e4f-bca8-ef52ea0157c1

company, generating about a quarter of its $30.8 billion revenue in 2022.[43] Anticipating the headwinds, Micron cautioned in its March 2023 quarterly report that "the Chinese government may restrict us from participating in the China market or may prevent us from competing effectively with Chinese companies."[44]

In June 2020, following a border clash with China, India banned dozens of Chinese apps citing national security and data privacy risks. The list included ByteDance's TikTok, which was the top downloaded app in India on the Android platform the previous year.[45] For ByteDance, India was among the largest markets outside China. Being shut out of this market meant the company faced financial losses of over $6 billion.[46]

Restricting market access for geopolitical advantage is not a new phenomenon. At one point in the 1980s, France required all imported video tape recorders to arrive through a small customs entry port that was both remote and poorly staffed. The nine-person customs depot was ostensibly ensuring that new taxes on video recorders were collected. However, the checks were done in such minute detail that virtually none of the machines ever reached the French market. The Trade Ministry called the restrictions to be "interpreted as a signal to Japan that it make the necessary efforts to re-establish the balance of trade with France, either by developing imports or moderating its exports."[47]

---

[43] China Bans Micron's Products from Key Infrastructure over Security Risk. *Financial Times*, May 22, 2023.

[44] Excerpt from the Quarterly Report on Form 10-Q filed by Micron Technology Inc. on March 29, 2023. Available at: https://investors.micron.com/static-files/e4bddac1-1670-4ed6-a5f0-9873340fdd41. China eventually banned Micron's products from key infrastructure.

[45] A Year since TikTok Ban, Indian TikTokers Narrate How Their Lives Were Impacted. *India Today*, July 2, 2021. Available at: www.indiatoday.in/technology/features/story/a-year-since-tiktok-ban-indian-tiktokers-narrate-how-their-lives-were-impacted-1823024-2021-07-02

[46] TikTok Expects over $6 billion Loss after India's Ban on App: Report. *NDTV*, July 3, 2020. Available at: www.ndtv.com/india-news/tiktok-expects-over-6-billion-loss-after-indias-ban-on-app-report-2256800

[47] French Lifting Curb on Japanese Video Recorders. *The New York Times*, April 29, 1983. Available at: www.nytimes.com/1983/04/29/business/french-lifting-curb-on-japanese-video-recorders.html

Level Playing Field

In May 2017, when the US government was reportedly seeking dramatic funding cuts to the State Department, a group of about 200 business leaders advocated for a robust diplomatic budget, noting that American companies depended on embassies and consulates around the world to ensure that they "competed on a level playing field."[48] The idea that firms from different countries would compete in global markets under the same rules was powerful, even if it was never fully true in practice. Bound by the same set of rules, competition between firms could be fair.

A level playing field needs both a commonly agreed upon set of rules and a mechanism by which those rules are arbitrated consistently. In the post-Cold War era, the rules of the game were mostly clearly defined, although they were driven by US and Western interests. There were also institutional arrangements to enforce these rules. For example, the World Trade Organization provided a forum to not only negotiate agreements reducing obstacles to international trade but also adjudicate disputes that would eventually arise. Similarly, foreign investment was governed by a set of international investment agreements that specified each country's obligations toward foreign investors, especially in terms of their treatment in a fair manner and on par with domestic investors. Importantly, these agreements allowed foreign firms to exercise those guarantees through an international legal mechanism.

When China joined the World Trade Organization in 2001, the US assumed that it would commit China to play by the rules of the international trading system. Twenty years later, many in the US believed membership in the World Trade Organization allowed China to participate in global markets on its own terms – benefitting from access to international markets but still playing by its own rules. At the same time, US support for the World Trade Organization's

---

[48] U.S. Global Leadership Coalition, 2017. Letter to Secretary of State Rex Tillerson, dated May 22, 2017. Available at: www.usglc.org/downloads/2017/05/Business-Letter-Tillerson-May-22.pdf

arbitration system was waning, and many countries began to opt out of international investment treaties.

With an eye on geopolitical competition, most governments seemed to have abandoned the idea of a level playing field. Support for "their" companies, often at the expense of "other" companies, was seen as essential if were to retain power and relevance in the international system. In the United States, industrial policy came back. A $280 billion CHIPS and Science Act and $370 billion Inflation Reduction Act aimed to expand US semiconductor and green energy industries and reduce American dependence on China. Korea passed its own bill to give "its" semiconductor firms tax breaks.[49] Germany planned an estimated €25–30 billion subsidy for power hungry industries in sectors such as chemicals, steel, metal, glass, solar panels, and semiconductors. The German Economy Minister was reported to have observed that these subsidies were needed to respond to the "tough international competition" that was "not taking place on a level playing field."[50] Indonesia banned exports of nickel ore to promote its electric-vehicle battery industry and looked to impose further restrictions on raw materials such as copper and bauxite.[51] China was long accused by the West of subsidizing its state-owned companies with unfair advantages and forcing foreign firms to share their technologies in exchange for access to the Chinese market. In the signature Belt and Road Initiative, the Chinese government was a key player in selecting projects, financing them with preferential loans from state-owned banks and relying on state-owned companies for their construction.[52]

---

[49] South Korea Passes Its "Chips Act" amid US-China Friction. *Bloomberg*, March 30, 2023. Available at: www.bloomberg.com/news/articles/2023-03-29/south-korea-to-pass-its-own-chips-act-amid-us-china-friction#xj4y7vzkg

[50] Germany Plans to Subsidise Power-Hungry Industries. *Financial Times*, May 5, 2023. Available at: www.ft.com/content/b4f6d51d-e023-4af0-bafc-b96650a0586d

[51] Indonesia to Allow Freeport, Amman Mineral to Ship Copper Concentrate until 2024. *Reuters*, April 29, 2023. Available at: www.reuters.com/markets/commodities/indonesia-allow-freeport-amman-mineral-ship-copper-concentrate-2024-2023-04-28/

[52] Li, J., Van Assche, A., Fu, X., Li, L., & Qian, G. 2022. The Belt and Road Initiative and international business policy: A kaleidoscopic perspective. *Journal of International Business Policy*, 66, 1–17.

Geopolitical competition also creates a second form of uneven playing field. Beyond supporting domestic firms against foreign competitors, state policy will also tend to treat foreign firms differently based on their corporate nationality, that is, whether they come from friendly or adversarial countries. In the US, for example, foreign companies such as Samsung Electronics and Taiwan Semiconductor Manufacturing Company were poised to receive tax breaks and subsidies from the CHIPS Act to bring their manufacturing to the country. These companies may have been the most sophisticated memory chip manufacturers in the world, but their success in the US was partly also because they came from South Korea and Taiwan, respectively, longstanding US allies. At the same time, a Chinese company's plan to build a corn mill in North Dakota was seen as a significant threat to national security.[53] Leading Chinese renewables firms rushed to open factories in the US after the country passed a landmark climate bill to support local clean energy manufacturing but remained worried about not getting the same treatment as their South Korean or European counterparts.[54] Similarly, India's 2020 FDI regulations explicitly stipulated the need for prior government approval for investments from countries that share a land border, a move seen as mainly targeting China.[55] This meant Chinese companies faced greater investment restrictions in the country than their peers from other countries.

A third form of uneven playing field is by company ownership. Compared to private sector firms, state-owned companies investing in foreign markets are especially sensitive to geopolitical tensions. State ownership generates the perception that the

---

[53] Air Force Says Proposed Chinese-Owned Mill in North Dakota Is "Significant Threat." *New York Times*, January 31, 2023. Available at: www.nytimes.com/2023/01/31/us/corn-mill-fufeng-china-north-dakota.html

[54] Biden's Landmark Climate Bill Lures China's Clean Energy Giants. *The Japan Times*, 2 April 2023.

[55] India Approves Investments Worth $1.79 Billion from Its Neighbors. *Reuters*, March 16, 2022. Available at: www.reuters.com/world/india/india-approves-investments-worth-179-billion-its-neighbours-2022-03-16/

company's investments reflect the controlling governments' political and geopolitical interests. National security externalities are exacerbated, and investment by state-owned companies generates more scrutiny, greater restrictions, and lower legitimacy. In one study with my collaborators, we examined the foreign acquisitions by sovereign wealth funds relative to private firms.[56] We found that despite sovereign wealth funds' expectation of limited managerial control of the acquired firms, state ownership was a red flag when geopolitical relations between two countries were adversarial. State ownership made companies' internationalization more sensitive to interstate relations.

Investment Security

In 2019, the World Bank conducted a survey of more than 2,400 business executives of multinational companies in 10 large middle-income countries.[57] They asked respondents to identify the top three factors influencing their investment decisions. In other words, they wanted to know what factors companies thought were important in choosing one country over another for an investment. Nearly nine in ten businesses considered political stability, macroeconomic stability, and a country's legal and regulatory environment to be important or critically important. For large firms, with more than 250 employees, legal and regulatory environment was the *top* investment consideration. Investors encountering major legal and regulatory obstacles were more likely to say that they will reduce or withdraw investment from the country.[58]

Why is the legal and regulatory environment so critical for foreign operations? Greater stability and consistency in these elements

---

[56] Wang, D., Weiner, R. J., Li, Q., & Jandhyala, S. (2021). Leviathan as foreign investor: Geopolitics and sovereign wealth funds. *Journal of International Business Studies*, 52(7), 1238–1255.

[57] In Brazil, China, India, Indonesia, Malaysia, Mexico, Nigeria, Thailand, Turkey, and Vietnam.

[58] Rebuilding Investor Confidence in Times of Uncertainty. Global Investment Competitiveness Report 2019/2020. World Bank Group.

allow firms to develop higher trust and closer collaborations with partners, buyers, and suppliers. Firms can focus on their operational and commercial activities with confidence that the system will ensure that they are paid and that their investments are secure. As countries competed for foreign investment in the post-Cold War era, they went to great lengths to convince foreign investors that their assets were safe in the country. Governments adopted new reforms, strengthened institutions, and even signed away some of their sovereignty through investment agreements.

Under heightened geopolitical competition, however, private firms' investment security will be secondary to leveraging those assets for geopolitical advantage. Governments worry less about whether firms believe their investments are protected and focus instead on how those investments can be used to improve their geopolitical position. The US passed a law that kicked off a 270-day countdown for TikTok, a Chinese app that was one of the most popular platforms in the United States, to either be sold or banned from US app stores and the internet hosting services that support it.[59] TikTok wasn't much different from other social media apps in its data collection and privacy policies, but its parent company's relationship to the Chinese government was raised as a cause for concern. China also turned up the heat on several western companies and industries. New sanctions have been slapped on US weapons companies Lockheed Martin and Raytheon, investigations launched into US chipmaker Micron, raids conducted on US due diligence firm Mintz, and fines slapped on the UK-based company Deloitte.[60] Chinese police visited Shanghai offices of the consulting company Bain & Co. and questioned employees at the

---

[59] Congress Passed a Bill That Could Ban TikTok. Now Comes the Hard Part. *New York Times*, April 23, 2024. Available at: www.nytimes.com/2024/04/23/technology/bytedance-tiktok-ban-bill.html

[60] China Starts "Surgical" Retaliation against Foreign Companies after US-Led Tech Blockade. *Financial Times*, April 17, 2023. Available at: www.ft.com/content/fc2038d2-3e25-4a3f-b8ca-0ceb5532a1f3

US management consulting firm.[61] An executive of the Japanese pharmaceutical company Astellas was detained.[62]

A particular form of investment security is the exit ban, which prevents a foreign executive from leaving a country if their company gets involved in a dispute. While some disputes may be purely commercial, others involved national security concerns. Courts or other regulators may impose restrictions on the movement of foreign executives, who sometimes only find out that they are subject to such a ban when they try to board an international flight.[63]

Amid western sanctions following the Russia–Ukraine conflict, European and American companies found their assets in Russia being seized.[64] A Russian court imposed the seizure of about $250 million in securities, real estate, and bank accounts of Deutsche Bank. A Presidential decree put the St Petersburg's Pulkovo Airport under the management of a Russian company, taking control from the German airport operator Fraport, Qatar's sovereign wealth fund, and other investors. The Dutch beer maker Heineken exited the country following a sale of its business there for a symbolic $1.[65]

At least some of these examples are striking because government actions are targeted at companies that are not in sectors such as oil, energy, defense, or advanced manufacturing – industries traditionally considered to be "strategic" for a country. Instead, these are levers to pull in a complicated set of intertwined competition. For multinational companies, the threat of being pulled into the conflict,

---

[61] Chinese Police Question Employees at Bain's Shanghai Office. *Financial Times*, April 26, 2023. Available at: www.ft.com/content/454ef0c7-cd2c-4cbc-a581-aed2bf8b186f
[62] Japanese Pharma Boss Rules Out China Exit after Executive's Arrest. *Financial Times*, April 9, 2023. Available at: www.ft.com/content/4fb65320-3c6a-4a8a-a56a-89a5cb40e069
[63] See Wroldsen, J., & Carr, C. (2024). The rise of exit bans and hostage-taking in China. *MIT Sloan Management Review*, 65(2), 5–7.
[64] See: Moscow Takes Control over Assets of Western Companies. *Reuters*, May 20, 2024. Available at: www.reuters.com/business/moscow-takes-control-over-assets-western-companies-2023-07-27/
[65] Heineken Sells Russian Business for $1 as It Completes Exit. *CNN*, August 25, 2023. Available at: https://edition.cnn.com/2023/08/25/business/heineken-exits-russia/index.html

even as a bystander, or a specter of hostage diplomacy dampens their ability and appetite to undertake global strategies. Managers will rightfully be asking many questions. Who will ensure that investments are protected? Can we guarantee the safety of our employees or expatriate managers? Should we invest in countries that limit the repatriation of profits? Will uncompensated expropriations increase? When the US Commerce Secretary Gina Raimondo visited China in the summer of 2023, these were some of the concerns she raised with her Chinese counterparts: "Increasingly I hear from businesses, 'China is uninvestible' because it's become too risky. There are the traditional concerns that they've become accustomed to dealing with. And then there's a whole new set of concerns, the sum total of which is making China feel too risky for them to invest."[66]

Institutional Alignment

Since the mid 2010s, India's Ministry of Corporate Affairs has been pushing forth new accounting standards to better align the reporting requirements of Indian companies with the International Financial Reporting Standards (IFRS).[67] The latter are designed as a common global accounting language so that company accounts are understandable and comparable across international borders. This has some big advantages for Indian companies expanding abroad: better access to global capital markets, easier cross-border listing, and minimizing reporting effort in multiple markets. Global standards – not just in accounting – are important for interoperability in international firms, to lower barriers to trade, and minimize costs for companies and customers. Thanks to these standards, a USB stick

---

[66] Raimondo Says US Businesses See China Becoming "Uninvestible." *Bloomberg News*, August 29, 2023. Available at: www.bloomberg.com/news/articles/2023-08-29/raimondo-says-us-firms-tell-herchina-is-becoming-uninvestable

[67] Indian Companies to Comply with International Financial Reporting Standards. *The Economic Times*, December 23, 2014. Available at: https://economictimes.indiatimes.com/news/economy/policy/indian-companies-to-comply-with-international-financial-reporting-standards/articleshow/45613879.cms?from=mdr

made by one company can fit into a USB port built by another. A laptop computer can connect to Wi-Fi anywhere in the world. Shipping containers can be neatly stacked, easily lifted, and quickly loaded onto ships. Websites communicate with servers around the world to show you content. Compare this to the frustration in charging your phone on different types of power outlets.

Yet, standards are another area of contestation in geopolitical competition. As Werner von Siemens, the founder of the eponymous German conglomerate noted: "He who owns the standards, owns the market."[68] You might remember the bruising standards wars between companies – Microsoft and Netscape over internet browsers, the video cassette recorder duel pitting Matsushita's VHS over Sony's Betamax formats, or Toshiba's HD-DVD versus Sony's Blue Ray. These companies fought tooth and nail because their very survival depended on the format and standards adopted in the market. If their format or technology became the de facto standard in the market, more customers would choose their products, and third parties would build apps, software, and technologies that were compatible with their standard, forcing even more customers to choose their products over competitors. The company also controls the intellectual property rights of certain features or applications related to the technology; so other companies have to obtain licenses and permissions for use. This means the firm has a technological advantage, with all other competitors playing catch up to their level of innovation.

The same dynamic is relevant in geopolitical competition.

In 2017, the United States withdrew from the United Nations Educational, Scientific and Cultural Organization (UNESCO), following years of reducing funding to this agency. After a six-year absence, however, the US wanted back in. While UNESCO is

---

[68] Quotes in "From AI to Facial Recognition: How China Is Setting the Rules in New Tech." *Financial Times*, October 7, 2020. Available at: www.ft.com/content/188d86df-6e82-47eb-a134-2e1e45c777b6

probably best known for designating world heritage sites (think of the Grand Canyon in the US, Angkor in Cambodia, or the Taj Mahal in India), it also plays a crucial role in setting standards on a range of issues, including artificial intelligence and technology education around the world. This important role was instrumental in bringing the US back. As reported in the *New York Times*, US officials worried about creating a vacuum that competing powers, especially China, were filling and undercutting US advantages.[69] By 2023, the US announced plans to rejoin the organization and increase its financial contributions.

Outside of UNESCO, there are hundreds of standards-setting organizations across industries where different specifications are discussed, and some endorsed. Historically, major American and European companies have dominated discussions at these organizations, where they generally tended to represent their own companies' interests. This reflects the core principles of most standards organizations, where decisions are industry-led and consensus-driven. The standards they endorse are also nonbinding. But there has been a steady increase in state participation and advocacy in these bodies. The Chinese government asks Chinese firms to vote as a bloc to support China's proposals and to support Chinese nationals for leadership roles at standards bodies.[70] As the number of Chinese technocrats, officials, and business leaders take over key leadership positions at these organizations, they have pushed for Chinese businesses' standards as the de facto international technical standards in crucial sectors.[71] Some have also argued that Beijing was also using

---

[69] U.S. Will Rejoin UNESCO in July, Agency Says. *The New York Times*, June 12, 2023. Available at: www.nytimes.com/2023/06/12/world/europe/us-china-unesco.html?searchResultPosition=4

[70] Government Should Take Bigger Role in Promoting US Technology or Risk Losing Ground to China, Commission says. *The Washington Post*, December 1, 2020. Available at: www.washingtonpost.com/technology/2020/12/01/us-policy-china-technology/

[71] China's "2035 Standards" Quest to Dominate Global Standard-Setting. Hinrich Foundation, February 21, 2023. Available at: www.hinrichfoundation.com/research/article/tech/china-2035-standards-project-restructure-global-economy/

its Belt and Road Initiative to promote Chinese standards in industries such as rail and power transmission; it uses Chinese standards to lock in partner nations who would face major switching costs to change to other international standards.[72] Chinese influence has, not surprisingly, led to significant concern in the US as the country looks at ways to counteract it.

The risk for global companies is that widely accepted, consensus-driven standards will be abandoned. This will make it much more difficult to operate across countries and markets. And it will increase costs as firms will have to adapt to different standards in different markets.

CORPORATE DIPLOMACY

In 2022, American and foreign carriers flew nearly 190 million passengers and carried 12.4 million freight tons between the United States and the rest of the world. That is roughly an increase of about 33% in passenger numbers and 50% in freight compared to the year 2000.[73] This increase was driven, in part, by international treaties negotiated by the American government called Open Skies Agreements. Since the 1990s, the US government, through a series of bilateral agreements, essentially eliminated government interference in the commercial decisions of air carriers about routes, capacity, and pricing. There was more competition in the aviation industry, and airlines were free to provide more affordable, convenient, and efficient air service for consumers. The agreements also removed restrictions on the number of designated airlines, capacity, frequencies, and types of aircraft that can service a route. Any fare offered by an airline could only be disallowed if both governments

---

[72] From Lightbulbs to 5G, China Battles West for Control of Vital Technology Standards. *The Wall Street Journal*, February 8, 2021. Available at: www.wsj.com/articles/from-lightbulbs-to-5g-china-battles-west-for-control-of-vital-technology-standards-11612722698

[73] US International Air Passenger and Freight Statistics. US Department of Transportation – International Aviation Development Series. Editions: December 2000 and December 2022.

to the agreement concurred (and for specific reasons). All carriers of both countries could establish sales offices in the other country, provide their own ground-handling services, and convert and remit earnings. Over two decades, US passengers witnessed greater competition in aviation, lower airfares, and more flights to hundreds of destinations such as Seoul, Singapore, Istanbul, Beijing, and Rio de Janeiro. One study found that a more competitive air transport market, driven by the Open Skies Agreements, reduced air transportation costs by about 9% and increased the share of imports arriving by air by 7% within 3 years after an agreement was signed.[74]

US carriers were initially enthusiastic supporters of Open Skies agreements as liberalization offered access to new markets, routes, and profits. But that enthusiasm waned as competition increased from Middle Eastern and Asian carriers. Since Russia's invasion of Ukraine, however, US carriers significantly changed their tune, demanding more government restrictions rather than openness.

In his 2022 State of the Union Address, the US President announced that the country would "join our allies in closing off American airspace to all Russian flights."[75] In retaliation, Russia banned US airlines from flying over Russian territory. But Russia's ban did not extend to many other countries, including China and India. As flight connectivity between China and the US increased, Chinese carriers took advantage of shorter routes to offer more attractive fares and shorter flying times to passengers. Not surprisingly, American carriers complained about facing an uneven playing field. But how could they fix this?

To make the playing level again, US carriers such as Delta, United, and American Airlines turned to their government and

---

[74] Micco, A., & Serebrisky, T. (2006). Competition regimes and air transport costs: The effects of open skies agreements. *Journal of International Economics*, 70(1), 25–51.

[75] Biden Says U.S. to Ban Russian Flights from American Airspace. *Reuters*, March 2, 2022. Available at: www.reuters.com/business/aerospace-defense/united-airlines-suspends-flying-over-russian-airspace-2022-03-01/

stepped up lobbying campaigns in Washington DC. But this time, they advocated for more restrictions. They pressed the White House and Congress to fix the problem by subjecting foreign carriers from countries not banned from Russian airspace to the same restrictions as US airlines. An industry representative demanded that the US government "take action to ensure that foreign carriers overflying Russia do not depart, land or transit through U.S. airports."[76] This effectively forced all international carriers to fly the same routes as their American competitors, even if they are able to offer faster flights at lower costs. And their lobbying was effective. When the US government negotiated an increase in round-trip flights with their Chinese counterparts, all new flights by Chinese carriers avoided Russian airspace.[77]

This is one example of a broader picture where managing geopolitical risks means CEOs and top managers spend more time and resources in lobbying the state for preferential treatment. US chip company executives lobbied against more restrictive China curbs.[78] The largest US technology and manufacturing companies lobbied their government to urge India to reconsider its new technology import licensing regime.[79] Chinese e-commerce and tech companies such as Shein and TikTok also stepped up their lobbying efforts to win government approval in global markets.[80] Companies around the

---

[76] Banned from Russian Airspace, US Airlines Look to Restrict Competitors. *New York Times*, March 17, 2023. Available at: www.nytimes.com/2023/03/17/us/politics/russia-us-airlines-ukraine.html

[77] Deal on China Flights Signals U.S. Airlines Stronger Hand. *The Wall Street Journal*, August 22, 2022. Available at: www.wsj.com/business/airlines/deal-to-double-china-flights-signals-u-s-airlines-stronger-hand-a789123a

[78] Chip Companies, Top US Officials Discuss China Policy. *Reuters*, July 18, 2023. Available at: www.reuters.com/technology/biden-administration-holding-meetings-with-chips-companies-source-2023-07-17/

[79] Top US Firms from Apple to Intel Decry India PC Import Curbs. *Bloomberg*, August 18, 2023. Available at: https://news.bloomberglaw.com/international-trade/top-us-firms-from-apple-to-intel-decry-india-pc-import-curbs

[80] Shein Spends $600,000 on US Lobbying as It Faces Washington Scrutiny. *Bloomberg*, 21 July 2023. TikTok Owner Spends Record $2.14 Million on US Lobbying. *Bloomberg*, 20 July 2022.

world sought personnel to assess and respond to geopolitical risks. More than 40 percent of chief legal officers in Asia and Europe and nearly a third in the US expected political developments to be their top challenge in business, while the function of providing legal advice to only be about a quarter of their roles.[81]

Increasingly, successful firms rely on government actions to support their market activity. This was always true. In a globalizing and liberalizing world, firms relied on governments to open markets and provide new avenues for growth. With increased geopolitical tensions, however, successful firms will be ones that are able to ensure preferential policies work in their favor. Managing governments is going to be critical for global businesses, and perhaps more important than market competition in some instances. One study, for example, found that politically connected American companies were more likely to receive exemptions from having to pay higher tariffs on Chinese imports.[82] McKinsey, a consulting firm, noted that geopolitical risk is at the top of CEO agenda,[83] and many clients "invest in their classic corporate affairs capabilities, their legal teams, and given the uptick in regulatory changes, their government affairs teams."[84] It calls for board members to upgrade their capabilities to conduct more nuanced discussions and decisions around managing geopolitical risk.[85] There are increasing calls for CEO diplomats, ones who can walk the fine line between managing business interests and

---

[81] Wanted: In-house Legal Leaders Who Can Interpret World Events. *Financial Times*, May 25, 2023. Available at: www.ft.com/content/100af542-9dec-4433-8a60-9f35e26753fa

[82] Fotak, V., Lee, H. S., Megginson, W. L., & Salas, J. M., (2023). The Political Economy of Tariff Exemption Grants. Available at SSRN: https://ssrn.com/abstract=3963039 or http://dx.doi.org/10.2139/ssrn.3963039

[83] Economic Conditions Outlook during Turbulent Times, December 2022. McKinsey Report, December 21, 2022. www.mckinsey.com/capabilities/strategy-and-corporate-finance/our-insights/economic-conditions-outlook-2022

[84] Geopolitical Risk: Navigating a World in Flux. McKinsey & Company Podcast, March 9, 2023. www.mckinsey.com/capabilities/risk-and-resilience/our-insights/geopolitical-risk-navigating-a-world-in-flux

[85] Geopolitical Resilience: The New Board Imperative. McKinsey & Company Commentary, August 8, 2023. www.mckinsey.com/capabilities/risk-and-resilience/our-insights/geopolitical-resilience-the-new-board-imperative

external governmental stakeholders. Overall, businesses are devoting more time and attention to dealing with global politics, its impact, and consequences. Large companies such as Microsoft have built a legal, policy, and influence staff of around 2,000 people and costs more than $1 billion a year to run.[86]

UNINTENDED CONSEQUENCES OF CORPORATE DIPLOMACY

Managing political and geopolitical tensions is increasingly a part of the job for many mangers, especially at higher levels of an organization. Yet, this comes at a cost. When firms are unable to determine which policies will endure or what form they will ultimately take, managers will tend to withhold or underinvest in key areas. When they do engage in nonmarket activities, they may be rewarded with better information and greater clarity, but these activities make significant demands on firms' managerial resources, which comes at the expense of other more routine activities.

The Norwegian telecommunications company Telenor, attracted by the growth potential in India, began operations there in the late 2000s by partnering with a local company and investing approximately $2 billion in the venture. Only a few years later, the company found itself in challenging circumstances. The Supreme Court of India concluded that the telecommunications license allocation process (that pre-dated Telenor's entry) was flawed and directed the State to cancel all 2G licenses issued in the arbitrary and capricious process. This was a major setback for Telenor – the company would lose all of its telecommunication licenses in the country and would have to bid for and acquire them in a new license allocation round. Not only was this going to be expensive, but it also threatened the company's survival in the market. In the weeks and months that followed the Court's decision, the company devoted significant time,

---

[86] How Brad Smith Used Microsoft's $1bn Law and Lobbying Machine to Win Activision Battle. *Financial Times*, October 14, 2023. Available at: www.ft.com/content/07c507bd-2ce7-4345-85bd-0c27f408afbe

expertise, and attention to diplomatic, legal, and strategic activities to contain the fallout. On the diplomatic front, the company emphasized the support of the Norwegian government, which owned 54 percent of the firm. Within days of the ruling, they pursued the Norwegian Embassy to raise the issue with the Indian government. The Norwegian Minister of Government Administration and Reform and the former Prime Minister and the United Nations Special Envoy met with Indian officials to raise the issue. A few weeks later, the CEO and other managers, along with the Norwegian Trade and Industry Minister, met Indian officials in the Finance Ministry, the Planning Commission, and the Communications and Information Technology Minister to urge the Indian government to protect the firm's investment. Separately, Telenor prepared a legal challenge to the license cancellation and investigated the possibility of a court review. They sent a formal notice of their "intent to invoke" international arbitration proceedings over what they saw as the Indian Government's failure to protect the company's investment and were seeking $14 billion in damages. At the same time, Telenor was also trying to shape the rules of the new licensing round. The firm planned to participate in the Court-directed reauction but wanted the Indian government to limit the auction to companies that lost licenses. They also lobbied to relax the stringent rules proposed by the Telecom Regulatory Authority of India (TRAI) regarding spectrum allocation, infrastructure requirements, and reserve pricing in the new auction.

All the nonmarket activities won the company some important concessions in the subsequent licensing process. However, the range of new and complex activities in the nonmarket domain also made extensive demands on the firm's managerial resources. Significant time, attention, and expertise of Telenor's management – which would otherwise have focused on the firm's operations – was spent dealing with political, legal, and diplomatic issues. The diversion of resources was reflected in the firm's relative operational and network performance. On the other hand, telecom companies that were not affected by the Court ruling – and hence presumably not diverting additional managerial resources to political, legal, and diplomatic actions – saw a significant improvement in their network performance. In other words, Telenor's operational performance declined but that of its unaffected peers improved in the same time period.[87]

With many balls in the air, something is bound to fall.

PREVIEWING THE PATH: CHAPTERS AHEAD

The rest of this book will unpack the many ways by which global politics shapes companies, managers, and work. In Chapter 2, I will first take a closer look at corporate nationality, a key element of geopolitical risk. Even though it is challenging to define a global company's nationality, it will shape how companies compete, the resources they have access to, and their relative advantage (or disadvantage) in global operations. For managers, an important question is whether and how to distance their companies from their home countries as well as shaping others' perceptions of their company's nationality.

Next, I focus on innovation as one of the central arenas of geopolitical tensions (Chapter 3). As geopolitical tensions increase, governments strive to keep innovations at home and increase barriers to cross-border flows of cutting-edge knowledge, technology, and information. Companies withdraw or scale back foreign innovation efforts and the flow of ideas, talent, and resources slows. The promise of global innovation – that unlikely combination of knowledge and information from different sources and locations – is challenged.

In the following section, I turn to questions that many may be concerned about, including chief executives and heads of business

---

[87] For Telenor, the ratio of calls terminated unwillingly to all call attempts, an important network performance measure, increased by 0.03 percentage points after the Court ruling (benchmark value of ≤2%). In contrast, the comparable value for firms unaffected by the Court ruling *decreased* by 0.19 percentage points. For a full analysis, see Blake, D. J., & Jandhyala, S. (2019). Managing policy reversals: Consequences for firm performance. *Strategy Science*, 4(2), 111–128.

units but also line managers and employees: What are the strategic and managerial implications of geopolitics for global companies? I highlight risk mitigation strategies and discuss how decisions regarding resources, competitive advantage, and firm organization will allow companies and managers to buffer against geopolitical risk (Chapter 4). But getting it done also means having the right skills, employees, and organizational setup. In Chapter 5, I offer a four-step process – scanning, personalizing, planning, and pivoting – that combines internal and external expertise to allow companies to be better prepared. Then, I examine how geopolitical tensions are reshaping the future of work, influencing who works, how work is performed, and where it takes place (Chapter 6).

Stepping back, in Chapter 7 I highlight the broader information revolution to examine some leading methodologies in assessing and quantifying geopolitical risk. Computational geopolitics is an attempt to integrate quantitative methods and geopolitical analysis to understand and predict trends, while taking advantage of the explosive growth of data, improvements in computational power, and access to cloud computing.

The ideas discussed in different sections are then brought together in two case studies – on e-commerce (Chapter 8) and green energy (Chapter 9). In each case, I highlight how geopolitical forces are fundamentally shaping industry pressures. National security concerns have led to governments adopting a range of policies to alter the behavior of companies in these sectors. Government actions influence market access, level playing field, investment security, and institutional alignment. In response, companies in these sectors have adopted various strategies to manage geopolitical tensions.

Finally, I wrap up the discussion in Chapter 10 by highlighting the main features of geopolitical risk for companies as well as its impact on managers, employees, and work. To respond effectively, global companies must recognize the systemic changes underway and develop capabilities to address them.

2   Corporate Nationality

"Where are you *really* from?" is a fraught and polarizing question for many individuals. And it can sometimes be the same for companies. As far back as the 1880s, the British were asking companies this question. As the country was being run over by copycat products from Germany, the British government – in an effort to protect British manufacturing – adopted the Merchandise Marks Act in 1887. For the first time, foreign manufacturers were required to indicate the geographical origin of their exports to Britain. The Act allowed British customs officials to seize goods with misleading indicators, which led to significant, and sometimes unintended, consequences. Some German products were poorly made or fraudulent, and the law helped customers become aware of their origin and potentially modify their purchasing behavior. Other products, however, were of high quality, often as good as or better than British products. Once the British consumers became aware of the amount of German merchandise they were actually buying, they willingly gravitated to excellent German made products. German exports continued to rise, and the "Made in Germany" mark developed into a mark of quality.[1]

ROOTLESS AND STATELESS COMPANIES?

Meta is the world's largest social media company, with over 3 billion users and a market value of over $1 trillion. It does not have a single headquarters or jurisdiction but functions out of several regional hubs and offices in different countries. About 90 percent of its users and many of its staff are outside North America. Its top executives

---

[1] Stusowski, D. (2017). A Manufacturing War between the UK and Germany in the 19th Century Set the Stage for Today's Trade Crisis. History Collection, June 5, 2017. Available at: https://historycollection.com/now-look-merchandise-marks-act/

function out of Hawaii, California, London, Israel, Spain, and New York. Depending on its operations, it has a tax obligation in different countries and complies with local laws wherever it operates. With its global spread, where is the company *really* from?

The influential political scientist Robert Reich argued in 1990 that corporate nationality was becoming irrelevant; that a company's country of origin was not evident, and its nationality did not determine its behavior.[2] Trends such as outsourcing and offshoring, shopping for headquarters locations based on low taxes, and companies employing more people outside their home countries strengthened the view that a company's nationality was not important; that multinational corporations have outgrown their home country identity. Some go further, arguing that not only is the home country irrelevant, but it is also mostly an obstacle to firms aiming to achieve their maximum efficiency.

Rather than worry about where a company was from, growing concerns in the 1990s and 2000s were about stateless companies that were not bound by geography. Firms were headquartered in one country, had their top management teams in another, operational assets in a third, and employees in many other countries. Allegiance to or even affiliation with a political state was considered unnecessary, a disadvantage, or irrelevant. In 2008, *The Economist* published an article titled "In praise of the stateless multinational" and went on to conclude that while such a corporation was not without flaws, it was "infinitely preferable to the state-bound version."[3]

CORPORATIONS BOUND TO A NATION

In 2023, Meta was fined a record $1.3 billion by the European Union for violating data privacy laws by transferring the personal data of Facebook users to servers in the United States. The root of the issue

---

[2] Reich, R. B. (1990). Does corporate nationality matter?. *Issues in Science and Technology*, 7(2), 40–44.

[3] In Praise of the Stateless Multinational. *The Economist*, September 18, 2008. Available at: www.economist.com/leaders/2008/09/18/in-praise-of-the-stateless-multinational

was a conflict of law between US rules on access to data and EU privacy rights. The firm's immediate response to the ruling came in the form of a statement from Nick Clegg, Meta's president of global affairs, and Jennifer Newstead, the company's chief legal officer arguing that the European Data Protection Board "chose to disregard the clear progress that policymakers are making to resolve this underlying issue," referring to continued efforts by EU and US policymakers to hammer out a new transatlantic data privacy framework.[4] For a company that was listed as one of the twenty-five multinational corporations more powerful than many countries, and vying with governments for global power,[5] it was ironic that they immediately turned to their home government's efforts to resolve their problems.

As early as 1990, Professor Stephen Cohen noted that global corporations were a myth. In testimony to the US Joint Economic Committee, he wrote[6]:

> Companies are not global: American MNCs are the most mature and the closest to global. Yet Commerce Department studies indicate that about ¾'s of the total assets of American MNCs are still accounted for by the parent operations in the U.S., with similarly high proportions for sales and employment. Despite much outbound investment these past years, that proportion has not changed much. For Japanese based MNCs, I would estimate the proportion of assets at the parent operation to be well over 90%. Even by these crude numbers, there is a long way to go before companies become global.

---

[4] Meta Slapped with Record $1.3 billion EU Fine over Data Privacy. *CNN Business*, May 22, 2023. Available at: https://edition.cnn.com/2023/05/22/tech/meta-facebook-data-privacy-eu-fine/index.html

[5] These 25 Companies Are More Powerful than Many Countries. *Foreign Policy*, March 15, 2016. Available at: https://foreignpolicy.com/2016/03/15/these-25-companies-are-more-powerful-than-many-countries-multinational-corporate-wealth-power/

[6] Cohen, S. (1990). Corporate Nationality Can Matter a Lot. Testimony to the Joint Economic Committee: September 5, 1990. Available at: https://escholarship.org/content/qt9fb548d6/qt9fb548d6.pdf?t=krn9ax (accessed on November 29, 2023).

Things have changed in recent years, but in some cases, not by much. Only about 14 percent of Fortune Global 500 companies have a CEO from outside the country where the company was headquartered, and as late as 2013 only one such company from the BRIC countries was led by a non-native.[7] At the other end of the spectrum, there is national bias in very small companies as well. Judges in accelerator programs to nurture the most promising startup ideas are less likely to recommend startups headquartered outside their home region by 4 percentage points, a discount that leads them to pass over one in twenty promising startups.[8] A home bias exists in virtual marketplaces for financial products,[9] and US investment managers exhibit a strong preference for locally headquartered firms.[10] In patent lawsuits adjudicated by federal district courts in the US, foreign patent holders are 14 percent less likely to win against US firms when compared to similar disputes against other foreign firms.[11]

The strong tendency to act in ways that protect domestic firms, often at the expense of foreign firms, is exacerbated by geopolitical tensions. In the new global order, corporate nationality may be one of the most significant factors for many companies, regardless of whether they have international operations or not. Because economic statecraft is a key element of geopolitics, policy choices are often driven to explicitly advantage some firms over others based on their nationality.

As highlighted in Chapter 1, *where* a company is from will determine the geopolitical risk it faces. A firm from a country that

---

[7] World's Biggest Companies: Still Xenophobic after All These Years. *Fortune*, June 24, 2013. Available at: https://fortune.com/2013/06/24/worlds-biggest-companies-still-xenophobic-after-all-these-years/ (accessed on November 29, 2023)

[8] Wright, N. L., Koning, R., & Khanna, T. (2023). Judging foreign startups. *Strategic Management Journal*, 44, 2195–2225.

[9] Lin, M., & Viswanathan, S. (2016). Home bias in online investments: An empirical study of an online crowdfunding market. *Management Science*, 62(5), 1393–1414.

[10] Coval, J. D., & Moskowitz, T. J. (1999). Home bias at home: Local equity preference in domestic portfolios. *The Journal of Finance*, 54(6), 2045–2073.

[11] Choudhury, A., Jandhyala, S., & Nandkumar, A. (2025). Economic nationalism and the home court advantage. *Strategic Management Journal*, 46(1), 242–272.

is a geopolitical rival will be perceived to create vulnerabilities in the nation's security. This may be due to the additional revenues that the company remits back to its home country, which could strengthen the economic and military capabilities of the rival country. Alternately, foreign control of the domestic economy, especially if the firm is from a rival country, raises concerns that the company will not act in ways that support local interests. Finally, rival governments could leverage the firm's operations to shape public opinion or spread propaganda in the country.

Because a rival foreign government is more likely to exploit security vulnerabilities than a friendly foreign government, foreign firms from rival countries are treated differently from companies that come from more friendly countries. As a result, a firm's country of origin will shape how it is treated, and the geopolitical risk it faces.

This is illustrated in the example of Hesai, a Shanghai-based manufacturer of advanced laser sensors for cars, which successfully managed markets and policies in the US for several years. It was one of the largest Chinese companies to go public in the US, with a $2.4 billion initial public offering in February 2023. The company also won a patent infringement case against the US rival Ouster. Despite its relative success in the US, the company shied away from opening a $60 million manufacturing plant in the US. Hostile attitudes toward Chinese investment contributed to this decision. Louis Hsieh, the company's chief financial officer, was quoted in the *Financial Times* attributing their decision to the perception of the company's nationality[12]:

> The temperature is so high. It doesn't matter what you want, if you're trying to be a global corporate citizen and help America, they don't care. The label China turns them off. [...]

---

[12] Shanghai Manufacturer Says US Has "Xenophobic" View of Chinese Investors. *Financial Times*, November 16, 2023. Available at: www.ft.com/content/55cd830b-6fb3-4696-ab03-2c9deeefbc18

> The US just seems to think that if it's a Chinese company bringing that technology, you must have an ulterior motive, you may be a threat to national security, which is not true.

As identified in prior research with my collaborators,[13] one of the most important implications of the argument is that a foreign firm cannot credibly reassure local stakeholders that it will not act to support its home government's actions. A foreign technology company, for example, can try to convince the local government that it would not share user data or technology developed locally with its home government. But such a claim would not be credible – even if it has the ability to keep user data or technology private, it does not have the incentive to act this way especially when the company's own home government controls the resources needed for the firm's success or can expropriate its assets.

CORPORATE NATIONALITY SHAPES GLOBAL BUSINESSES

By design or default, companies can no longer overlook their nationality. Whether they have international operations or not, corporate nationality may be one of the most significant factors for many companies. It will shape how companies compete, the resources they have access to, and will be a source of advantage (or disadvantage) in global operations.

Corporate Nationality versus Market Capabilities

A fundamental question for any firm is where to operate; which location, area, or geography offers the best option for the firm to set up operations? This is especially the case for internationalizing firms who have to carefully consider different countries and evaluate the trade-offs among them. In most of the last thirty years, these decisions were primarily driven by economics: size of the market, cost of operations,

---

[13] See Blake, D., Jandhyala, S., Beazer, Q., & Cunha, R. (2024). Geopolitical Liability of Foreignness and Global Strategy. Working Paper. Blake, D., Jandhyala, S., Beazer, Q., & Cunha, R. (2024). Managing Geopolitics in the Digital Age. Working Paper.

ease of transportation, connectivity, labor force sophistication, and raw material availability. These calculations tended to be somewhat similar for firms from different home countries. For instance, mining companies from around the world evaluated potential mining assets using similar valuation methods in technical reports and feasibility studies.

With rising geopolitical tensions, however, where a firm can operate depends on its corporate nationality. The hostility firms face in foreign markets, whether from policymakers or the public, may be less about their corporate actions and more about their corporate nationality. No company exemplifies this more than TikTok in recent times. The Chinese-owned video sharing platform has been under immense scrutiny in many countries over concerns around security of user data and potential control by the Chinese government. The worry was that the Chinese government could use the app to extract sensitive user data to advance its interests, for example, by promoting a view that is against the country's foreign policy goals. The app was either banned entirely, banned in some circumstances (such as on government devices), or under evaluation in countries such as the US, Britain, India, Nepal, Pakistan, Philippines, Australia, France, the Netherlands, New Zealand, Canada, Taiwan, and Afghanistan.

But in all these countries, TikTok was a very popular app. About 150 million Americans used the app each day, and millions of people around the world generated livelihoods on the app. Across the world, TikTok had over a billion monthly users by 2021, and surpassed 2 billion global downloads in 2020.[14] The company had clearly figured out how to compete in the market. But resistance began to climb because of its corporate nationality.

TikTok itself was incorporated in the United States, and the app was not even available in mainland China. The company was headquartered in Los Angeles and led by an executive team in the United States and Singapore. Its global offices span the world, including

---

[14] TikTok Hits 1 Billion Monthly Active Users Globally – Company. *Reuters*, September 27, 2021. Available at: www.reuters.com/technology/tiktok-hits-1-billion-monthly-active-users-globally-company-2021-09-27/

in Los Angeles, Silicon Valley, Nashville, New York, Washington DC, Dublin, London, Paris, Berlin, Dubai, Singapore, Jakarta, Seoul, and Tokyo. However, ByteDance, TikTok's parent company, was founded by Chinese entrepreneurs and this origin story continues to be the sticking point.

ByteDance has since evolved into a privately held global enterprise, with roughly 60% owned by global institutional investors, about 20% owned by the company's founders, and approximately 20% owned by its employees.[15] Despite its diffused corporate structure, the questions that Shou Chew, CEO of TikTok faced in a five-hour hearing by dozens of US House Energy and Commerce Committee members repeatedly went back to its nationality. Committee Chair Cathy McMorris Rodgers shared concerns about the security of US users' data, noting[16]:

> To the American people watching today, hear this: TikTok is a weapon by the Chinese Communist Party to spy on you and manipulate what you see and exploit for future generations.

Assurances from the CEO that new policies will ensure American data is stored on American soil, by an American company, and overseen by American personnel, failed to convince lawmakers. Frank Pallone, the top Democrat on the Committee commented:

> I still believe that the Beijing communist government will still control and have the ability to influence what you do.

Taking another approach, Shou Chew pointed out that American social media companies did not have a good track record with data privacy and user security. He reminded everyone that Facebook users' personal data was used for political advertising in the Cambridge Analytica scandal. But lawmakers went back to their

---

[15] Testimony of Shou Chew, Chief Executive Officer of TikTok. Testimony before the U.S. House Committee on Energy and Commerce, March 23, 2023.

[16] Lawmakers Grilled TikTok CEO Chew for 5 Hours in a High-Stakes Hearing about the App. *NPR*, March 23, 2023. Available at: www.npr.org/2023/03/23/1165579717/tiktok-congress-hearing-shou-zi-chew-project-texas

central concern: As long as TikTok was connected to its Chinese parent company, data security could not be trusted.

TikTok's experience in India followed a similar trajectory. In the aftermath of a military clash along the border between India and China, more than 300 Chinese apps were banned in India. Prominent among them was ByteDance's TikTok. But the app itself was hugely popular in the country prior to the ban. In 2019, it was the top downloaded app in India on the Android platform.[17] For ByteDance, India was one of the largest markets outside China. They knew how to compete in the Indian market and were arguably doing a very good job. The fact that TikTok was no longer available to Indian users had little to do with market factors and everything to do with its corporate nationality.

A similar narrative was evident in the case of the American chip maker, Qualcomm. In 2018, the company walked away from a $44 billion deal – the biggest semiconductor deal globally – to buy the Dutch company NXP Semiconductors. Regulators in most jurisdictions had signed off on the deal, but there was one holdout. The deal was ultimately derailed when Qualcomm failed to secure Chinese regulatory approval, where it earned more than two-thirds of its revenues. This proved expensive as Qualcomm had to cough up a $2 billion break-up fee. CEO Steve Mollenkopf attributed this to rising geopolitical tensions. In perceived tit-for-tat measures, China's actions followed US policies to block a $117 billion takeover of Qualcomm, crippling sanctions on the Chinese telecommunications company ZTE, and additional tariffs on several Chinese goods. Mollenkopf, quoted in a Reuters report, acknowledged their liability: "We obviously got caught up in something that was above us, so I don't know if I would conclude anything about our business, our ability to invest [in China] or partner with Chinese companies."[18]

---

[17] www.indiatoday.in/technology/features/story/a-year-since-tiktok-ban-indian-tiktokers-narrate-how-their-lives-were-impacted-1823024-2021-07-02

[18] https://in.reuters.com/article/nxp-semicondtrs-m-a-qualcomm-mollenkopf/qualcomm-ceo-in-the-ring-alone-after-u-s-china-spat-kills-deals-idINKBN1KH0EL

Another example is the US ban of the popular antivirus software made by Moscow-based Kaspersky Labs. In adopting the first US ban of cybersecurity products, the Department of Commerce was clear that their action had nothing to do with the effectiveness of the product. As they noted in their assessment[19]:

> The risks to U.S. national security addressed in this Final Determination stem not from whether Kaspersky's products are effective at identifying viruses and other malware, but whether they can be used strategically to cause harm to the United States.

Kaspersky argued that the decision of the US Department of Commerce reflected geopolitical tensions rather than business issues. The company's press release countered[20]:

> Despite proposing a system in which the security of Kaspersky products could have been independently verified by a trusted 3rd party, Kaspersky believes that the Department of Commerce made its decision based on the present geopolitical climate and theoretical concerns, rather than on a comprehensive evaluation of the integrity of Kaspersky's products and services. Kaspersky does not engage in activities which threaten U.S. national security and, in fact, has made significant contributions with its reporting and protection from a variety of threat actors that targeted U.S. interests and allies.

The problem, of course, is that while Kaspersky can have good intentions about not threatening US national security interests, this is not a credible statement as far as American regulators and policymakers are concerned. From their perspective, as long as there

---

[19] Final Determination: Case No. ICTS-2021-002, Kaspersky Lab, Inc. A notice by the Industry and Security Bureau on June 24, 2024. Available at: www.federalregister.gov/documents/2024/06/24/2024-13532/final-determination-case-no-icts-2021-002-kaspersky-lab-inc

[20] Kaspersky Statement on the U.S. Commerce Department Determination. Company Press Release, June 21, 2024. Available at: https://usa.kaspersky.com/about/press-releases/2024_kaspersky-statement-on-the-us-commerce-department-determination

is any connection between the company and its country of origin, Kaspersky could be coerced by the state to act in ways that undermine American interests.

Corporate Nationality and Government Support

In 2009, a small California-based company called Solyndra was on the US government's radar. The firm was being considered for a government lending program aimed at supporting ventures that needed a boost in commercializing clean energy technology. Solyndra was an innovative manufacturer trying to produce solar panels by minimizing the use of silicon, which at the time was a key but expensive ingredient in most panels. Their technology allowed the company to change the shape of conventional solar panels so that they could get the same performance using significantly less silicon. Just the previous year, the company announced $1.2 billion in long-term contracts. They were looking for additional funding to step up their manufacturing. With much fanfare, the company received a $535 million federal loan guaranteed by the Obama Administration as part of its stimulus efforts. Solyndra was riding high.

And then things began to fall apart.

Three years after announcing attractive long-term contracts, cumulative sales of the company were a mere $330 million.[21] The market had changed dramatically. A sudden silicon mining boom caused the price of the raw material – silicon – to drop precipitously. Pure crystalline polysilicon needed to make solar panels fell from about $400 a kilogram in 2008 to just $30 a few years later.[22] At this price, conventional flat solar panel manufacturers were very competitive and Solyndra's new technology that used minimal

---

[21] Solyndra: $1.2 Billion in Contracts undercut by China. *Reuters*, October 19, 2011. Available at: www.reuters.com/article/us-solyndra-bankruptcy-idUSTRE79H5YI20111018/

[22] How US Manufacturing, Not Chinese Dumping, Killed Solyndra. *Quartz*, October 15, 2012. Available at: https://qz.com/15775/how-us-manufacturers-not-chinese-dumping-killed-solyndra

silicon didn't justify the additional cost. In addition, China began to invest billions of dollars in subsidies for solar panel manufacturing. Over just eighteen months, the Chinese Development Bank extended more than $34 billion in credit lines to Chinese solar companies.[23] The price of solar panels fell 70 percent in two and a half years and a global glut of panels soon followed. At the same time, countries in cash-strapped Europe began to cut incentives for installing solar power projects, and European demand for solar panels began to soften. It seemed like the perfect storm. Solyndra ran out of money, filing for bankruptcy in 2011 and defaulting on a loan of over $500 million.

In the political fallout that ensued, Solyndra became the poster child for well-meaning but ineffective and expensive government failure. Some critics questioned whether decisions about Solyndra's loans reflected political favors to supporters.[24] Others challenged the efficacy of the industrial policy approach, where governments supported industries deemed strategically important. Were targeted interventions, such as in Solyndra, the most efficient way to allocate public resources? Further skepticism was driven by failures of government attempts to achieve objectives, the potential anticompetitive effects, and concerns about crowding out private investments.

Industrial policy largely fell out of favor among many industrialized nations during the era of globalization. But the pendulum is swinging back, with renewed interest in it. Some industrial policies are focused on creating jobs, but with heightened geopolitical competition, many emphasize strategic competition with geopolitical rivals and the ability to influence international trade. Examples include the Inflation Reduction Act and the CHIPS and Science Act in the United States, Made in China 2025 policies in China, the Green Deal

---

[23] Solyndra: Soft Markets and Chinese Subsidies. *Scientific American*, November 18, 2011. Available at: https://blogs.scientificamerican.com/plugged-in/solyndra-soft-markets-chinese-subsidies-no-apologies/

[24] Steven Chu Takes Heat on Solyndra at Hearing. *CNET*, November 17, 2011. Available at: www.cnet.com/culture/steven-chu-takes-heat-on-solyndra-at-hearing/

Industrial Plan in the EU, K-Chips Act in Korea, and the Production Linked Incentive Scheme in India.

Companies are at the center of these industrial policy debates. By one estimate, as much as 60 percent of industrial policies are targeted at specific firms.[25] In other words, industrial policy is about governments carefully considering which firms they will support, and the specific policy measures such as trade financing, state loans, and financial grants to support the chosen firms. And here, a clear distinction emerges for governments between "our" companies and "their" companies.

Corporate nationality determines who receives government support. At a basic level, governments support national firms over foreign ones. The Australian Industry Growth Program offers one example. The $393 million program, part of a larger $15 billion National Reconstruction Fund, aimed to scale up small businesses into medium-sized entities, with a particular emphasis on home grown companies. The Industry and Science Minister emphasized this in stating[26]: "The Industry Growth Program is designed to commercialise great ideas and know-how, build stronger, Australian businesses and put them on a pathway for potential support by the National Reconstruction Fund."

But governments also make strategic calculations about subsidizing foreign companies with their tax-payer dollars. In general, they are more likely to provide subsidies, grants, loans, and tax benefits to companies from partners or allies. Companies from rival countries are less likely to receive such support, even if they are as capable as their peers who come from friendly countries.

---

[25] Juhasz, R., Lane, N., Oehlsen, E., & Perez, V. (2023). Global Industrial Policy: Measurements and Results. United Nations Industrial Development Organization Policy Brief Series: Insights on Industrial Development, Issue No. 1, March 2023.

[26] Australian Government Launches $393 million Industry Growth Program to Benefit Life Sciences among Others. ProactiveInvestors, December 3, 2023. Available at: www.proactiveinvestors.co.uk/companies/news/1034991/australian-government-launches-392-million-industry-growth-program-to-benefit-life-sciences-among-others-1034991.html

Examining data on US subsidies is illuminating.[27] During the period 2021–23, various US government agencies at the federal, state, and local levels offered some type of support to several foreign companies in the United States. However, the nationality of foreign companies appears to determine who received those subsidies. Table 2.1 highlights the number of subsidies to foreign companies from a selected group of countries offered by the US as well as the number of megadeals – where subsidy packages worth $100 million or more were offered.

Some trends are evident. There were no instances of Russian firms receiving US subsidies, while there were only twenty-one instances of Chinese firms receiving any sort of assistance from the US. Importantly, there were no megadeals – or subsidy packages of more than $100 million – for Chinese firms, but companies from India and Vietnam received them. Fifty-one Korean firms received some type of government support, including five instances of megadeals. Companies from the UK and Japan – longstanding allies of the US – received the most.

Rather than simply looking at the number of foreign investments receiving subsidies, we can further benchmark this with the total foreign investment in the US coming from these countries (Table 2.2). Chinese investments in the US were roughly double that of Taiwan, but a similar number of investments from both countries received subsidies (twenty-one for China and seventeen for Taiwan). This suggests Taiwanese companies were more likely on average to receive some support from the US government. India and Russia had about similar levels of investment in the US, but while Russian firms received absolutely no subsidies, Indian firms even managed to find a megadeal.

---

[27] Data are drawn from Subsidy Tracker, a database that aggregates information on subsidies and other forms of financial assistance offered by federal, state, or local government agencies to companies in the United States. See: https://subsidytracker.goodjobsfirst.org/

Table 2.1 US subsidies for foreign companies from selected locations

Country	2023		2022		2021	
	# companies	# megadeals	# companies	# megadeals	# companies	# megadeals
China	4	0	10	0	7	0
Russia	0	0	0	0	0	0
UK	23	0	72	0	98	0
Japan	46	0	128	4	152	2
Korea	11	2	21	2	19	1
Taiwan	2	0	5	0	10	0
India	2	0	5	1	9	0
Brazil	2	0	3	0	6	0
Vietnam	0	0	1	1	0	0
Total	90	2	245	8	301	3

Source: Author's calculations based on data from Subsidy Tracker (https://subsidytracker.goodjobsfirst.org/)

Table 2.2 *Foreign investment in the US, selected nationalities*

Country	2023	2022	2021
China	28,043	29,907	31,831
Russia	4,065	4,057	4,010
UK	630,551	683,382	627,312
Japan	688,054	663,427	653,548
Korea	76,689	65,009	66,141
Taiwan	15,643	15,739	15,704
India	4,664	3,830	3,496
Brazil	6,514	4,813	3,887
Vietnam	627	328	337

Source: Bureau of Economic Analysis.
Notes: historical cost basis, in millions of dollars.

Electric vehicles offer an intriguing story where corporate nationality is a focal issue. Since 2009, the Chinese government has carefully cultivated an effective electric vehicle ecosystem through subsidies, grants, tax breaks, and local contracts.[28] In the early stages of the industry, these subsidies helped Chinese EV companies invest in the technology needed to improve their models. At the same time, government procurement contracts provided a steady stream of revenue for companies as well as experience in building, testing, and running electric vehicles. Crucially, the Chinese government's subsidies were not restricted to domestic firms early on. Tesla, an American company, benefited from the financial incentives and was even actively courted by local Chinese officials.

Fast forward a few years, and the electric vehicles industry is squarely in the midst of geopolitical tensions. Chinese electric vehicle companies faced headwinds in Europe – their most successful export markets. The European Union launched an anti-subsidy

---

[28] For more details, see "How Did China Come to Dominate the World of Electric Cars?," *MIT Technology Review*, February 21, 2023. Available at: www.technologyreview.com/2023/02/21/1068880/how-did-china-dominate-electric-cars-policy/

investigation into electric vehicles from China and imposed higher tariff rates.[29] This investigation was notable in that it was preemptively initiated by the European Commission itself, rather than in response to industry complaints.[30] The founder of Nio, a large and successful Chinese electric vehicle maker, had indeed presciently warned a few months earlier that Chinese firms, which had as much as a 20 percent cost advantage over rivals thanks to China's control of the supply chain and raw materials, could expect protectionist policies by foreign governments. William Li, the CEO, commented on the sidelines of the Shanghai Autoshow that[31]:

> After exports grow and grow, market protectionism will definitely happen. It is not a good thing for global sustainable development, but we must respect that every country has considerations for protecting local industries. This is the reality we must face.

Across the ocean, American officials also proposed new rules aimed to shift more production of electric vehicles, batteries, and raw materials that power them to the United States. This included $7,500 in tax credits to Americans who buy electric vehicles, as long as those cars did not use critical minerals or other components used in the battery from "a foreign entity of concern."[32] In other words, they discouraged companies seeking federal funding from sourcing materials from China or Russia.[33]

---

[29] Europe Is Slapping Tariffs on Chinese Electric Vehicles – for Now. Here's What to Know. Associated Press, July 4, 2024. Available at: https://apnews.com/article/europe-china-electric-vehicles-customs-trade-705e8f18964b2e77ec076675522bcc83

[30] The investigation also covers non-Chinese brands such as Tesla, Renault, and BMW which have production facilities in China.

[31] Chinese EV Makers Should Brace for Protectionist Policies Abroad – Nio CEO. *Reuters*, April 18, 2023. Available at: www.reuters.com/markets/asia/chinese-ev-makers-should-brace-protectionist-policies-abroad-nio-ceo-2023-04-18/

[32] US Debates How Much to Sever Electric Car Industry's Ties to China. *New York Times*, November 29, 2023.

[33] Lawmakers defined a foreign entity of concern to be any firm that is owned by, controlled by or subject to the jurisdiction of North Korea, China, Russia, or Iran.

Across the board, the narrative of "our companies" versus "their companies" is evident. Corporate nationality is a key element to benefiting from government support.

Corporate Nationality as an Advantage (or Disadvantage) in Global Competition

Another implication is that some firms will have new opportunities at the expense of others because of their corporate nationality. And perceptive firms might even go so far as to prominently advertise their corporate nationalities to take advantage of a real or perceived national advantage.

When the US Congress passed the CHIPS Act, it was meant to bolster domestic industry. But foreign companies such as Samsung Electronics and Taiwan Semiconductor Manufacturing Company were also in the mix to receive tax breaks and subsidies as long as they manufactured their products in the US. These companies were no doubt some of the most sophisticated memory chip manufacturers in the world, but their success in the US, especially in receiving favorable government treatment, was also partly driven by the fact that they come from South Korea and Taiwan, respectively, which were long-time US allies.

As in the previous discussion, the electric vehicle sector again highlights this dichotomy. Even as China's leading electric vehicle maker, BYD, set new sales records and scaled up operations in countries such as Thailand, Brazil, and Colombia, India remained a prized market, with its potential for large volume sales and the ability to serve as an export base. The company had been operating in India since 2007, including under a joint venture with a local company Megha Engineering. In 2023, as interest and competition in electric vehicles grew around the world, the company proposed a $1 billion investment to build electric cars and batteries and had a longer term vision of expanding to a full line up of BYD brand electric cars in India.[34] BYD

---

[34] BYD Proposes $1 Billion Plan to Build EVs, Batteries in India. *Asia Financial*, July 14, 2023. Available at: www.asiafinancial.com/byd-proposes-1-billion-plan-to-build-evs-batteries-in-india

submitted a proposal to the Indian regulators along with its long-time partner Megha Engineering that included plans for charging stations, R&D facilities, and training centers in the country. But in 2023, BYD faced a very different geopolitical situation than in 2013. Following border conflict in 2020, India had stricter investment rules and tightened scrutiny of Chinese investments in the country. The country's rules on foreign direct investment were updated in 2020 such that any proposed investment from countries that share a land border with India – largely viewed as targeting China – required explicit government permission. When BYD's proposal reached the regulators, it was widely debated and ultimately rejected. One official was reported as expressing concerns about the company's nationality, noting[35]: "Security concerns with respect to Chinese investments in India were flagged during the deliberations."

Another official said that India was "uncomfortable with Chinese automakers."[36] In other words, the fact that BYD was a Chinese company counted against it. It appeared that it was the company's corporate nationality rather than the investment proposal itself that was viewed unfavorably.

BYD's experience was in stark contrast with that of Tesla, its biggest and most consequential rival. Days after BYD's proposal was rejected, Tesla had a "red-carpet welcome from India for its proposal to invest in the country."[37] Following an initial meeting between Tesla's Elon Musk and the Indian Prime Minister during the latter's visit to New York a few months earlier, Tesla worked behind closed doors to fast track its proposed investment in the country. Although the specific details of the investment were not available,

---

[35] Modi Govt Rejects Chinese EV Maker BYD's $1b Mfg Plant Proposal in India! *The Times of India*, July 22, 2023. Available at: https://timesofindia.indiatimes.com/auto/news/modi-govt-rejects-chinese-ev-maker-byds-1b-mfg-plant-proposal-in-india/articleshow/102036056.cms?from=mdr

[36] In India, It's Advantage Tesla as Chinese Automakers Face Heat. *Reuters*, August 3, 2023. Available at: www.reuters.com/business/autos-transportation/india-its-advantage-tesla-chinese-automakers-face-heat-2023-08-02/

[37] Ibid.

the government had indicated it was open to expedite the approval process and welcome Tesla in the country.[38] This included discussions on significantly lowering the tax on imported cars of high value and allowing some of Tesla's Chinese suppliers to set up base in the country in partnership with local firms.

In this case, Tesla's advantage was again linked to its corporate nationality. With India building closer ties with the US, Tesla was seen as a safe bet for the country.

The other side of the coin is also in play. In some cases, Indian firms' corporate nationality could work to their advantage. In the pharmaceutical industry, China had long been the preferred destination for research and manufacturing services due to the relatively low cost and the speed offered by Chinese companies. But as rising geopolitical tensions have prompted calls from Western governments to "de-risk" supply chains and limit exposure to China, some biotech companies began to look to Indian manufacturers to produce active pharmaceutical ingredients for clinical trials and other work. One investment banker was quoted as saying[39]:

> Today you're probably not sending an RFP (request for proposal) to a Chinese company ... It's like, "I don't want to know, it doesn't matter if they can do it for cheaper, I'm not going to start putting my product into China."

In contrast, as US-based Glyscend Therapeutics explicitly observed, Indian contract development and manufacturing organizations would be preferred over Chinese ones. Consequently, some Indian

---

[38] Tesla's India Investment: Key Ministries Collaborate for Swift Entry of EV Maker. *Mint*, November 7, 2023. Available at: www.livemint.com/companies/news/teslas-india-investment-key-ministries-collaborate-for-swift-entry-of-ev-maker-11699338642955.html

[39] Indian Drug Manufacturers Benefit from Big Pharma Interest beyond China. *Reuters*, November 27, 2023. Available at: www.reuters.com/business/healthcare-pharmaceuticals/indian-drug-manufacturers-benefit-big-pharma-interest-beyond-china-2023-11-27/

companies have seen their sales grow 25–30 percent over a few years and doubled their workforce to keep up with new contracts from Western companies.

Corporate nationality is an advantage (or disadvantage) in global competition.

WHAT IS CORPORATE NATIONALITY ANYWAY?

When US authorities introduced new rules aimed at keeping Chinese components out of American electric cars, they excluded foreign made cars from federal grants and benefits. The law also excluded cars with battery components manufactured or assembled by a foreign entity of concern as well as cars that contain critical materials extracted, processed, or recycled by those entities.

US officials then quickly realized they faced a rather thorny problem. For the law to have any effect, they have to carefully define what a foreign entity of concern is. This is much harder than it seems.

What really is a foreign firm? Which country does a firm come from? How do we define corporate nationality? Is it based on where the firm has its headquarters or the location of incorporation? Or where most of its workforce is located? Perhaps a company's nationality reflects the country where its CEO and top management teams are based. What about board seats or voting rights? Who provides the funding? Maybe the location of shareholders matters. Or where the firm pays taxes. Perhaps where the company's meetings are held is an indicator. Others may point to the location where the firm's intellectual assets are produced and controlled.

In an attempt to seem more "American" than "Chinese," TikTok hired former Disney executive Kevin Mayer in 2020 as its new Chief Executive Officer and to serve as the Chief Operating Officer of the parent company ByteDance. The company stressed that TikTok was not owned by a Beijing-based entity because its parent company was incorporated in the Cayman Island, a tax haven.[40] But

---

[40] Disney's Head of Streaming Is New TikTok C.E.O. *The New York Times*, May 18, 2020.

this claim did not square with Beijing rolling out export control rules that would require ByteDance to seek approval from the Chinese government before it could reach a deal with foreign buyers.[41]

Or take the case of Paytm, India's largest payment platform with more than 300 million registered customers and over 20 million merchants. It was founded in India in 2010 and the digital payment gateway was developed in the country by Indian developers. The company hired over 7,000 people in the country. Yet, it faced scrutiny for being "Chinese" because it was backed by Alibaba and Ant group.[42] Since it also had other big name foreign investors such as Softbank and Warren Buffet's Berkshire Hathaway, should it be treated as a "foreign" company?

The issue of nationality is often contested in international legal proceedings. Trade and investment treaties negotiated by pairs or groups of countries often include a provision by which investors from one signatory country can take legal action against the other signatory state if the firm believes that the foreign government's actions harmed its investment in that country. The treaties are almost always exclusionary, that is, only "their" firms can potentially benefit from the treaty but not "other" firms from countries that are not signatories to the treaty. However, some countries have a very generous interpretation of "their" companies. The Netherlands is a prominent example. There are nearly 100 Dutch bilateral treaties with strong investment protection terms, so Dutch investors have it pretty good. But who is a Dutch investor? Many Dutch claims are by "foreign" investors, or companies whose ultimate or controlling parent is not based in the Netherlands. Shell companies are set up in the jurisdiction of the

---

[41] China's Maneuver Means TikTok's US Suitors Could End Up with a Shell Company. *Quartz*, August 31, 2020. Available at: https://qz.com/1897682/beijing-interrupts-tiktok-sale-talks-with-new-export-rules

[42] Is PayTM Chinese? Here Is the Real Reason Why It Was Taken Down from Google Play Store. *India Times*, September 18, 2020. Available at: www.indiatimes.com/technology/news/paytm-app-which-country-chinese-or-indian-523119.html

Netherlands with the sole objective of leveraging generous tax breaks and investment protection. Such mailbox companies have initiated claims of over $100 billion against other governments for alleged damages to their profitability.

In one case, *Saluka Investment* v. *The Czech Republic*,[43] the arbitration tribunal explicitly expressed sympathy "for the argument that a company which has no real connection with a State party to a BIT [Bilateral Investment Treaty], and which is in reality a mere shell company controlled by another company which is not constituted under the laws of the State, should not be entitled to invoke the provisions of that treaty. [...] Such a possibility lends itself to abuses of the arbitral procedure, and to practices of 'treaty shopping' which can share many of the disadvantages of the widely criticized practice of 'forum shopping'."

As the above examples show, defining corporate nationality is indeed a tricky business.

In the case of US rules on electric cars, the American government provided some guidelines: A foreign entity of concern is a company headquartered in or owned or controlled by China, Russia, Iran, or North Korea. Additionally, any company in which the government of these countries holds 2 percent or more of a board's seats, voting rights, or shares would fall under the rules.[44] But expect more debate on this.

SHAPING CORPORATE NATIONALITY

In global competition, *where* a firm is from shapes the opportunities it has, the strategies it can adopt, and its financial performance. But while firms can't change their country of origin, or where they were founded, they can shape others' perceptions of their nationality.

---

[43] Quoted in "The Netherlands: A Gateway to 'Treaty Shopping' for Investment Protection," *Investment Treaty News*, January 12, 2012. Available at: www.iisd.org/itn/en/2012/01/12/the-netherlands-treaty-shopping/

[44] US Aims to Limit China's Role in Electric Cars. *BBC*, December 2, 2023. Available at: www.bbc.com/news/business-67593199

Masking Country of Origin

In the twentieth century, "cloaking" was a common strategy among German firms. They changed their organizational structure to camouflage ownership or relocated to neutral countries to avoid political risk. As a result, they were able to avoid taxation, circulate capital and products, and importantly, protect their assets from interference by governments.

The German company Beiersdorf is an interesting example.[45]

Founded in Hamburg, Germany in 1882, Beiersdorf quickly found fame with its innovative products such as band-aids, Pebeco toothpaste, and Nivea skin cream. Its marketing efforts persuaded consumers to pay a premium for its products and investment in distribution channels supported these initiatives. The company was eager to expand abroad. They extended production and sales, especially for their toothpaste brand, to markets such as the US, Great Britain, Austria, Mexico, Denmark, Argentina, Russia, France, and Australia. By 1914, exports accounted for 42 percent of the company's total sales. But World War I threw a spanner in the works for international activities. The planned international rollout of the Nivea skin cream was put on hold. By the end of the war, German assets were expropriated, sold, or seized for reparations. Beiersdorf's foreign businesses ceased to exist. Their brands and trademarks found their way to competitors' hands.

After the war, the company tried to pick up the pieces and continue its international expansion. The company was focused on strategies to protect the firm in case of future political risks. To this end, they founded new companies in two countries that had stayed neutral in World War I: Switzerland and the Netherlands. The Swiss firm held Beiersdorf's trademarks in Switzerland and other countries where a Swiss owner was politically preferable to a German one. The Dutch company was created to retrieve trademarks that

---

[45] This section draws on Jones, G., & Lubinski, C. (2012). Managing political risk in global business: Beiersdorf 1914–1990. *Enterprise & Society*, 13(1), 85–119.

had been lost in Great Britain, something that a German company would not have been allowed to do. In the 1930s, after the Nazis came to power, the firm's Jewish heritage, ownership, and management introduced new political challenges. Using its foreign affiliates, Beiersdorf transferred its Jewish employees outside of Germany. When Germany's subsequent foreign exchange controls increased the tax obligation and repatriation requirements for the German-based Beiersdorf, based on its control of international affiliates, it became necessary to separate foreign affiliates from the parent company and limit the German state's influence. In 1934, they established a ring structure, where Amsterdam was in the middle of a ring of foreign affiliates. The Dutch company was responsible for raw material acquisition, quality control, R&D, advertising, and general administration. Other foreign affiliates in the ring contributed a fee to finance the central operations in the Netherlands. The local operations in countries such as Switzerland, France, and the US only held trademarks, and occasionally plant and equipment, while the actual business was contracted to local companies in those countries on a profit-sharing basis. The parent company in Germany received a license fee based on turnover. Beiersdorf became two legally separated entities, the German business and the foreign business.

Fast forward several decades, and a similar strategy is being used by firms in the midst of geopolitical tensions. Several consumer facing Chinese companies in the US are trying to distance themselves from their roots and shape perception of their corporate nationality. PDD – the owner of the online superstore Temu – moved its headquarters nearly 6,000 miles to Ireland.[46] Other approaches include switching to overseas cloud centers and relocating executives abroad.

---

[46] These Hugely Successful Companies Came from China. But You'd Never Know. *CNN Business*, May 5, 2023. Available at: https://edition.cnn.com/2023/05/04/business/china-born-companies-downplay-roots-dst-intl-hnk/index.html

Localization

The year was 2020. People were encountering a head spinning number of changes to daily life, thanks to the COVID-19 pandemic. By April, about 3 billion people were living in countries where borders were closed to nonresidents and noncitizens.[47] More than half of humanity was restricted in some form. And Zoom became the lifeline for millions. The company began trading on the stock market just a year earlier. During lockdowns, Zoom went from a niche business to a daily necessity. There were Zoom meetings, of course, but also Zoom birthdays, weddings, and baby showers. Zoom became a verb.

But Zoom, the noun, was also facing stiff opposition from governments. In the US, the House Speaker Nancy Pelosi referred to Zoom as "a Chinese entity" in a television interview.[48] Although the company was founded in the US and run by an American CEO, it had a product development team that was largely based in China. Hence, the concern.

Halfway across the world, Indian regulators were considering banning the service as part of a larger effort to limit Chinese apps in the country following border clashes. Zoom had to go the extra mile to establish its credentials. And one way was to showcase its top management with Indian roots; Aparna Bawa, the Chief Operating Officer; Sunil Madan, Corporate Chief Information Officer, and Velchamy Sankarlingam, the President. Bawa referred to growing up in India, studying grade school in Bengaluru before moving to the US during her teens. Sankarlingam highlighted his own Indian roots, saying[49]:

---

[47] Nearly 40% of World's Population Living in Countries with Closed Borders amid Coronavirus Outbreak, Analysis Finds. *Newsweek*, April 2, 2020. Available at: www.newsweek.com/nearly-40-living-countries-closed-borders-amid-covid-19-outbreak-1495697

[48] Nancy Pelosi Called Zoom "a Chinese Entity," but It's an American Company with an American CEO. *CNBC*, April 15, 2020. Available at: www.cnbc.com/2020/04/15/nancy-pelosi-calls-zoom-a-chinese-entity.html

[49] Is Zoom American or Chinese? App's Indian President Clears the Air. ETNowNews.com, July 8, 2020. Available at: www.timesnownews.com/business-economy/companies/article/is-zoom-american-or-chinese-the-apps-indian-president-clears-the-air/618486

"I grew up in Virudhunagar, a place known for K Kamaraj. I studied in Montfort in Yercaud and then Anna University. I still have connections in Virudhunagar and am a member of the Golf Club of Kodaikanal."

And the company emphasized its goal of becoming more embedded in the country. The President described the company's offices and data centers in India and alluded to further investment. "We also have plans for significant investment in the country over the next five years and beyond, including expanding our footprint and hiring more top talent in the region."

In the end, Zoom did not join the list of banned Chinese apps/companies. Rather, by 2021, India was Zoom's largest market in terms of mobile downloads.[50] Whether the company's attempts to showcase its "Indianness" had anything to do with their rapid growth in the country is debatable. But it points to a common strategy to shape perceptions of corporate nationality: localization. When firms face disadvantages due to their country of origin, or perceptions thereof, localization can be an effective strategy to minimize their liability. Research has suggested that actions such as corporate political activity, corporate social responsibility (CSR), local sourcing, or other types of embeddedness can be particularly critical to bridge legitimacy gaps.

In one study, researchers tracked 157 of the largest multinational firms from emerging markets.[51] These companies, they reasoned, faced a liability of origin, that is, negative perceptions in foreign markets about the willingness and ability to conduct legitimate business because of where they are from. The researchers argued that one way to overcome this liability of origin is to report

---

[50] India Is Zoom's Largest Market in Terms of Mobile Downloads: Report. *The Hindu Business Line*, July 11, 2021. Available at: www.thehindubusinessline.com/info-tech/india-is-zooms-largest-market-in-terms-of-mobile-downloads-report/article35261413.ece

[51] Marano, V., Tashman, P., & Kostova, T. (2017). Escaping the iron cage: Liabilities of origin and CSR reporting of emerging market multinational enterprises. *Journal of International Business Studies, 48*, 386–408.

about their CSR initiatives, or activities that create social value and reduce firms' negative externalities. Corporate social responsibility reporting allows firms to position themselves as adhering to widely accepted global norms of good corporate behavior rather than being associated with the weak institutions and reputations of their home countries. So, CSR reporting can help emerging market multinational firms to disassociate themselves from their home countries. When they examined the data, they found that the worse the liability of origin was the more likely emerging market multinational firms were to report their CSR activities.

In a different study, researchers focused on publicly traded firms in the US with foreign institutional ownership.[52] These are firms where foreign entities have the power to influence the management or operations of the company, through ownership of the US company's securities, contractual agreement, or other means. The researchers argued that these firms were subject to heightened regulatory scrutiny, such as review by the Committee on Foreign Investment in the United States (CFIUS) – a federal interagency committee with broad authority to investigate controlling and non-controlling foreign investment stakes in US companies and to intervene as necessary. This agency can force divestments, such as when they forced the transfer of a minority investment stake in the US cybersecurity company Cofense from a Russia-linked private-equity firm to a fund managed by the American company BlackRock. US firms with foreign institutional ownership also face indirect scrutiny and criticism from politicians and regulators, who are looking to advance their own political agendas. The researchers argued that firms susceptible to such pressures resort to lobbying and donations to political action committees. These actions allow firms to monitor and engage with government officials and shape the narrative

---

[52] Shi, W., Gao, C., & Aguilera, R. V. (2021). The liabilities of foreign institutional ownership: Managing political dependence through corporate political spending. *Strategic Management Journal*, 42(1), 84–113.

influencing policymaking. When they examined the data, they found that a US firm's level of foreign institutional ownership was in fact related to its corporate political spending.

Transferring Control Rights

A firm's ability to shape and influence its systems, methods, and decision with the goal of achieving specific outcomes are commonly referred to as its control rights. When these rights are located in a particular jurisdiction, the firm itself is subject to influence from that country's institutions and authorities. But if the firm were to move its control rights and decision-making power to a different jurisdiction, it could potentially reshape perceptions of its corporate nationality.

A firm could do this in two ways. First, it can relocate the company's headquarters and top management team to a friendly country. Second, it can transfer ownership and control of foreign country operations to a local partner. In one study, my collaborators and I examined whether such strategies are helpful in reshaping perceptions of nationality.[53] Our study focused on Shein, one of several dozen Chinese apps that were banned by the Indian government in 2020 following border clashes and worsening geopolitical ties between China and India. Subsequently, Shein moved its headquarters from China to Singapore, a country with more cooperative geopolitical ties with India than its home country.[54] Shein's CEO and founder also chose to relocate to Singapore and obtain permanent residency there. In May 2023, Shein concluded an agreement to reenter India in partnership with Reliance, an Indian conglomerate.[55] Under this partnership, Reliance would retain full equity control and pay Shein a licensing

---

[53] Blake, D., Jandhyala, S., Beazer, Q., and Cunha, R. (2024). Geopolitics and the Location Strategy of Multinational Enterprises. Working Paper.

[54] Chinese Companies Set Up in Singapore to Hedge against Geopolitical Risk. *Financial Times*, November 30, 2022. Available at: www.ft.com/content/a0c11e3e-ab72-4b4b-a55c-557191e53938

[55] Shein Is about to Return to India in a Big Way. *CNN*, 26 May 2023. Available at: https://edition.cnn.com/2023/05/26/business/shein-reliance-india-return-intl-hnk/index.html

fee. In addition, Shein would provide production support and training for local apparel suppliers, source materials locally, and develop an export hub. In granting Shein the right to reenter the Indian market, the Indian government reportedly considered the company to be a "non-Chinese entity."[56]

However, we should consider how footloose a company's headquarters can be. Some argue that headquarters of multinational corporations can be relocated with relative ease as they tend to have low costs compared to the overall cost structure of the firm and that location of finely sliced activities are constantly reassessed in large multinational corporations. This means companies instrumentally choose specific locations for their headquarters.[57] Others, however, challenge this view and argue that "inertial forces are strong, making this a rare event." Most headquarters continue to be in the same location as the one in which the company was founded.[58]

Partnerships with Foreign Firms

Another potential pathway to reshaping corporate nationality is to purposefully delink the company from its home country. As we discussed in other research, this could be achieved through extensive partnerships or mergers and acquisitions with foreign firms.[59]

One example is that of Da Jiang Innovations (DJI). It is the largest manufacturer of consumer drones, which are used in a variety of applications, including by emergency responders, in agriculture, and video production. The company accounted for about 70% of the global commercial drone market and about 80% of the US market in

---

[56] Fashion Giant Shein to Diversify Supply Chain beyond China with Indian Fabrics. *The Wall Street Journal*, May 19, 2023. Available at: www.wsj.com/articles/shein-makes-a-comeback-in-india-teams-up-with-reliance-retail-f4826338

[57] Coeurderoy, R., & Verbeke, A. (2016). The unbalanced geography of the world's largest MNEs: Institutional quality and head office distribution across countries. *Global Strategy Journal*, 6(2), 127–148.

[58] Meyer, K., & Benito, G. (2016). Where do MNEs locate their headquarters? At home! *Global Strategy Journal*, 6(2), 149–159.

[59] Blake, D., Jandhyala, S., Beazer, Q., & Cunha, R. (2024). Managing Geopolitics in the Digital Age. Working Paper.

2024. But its business was overshadowed by a bipartisan bill in the United States House to significantly limit its access to the US communications infrastructure on which its products run.[60] The fact that DJI did not manufacture military grade equipment or pursue business opportunities for combat use did not prevent it from being seen as a threat in the US. The main concern remained that collection of private and public data could strengthen Chinese efforts in technological and military dominance.

Da Jiang Innovations first invested heavily in lobbying and raising grass roots support from drone operators. Through the Drone Advocacy Alliance,[61] they aimed to collaborate with other drone manufacturers and lawmakers. This effort also provided resources for drone users to make their voices heard and offered resources for contacting elected officials.

But it also took another path to "somehow cleanse its Chineseness from their technology to make it so that there was still an avenue" for sales in the United States.[62] Meet Anzu Robotics, a one-man start-up that believed it could answer US government concerns. Anzu was an independent company that was founded by Randall Warnas, an American citizen, and former DJI employee. The company licensed DJI design for its drones and used a plant in Malaysia to assemble products, although some parts still came from China. In the United States, these drones began to be operated by flight-control software and a user app that originated with DJI but was modified by Anzu's US based data security partner Aloft. All data from drones were encrypted and stored on servers based in Virginia while a US-based cybersecurity firm verifies safety. With these safeguards in place, Anzu argues that the American public

---

[60] What You Need to Know about the DJI Ban in the United States. Associated Press, June 21, 2024. Available at: https://apnews.com/buyline-shopping/article/dji-drone-ban-in-the-us

[61] See https://droneadvocacyalliance.com/

[62] Are These Drones Too Chinese to Pass U.S. Muster in an Anti-China Moment? *The New York Times*, May 24, 2024. Available at: www.nytimes.com/2024/05/24/business/china-drones-anzu-dji.html

can use "the world's best drone technology" while "complying with country-of-origin ownership concerns."[63]

In another example, Seafile, a low-code application developer from China, expanded internationally through a joint venture with the German company.[64] The joint venture company then successfully signed up hundreds of thousands of users for its products, including the German Armed Forces.

CLOSING REFLECTIONS ON CORPORATE NATIONALITY

Today's multinational firm may have a distributed value chain across locations, hold portfolios of brands in different countries, have a diverse top management team and dispersed shareholders, serve customers of different nationalities, and engage governments around the world. Yet, the question is still relevant: where are you *really* from?

In the Spring of 2020, as the world tried to navigate the COVID-19 pandemic, the Edelman Trust Barometer surveyed individuals across eleven countries.[65] Among other issues, individuals were asked whether they agree with the statement: "A global CEO's first priority should be to use the power and resources of their companies to help the people of the country where they are headquartered before helping people in other countries where they do business."

An average of 60% of the respondents agreed with the statement. And that share was as high as 86% in China, 75% in India, and 73% in Mexico. The nationality of a firm is front and center, whether it wants it to be or not. It has a major influence on what the firm can do, and how it can achieve its objectives. And this seems to be growing with geopolitical tensions.

---

[63] China's Dominant Drone Industry Is a Step Ahead of Congress. *The Hill*, June 12, 2024. Available at: https://thehill.com/policy/defense/4714269-chinas-dominant-drone-industry-is-a-step-ahead-of-congress/

[64] How SeaTable Navigates the China Backlash as It Goes West. *TechCrunch*, May 26, 2023. Available at: https://techcrunch.com/2023/05/26/seatable-seafile-profile/

[65] Edelman Trust Barometer 2020, Spring Update: Trust and the COVID-19 Pandemic. Available at: www.edelman.com/sites/g/files/aatuss191/files/2020-05/2020%20Edelman%20Trust%20Barometer%20Spring%20Update.pdf

3   Geopolitics and Innovation

Take a moment to think about the big challenges facing our world. Pause, close your eyes, and contemplate the biggest problems humanity faces. From conflicts, climate change, and pandemics to food security, migration, and jobs, the challenges are immense. And we need innovative solutions to overcome them. New ideas, products, processes, business systems, organizational forms, and bold reforms play a central role in shaping our societies and worlds.

But where do pathbreaking new ideas come from[1] In the popular press, radical innovation is often characterized as the work of the lone genius; as a single, simple observation, a flash of brilliance, and – eureka – a new world is born. The reality could not be further from that. What starts as an idea for a new product or service depends on thousands of forces, seen and unseen, to be transformed into its functional form.

An article in the *Harvard Business Review* offers a very informative story of innovation at a large technology company.[2] The company won a multimillion-dollar contract to design a sensor that could detect pollutants at very small concentrations underwater. It was an unusually complex problem, so the firm set up a team of crack microchip designers, and they started putting their heads together. About forty-five minutes into their first working session, the marine biologist assigned to their team walked in with a bag of clams and set them on the table. Seeing the confused looks of the chip designers, the biologist

---

[1] Parts of the following sections draw on my talk at the 2019 India Conference on Innovation, Intellectual Property and Competition as well as the article "Diplomacy and Innovation", Council on Business and Society Insights 21 November 2019. Available at: https://cobsinsights.org/2019/11/21/diplomacy-and-innovation/

[2] Satell, G. (2017). The 4 types of innovation and the problems they solve. *Harvard Business Review*, 11, 2–9. Available at: https://hbr.org/2017/06/the-4-types-of-innovation-and-the-problems-they-solve

explained that that clams can detect pollutants at just a few parts per million, and when that happens, they open their shells. As it turned out, this company didn't really need a fancy chip to detect pollutants – just a simple one that could alert the system to clams opening their shells. So, the company could save $999,000 and eat clams for dinner!

That, in essence, is the value of knowledge and information from different sources. To solve a really difficult problem, it is often helpful to expand skill domains beyond the specialists in a single field. It is just these kinds of unlikely combinations that are key to coming up with breakthroughs. In fact, a study analyzing 17.9 million scientific papers found that the most highly cited work tended to be generally rooted within a traditional field, with just a smidgen of insight taken from some unconventional place. The highest-impact science is primarily grounded in exceptionally conventional combinations of prior work, yet simultaneously features an intrusion of unusual combinations.[3]

THE INTERNATIONAL FACE OF INNOVATION

Innovation and Foreign Knowledge Sources

In July 2017, a farmer in Maharashtra walked into the local police station with a rather peculiar problem – he wanted to file a complaint against the Indian Meteorological Department for a "wrong monsoon forecast."[4] Monsoon rain had commenced by the end of May, and after a brief spell of heavy showers in early June, the sky had turned completely dry for over a month decimating the farmer's cotton and jowar crop. He lost nearly Rs. 50,000 (approximately USD 602) per hectare. He contended that Marathi newspapers had published monsoon forecasts predicting good rains for two months, and asked, "why are we spending lakhs of rupees on people and satellites to make those predictions?." The police, in the end, did not register this complaint.

---

[3] Uzzi, B., Mukherjee, S., Stringer, M., & Jones, B. (2013). Atypical combinations and scientific impact. *Science, 342*(6157), 468–472.

[4] The Art of Monsoon Forecasting in India, and the Science behind It. *Live Mint*, August 2, 2018, Available at: www.livemint.com/Politics/Z10z9lZHnne1RgoRtVvUEK/The-art-of-monsoon-forecasting-in-India-and-the-science-beh.html

But the Indian Met Department, like others around the world, has a very challenging task in predicting patterns of rainfall or other weather patterns around the country. Climate models are difficult to build, and microlevel predictions that focus on small areas are even harder. Increasingly, these predictions rely on supercomputer simulation-driven methods. The key to this approach is high quality data to train the models; relevant data points are not only from within a country but also from around the world. Ocean temperatures, El-Nino effects, sea ice conditions, sea levels, salinity, and wind speeds from across the globe are important parameters. Collecting and reporting such information requires global coordination.

India, like many other countries, gets a large chunk of global weather data through systems put in place by the United Nations. The World Meteorological Organization – a UN organization where India has been a member since 1949 – facilitates international cooperation for the delivery and use of high-quality, authoritative weather, climate, hydrological and related environmental services for use by all its members. They coordinate daily observations from about 10,000 weather stations, 7,000 ships, and 3,000 aircraft to measure the key parameters of the atmosphere, land, and ocean surface. In the ocean alone, they oversee nearly 9,000 observing platforms around the world and 170 satellites that continually monitor the global ocean and atmosphere. They standardize the instrumentation, observation practices, and timing of these observations worldwide. Weather models are initialized using this observed data. Thus, international knowledge sources are important in our preparations for adverse weather events such as floods, heat waves, cold waves, and lightning.

Traditional models of innovation assumed companies in the most advanced countries developed innovative solutions that they subsequently rolled out to other regions of the world. But more recent work has challenged this assumption and highlighted how societies and organizations can access, utilize, and assimilate knowledge from around the world to develop innovative solutions.

During the COVID pandemic, for example, a key challenge was how to screen and treat the population without infecting medical staff or compromising the health system. Inspired by the drive through counters at American companies such as McDonalds and Starbucks, the Kyungpook National University Chilgok Hospital in Daegu, South Korea, first introduced a drive through testing center. Patients did not leave their cars during the medical exam that included a nasopharyngeal and oropharyngeal swab. Healthcare workers attired in personal protective equipment (PPE) minimized their contact with potentially infectious patients. This procedure was further modified into a walk-through screening center. The two innovations were subsequently adopted in the United States, Italy, Denmark, Australia, and other countries.[5] As this example highlights, there is no monopoly on good ideas; they can come from anywhere in the world.

Multinational companies know this. They scanned the globe for fresh knowledge and innovative ideas. When a firm operates in multiple countries, it has access to local knowledge networks in different geographic locations. It is precisely by leveraging these different knowledge sources that innovative solutions can be found.

Take, for example, General Electric's (GE) experience with ultrasound machines.[6] The American company launched high-end and high-priced ultrasound machines in the United States in 1979. Looking for additional markets overseas, the company targeted China. However, after more than a decade of operations there, GE's annual sales in 1995 were only $5 million and growing slowly. But the company managed a turnaround. By 2009, GE was the market leader with a 30 percent market share. How they managed to

---

[5] Cannavale, C., Claudio, L., & Simoni, M. (2021). How social innovations spread globally through the process of reverse innovation: A case-study from the South Korea. *Italian Journal of Marketing*, 2021(4), 421–440. https://doi.org/10.1007/s43039-021-00027-8

[6] Excerpted from Govindarajan, V., & Ramamurti, R. (2011). Reverse innovation, emerging markets, and global strategy. *Global Strategy Journal*, 1, 191–205. https://doi.org/10.1002/gsj.23

achieve it is an illuminating story of global ties, local knowledge, and innovative partnerships.

GE learnt that while in the US, performance mattered most followed by features, it was different in China. Here, price was most important followed by portability. This was because more than 90 percent of China's population relied on poorly funded, low-tech hospitals or basic clinics in rural areas. Ultrasound machines had to travel to patients, not the other way around. And rural doctors had to be trained in using the machines. Rather than trying to modify the existing product, GE's China team started from scratch. They used miniaturized hardware from standard laptop computers and shifted most of the muscle inside the ultrasound machine from hardware to software. Importantly, the team in China remained under local control, retaining profit and loss responsibility along with the power to set its own strategy. At the same time, the Chinese team also benefited from accessing GE's global resource base. Team leaders met with other worldwide ultrasound leaders within GE to periodically share engineering and business insights. Software expertise came via experts from Israel. Relevant software modules developed by other global research and development (R&D) centers were incorporated. Together, they were able to compact ultrasound machines.

As it turned out, those compact machines also had a market elsewhere, including in the United States where they were used in emergency rooms and to guide anesthesiologists' placement of needles and catheters. Compact ultrasounds were a $278 million global product line for GE within six years of launch and growing at 50 to 60 percent per year.

Challenges in Integrating Foreign Knowledge

As the examples earlier in this chapter indicate, innovative solutions can emerge when combining knowledge and information from different technologies, expertise, and regions of the world. But those are the success stories, and doing so is very challenging, for a variety of reasons. Knowledge and information don't exist in a vacuum; and how it is perceived, interpreted, understood, and evaluated is shaped by national systems, government policies, funding and regulation, education and research systems, and the patterns and attitudes of workers and investors.

As an example, what is the first thing that comes to your mind when I say "windows"? Perhaps you thought of structures in buildings that you can open to let the air in. Or you might have thought of the operating system that is running on your computer. Or something else entirely. The point is we don't all perceive the same information in similar ways, we perceive it as we are or what our experiences primed us to do. This creates challenges for actors trying to combine knowledge across contexts in innovative ways. Collaboration is hard because individuals have assumptions.

Another challenge is the "not-invented-here" syndrome where individuals and groups reject ideas from outsiders or view initiatives from other locations with suspicion and hostility. Inventors who are far away from corporate headquarters or lack collaborative networks within the firm have their inventions disregarded even when those inventions are of higher quality.[7] Alternately, individuals and firms worry about knowledge leakage to competitors and are thus less likely to share even if innovations are possible.

These issues create real challenges in spurring cross-border collaboration in innovation. Given these constraints, it is perhaps not surprising that only around 20% of scientific articles were published with international coauthors and less than 10% of patents filed in a country were with foreign coauthors.[8]

Take the example of climate change. Limiting temperature rise through the reduction of greenhouse gas emissions is a major global challenge. Although it is a global problem that requires a globally

---

[7] Kumar, A., & Operti, E. (2023). Missed chances and unfulfilled hopes: Why do firms make errors in evaluating technological opportunities?. *Strategic Management Journal, 44*(13), 3067–3097.

[8] Ghemawat, P. (2018: 20). *The new global roadmap: Enduring strategies for turbulent times*. Boston, MA: Harvard Business Review Press.

coordinated solution, different levels of development, technological sophistication, regulations, and expectations around the world make globally coordinated actions difficult. For instance, while scientists have been working on many different technological solutions, there is significant disagreement over which ones will be the most likely winners and hence deserving of support and attention.

In one approach, much emphasis remains on scaling up renewable energy production. Others propose capturing and storing industrial carbon emissions, though countries have historically focused on different methods to do this: The US has emphasized injecting captured emissions into the ground, but India has eschewed storage for turning carbon-rich materials into synthetic gas.[9]

One solution to overcoming the challenges of cross-border knowledge transfer is countries' participation in intergovernmental organizations. National governments sign treaties to participate in organizations such as the United Nations, the World Bank, and the World Trade Organization.

One such organization dealing with climate change is the Carbon Sequestration Leadership Forum.[10] Launched in 2003, it aims to enable coordinated action on carbon capture and storage, develop cost effective technologies, and promote the implementation of these technologies with an appropriate regulatory framework. Participating governments have noted that the international forum allows them to coordinate data on important policy initiatives as well as regulatory and legal developments. For instance, there is sharing of information on how governments can approach liability for the release of stored carbon dioxide, ownership of injected carbon dioxide, intellectual property protection for the transfer of technology, and the establishment of a sound regulatory framework.

---

[9] IEA Calls for Fast Action on Carbon Storage in Developing World. *New York Times*, October 12, 2009. Available at: www.nytimes.com/cwire/2009/10/12/12climatewire-iea-calls-for-fast-action-on-carbon-storage-50514.html?pagewanted=all

[10] Drawn from Jandhyala, S., & Phene, A. (2015). The role of intergovernmental organizations in cross-border knowledge transfer and innovation. *Administrative Science Quarterly*, 60(4), 712–743.

In addition to policy initiatives, the Carbon Sequestration Leadership Forum also provides technological direction. A technical group identifies and recognizes projects from member countries that show significant advancement toward commercialization and large-scale development. Cutting-edge projects get greater global visibility and information about their technical performance and financial viability are widely shared among members. The Forum has also been instrumental in generating technical reports on the state of carbon capture and storage technologies. These reports provide useful information for companies and other laboratories to leverage in their own R&D. Further opportunities for knowledge transfer are created by organizing a variety of meetings, conferences, and workshops in cities across the globe.

Global initiatives like this one facilitate cross-border knowledge transfer and spur domestic innovation. We examined the consequences of a country's participation in intergovernmental organizations that focus on knowledge sharing. Data on eighty-three countries over the time period 1996–2006 showed that countries participating in a greater number of intergovernmental organizations were associated with a larger number of domestic patents. For example, participating in twelve additional intergovernmental organizations was associated with approximately sixty additional patents per year for a country like Spain or seventeen additional patents a year for a country like Mexico.

INNOVATION AS THE BATTLEFIELD OF GEOPOLITICAL TENSIONS

Notwithstanding efforts to facilitate cross-border transfer of knowledge, geopolitical tensions tend to exacerbate challenges to international coordination in significant ways. On the face of it, far-away conflicts or tensions between states may not have much to do with private-sector companies and their daily operations including patenting and R&D functions. Yet, when one study examined the innovative output of more than 4,600 US publicly listed companies in relation to a geopolitical risk index that includes events such as the

US bombing of Libya, conflicts in Iraq, and the 2016 terrorist attacks in Paris, they came to a surprising conclusion.[11] Rising geopolitical risk stifles innovation. A 1% increase in risk is associated with 0.24% decrease in financial value of patents granted to firms, and the greatest impact is on companies with more foreign customers.

The landscape of global innovation is shifting in significant ways because innovation is seen as the central arena of geopolitical tensions. Countries around the world see leadership in scientific and technological innovation as the central tenet of international competition. In 2008, China spent only a third as much as the US on R&D. By 2014, it had surpassed Europe's spending on R&D, and by 2020 was spending 85 percent of America's.[12]

Correspondingly, China's share of patents has been rising over the years and by 2022 the country was leading the world in highly cited academic research.[13] In 2023, the Chinese President urged the country to step up the pace of technological breakthroughs.[14] In response, Western countries are trying hard to retain their technological edge with increased research spending coupled with restrictions on exporting and sharing technology. These developments are changing the face of innovation.

Why is cutting-edge technology the center of geopolitical tensions? Governments aim to have a leg up in the innovation contest for at least two related reasons: national security and economic competitiveness.

---

[11] Astvansh, V., Deng, W., & Habib, A. (2022). When Geopolitical Risk Rises, Innovation Stalls. *Harvard Business Review* (HBR.org), March 3, 2023. Available at: https://hbr.org/2022/03/research-when-geopolitical-risk-rises-innovation-stalls

[12] China and the West Are in a Race to Foster Innovation. *The Economist*, October 13, 2022. Available at: www.economist.com/briefing/2022/10/13/china-and-the-west-are-in-a-race-to-foster-innovation

[13] China Tops US in Quantity and Quality of Scientific Papers. *Nikkei Asia*, August 10, 2022. Available at: https://asia.nikkei.com/Business/Science/China-tops-U.S.-in-quantity-and-quality-of-scientific-papers

[14] Step up Pace of Technological Breakthroughs, Chinese President Xi Jinping Urges. *South China Morning Post*, September 25, 2023. Available at: www.scmp.com/news/china/politics/article/3235764/step-pace-technological-breakthroughs-chinese-president-xi-jinping-urges

Countries that control the most advanced technologies tend to have superior strategic advantages, including military advantages. In other words, innovation sustains military power. The Department of Defense in the US explicitly noted that their ability to accelerate innovation and adopt key technologies was critical to building an enduring military advantage.[15]

If rival countries had access to the same (or superior) technologies, they would be able to catch up or surpass a country's military capabilities, undermining its national security. As a result, even dual-use technologies, that is, those which can be employed for both civilian and military purposes will be tightly restricted.

Second, economic factors play a role. By limiting foreign access to cutting-edge innovations, governments seek to protect their domestic industries and maintain leadership in critical technology sectors. A classic example is that of semiconductor chips. In *Chip War*, the economic historian Chris Miller documented how better and faster chips, often developed by Silicon Valley firms, allowed the US to render Russian's arsenal of precision guided weapons obsolete during the Cold War.[16] As semiconductor chips become more ubiquitous (they are embedded in military equipment, cars, planes, electric grids, communication devices, and virtually everything else), the US has a strong incentive to maintain the technological lead.

Ukraine offers another example of technology competence leading to military advantage. Eric Schmidt, the former CEO of Google, writing in *Foreign Affairs* observed[17]:

---

[15] DOD Harnessing Emerging Tech to Maintain Enduring Advantage. DOD News, US Department of Defense, September 21, 2023. Available at: www.defense.gov/News/News-Stories/Article/Article/3532946/dod-harnessing-emerging-tech-to-maintain-enduring-advantage/

[16] Miller, C. (2022). *Chip war: The fight for the world's most critical technology*. Simon & Schuster.

[17] Schmidt, E. (2023). Innovation power: Why technology will define the future of geopolitics. *Foreign Affairs, 102*, 38.

When Russian forces marched on Kyiv in February 2022, few thought Ukraine could survive. Russia had more than twice as many soldiers as Ukraine. Its military budget was more than ten times as large. The U.S. intelligence community estimated that Kyiv would fall within one to two weeks at most.

Outgunned and outmanned, Ukraine turned to one area in which it held an advantage over the enemy: technology. Shortly after the invasion, the Ukrainian government uploaded all its critical data to the cloud, so that it could safeguard information and keep functioning even if Russian missiles turned its ministerial offices into rubble. The country's Ministry of Digital Transformation, which Ukrainian President Volodymyr Zelensky had established just two years earlier, repurposed its e-government mobile app, Diia, for open-source intelligence collection, so that citizens could upload photos and videos of enemy military units. With their communications infrastructure in jeopardy, the Ukrainians turned to Starlink satellites and ground stations provided by SpaceX to stay connected. When Russia sent Iranian-made drones across the border, Ukraine acquired its own drones specially designed to intercept their attacks while its military learned how to use unfamiliar weapons supplied by Western allies. In the cat- and-mouse game of innovation, Ukraine simply proved nimbler. And so what Russia had imagined would be a quick and easy invasion has turned out to be anything but.

Techno-nationalism and Keeping Innovations at Home

A growing sentiment of techno-nationalism broadly alludes to the idea of retaining a domestic technological edge in sectors that are key to national security. Foreign firms should not undermine domestic innovation efforts and the local edge. In some ways, this is not much different from traditional approaches to national security. The US, for instance, had rules since 1950, that can be used to reject foreign investments that threaten national security. There have long been restrictions on sharing of technologies that were seen as crucial to national security, such as military and defense-related innovations as well as those in aerospace, energy, and space systems. Developing countries widely used this policy tool prior to the 1990s.

Nonetheless, over the last thirty years, many countries removed requirements for screening and approval as a part of the general policy shift toward greater openness to foreign investment. There has been a significant growth in cross-border collaborations and technology transfer outside of highly specialized areas seen as critical to national security.

Many developing and emerging markets welcomed foreign investment as a way to bridge the gap with the global technological frontier. Home governments had few export restrictions that prevented firms from sharing technology with foreign partners. And Western governments largely kept away from industrial policy; rather than choosing which companies received government subsidies or aid, they preferred to invest in fundamental R&D.

Geopolitical tensions have changed those calculations. Governments around the world have increased scrutiny of foreign firms and carefully assess whether foreign acquirers will pose national security threats.

Only a handful of countries had national investment screening policies prior to 2005; but by 2022 at least thirty-seven countries had introduced new regulatory frameworks for screening of foreign investments that include national security concerns.[18] These policies generally expanded the scope of sectors targeted by the screening mechanism, indicating that governments are concerned about foreign firms operating in new services that are perceived as strategic.

---

[18] The Evolution of FDI Screening Mechanisms – Key Trends and Features. UNCTAD Investment Policy Monitor, Issue 25, February 2023. Available at: https://unctad.org/system/files/official-document/diaepcbinf2023d2_en.pdf (accessed on November 9, 2023).

For example, between 2018 and 2022, new subsectors that have come under greater scrutiny include information technology, medical devices, and internet domains. In addition, there is greater scrutiny of companies that collect or access sensitive personal information of citizens or that have the ability to shape public opinion.

Such policy restrictions can dramatically lower the likelihood of foreign transactions and limit exchange between foreign and domestic firms. In one study, researchers examined the consequences of a US national security-related foreign investment screening law in the US – the Foreign Investment and National Security Act of 2007. This law empowered a regulator known as the Committee on Foreign Investment with broad new powers to revise or reject foreign acquisition of domestic firms in national security related industries. There was a significant decline in foreign takeovers of US firms following the adoption of this law, especially among research intensive national security firms.[19]

In addition to foreign investment scrutiny, governments provide a range of other incentives and subsidies to keep innovation at home. The US CHIPS and Science Act is designed to solidify the country's advantage in the semiconductor industry and includes US $52 billion specifically allocated to subsidies, tax credits, and R&D incentives. Not to be left behind, the European Union has announced a $20–35 billion plan, Korea a $55–65 billion plan, and China a $150 billion plan over different time periods.[20]

The other side of the equation is export restrictions, which have expanded. In the US, for example, the Commerce Department maintains an Entity List or a blacklist of people and organizations to which US companies cannot export technology without first

---

[19] Godsell, D., Lel, U., & Miller, D. (2023). US national security and de-globalization. *Journal of International Business Studies*, 1–24.

[20] Meng, J. (2021). Global Governments Ramp up Pace of Chip Investments, Semiconductors.org blog, June 2, 2021. Available at: www.semiconductors.org/global-governments-ramp-up-pace-of-chip-investments/

securing a license. In 2023, there were more than 600 Chinese entities on that list, an increase of about 50 percent from 2021.[21] China, in apparent retaliation to American and European export restrictions on semiconductors, announced its own export controls of Gallium and Germanium, two rare earth elements used in a variety of products including computer chips and solar panels, to protect "national security and interests."[22]

However, it is difficult to disentangle innovations and cleanly distinguish between "our" innovations and "their" innovations. Take the example of WuXi AppTec, a Chinese biopharmaceutical company that generated about 66 percent of its sales from US clients in the first half of 2023.[23]

US lawmakers identified potential threats to the security of individual Americans' genetic information and US intellectual property. At the same time, this company was also responsible for blockbuster drugs available in the American market, including advanced drugs for the treatment of cancers, obesity, and debilitating illnesses such as cystic fibrosis.[24]

WuXi companies had a reputation for low-cost and reliable work by thousands of chemists who could create new molecules and operate complex equipment needed to make them in bulk. It was the main supplier of important ingredients for multimillion-dollar therapies treating some types of leukemia, lymphoma, and HIV. A leukemia treatment sold by American firms Janssen Biotech and

---

[21] US Boosts Enforcement of Export Controls to Contain China, Russia. *Bloomberg*, May 24, 2023. Available at: www.bloomberg.com/news/newsletters/2023-05-24/supply-chain-latest-us-export-controls-on-china-russia

[22] China Hits Back in the Chip War, Imposing Export Curbs on Crucial Raw Materials. *CNN*, July 3, 2023. Available at: https://edition.cnn.com/2023/07/03/business/germanium-gallium-china-export-restrictions/index.html

[23] WuXi Companies' Shares Fall amid Renewed U.S. Sanctions Concerns. *Morningstar*, May 7, 2024. Available at: www.morningstar.com/news/dow-jones/20240307116/wuxi-companies-shares-fall-amid-renewed-us-sanction-concerns

[24] Chinese Company under Congressional Scrutiny Makes Key U.S. Drugs. *New York Times*, April 15, 2024. Available at: www.nytimes.com/2024/04/15/health/wuxi-us-drugs-congress.html

AbbVie that brought in $5.9 billion in worldwide revenue in 2023 had a core ingredient that was made by WuXi factories in Shanghai and Changzhou.

Decoupling and Limiting International Exchanges

Neural tube defects are worrying birth defects of the brain, spine, or spinal cord that develop in fetuses within the first month of pregnancy. But scientists discovered a simple intervention that can lower the incidence of neural tube defects in babies: giving women folic acid before and during early pregnancy.

Nowadays, folic acid is routinely added to flour, bread, and other staple foods. The path-breaking study that made this intervention possible came from the mid 1990s, when a group of scientists from the US Centers for Disease Control and Prevention collaborated with those at the Peking University Health Science Center to run a large-scale community study.[25]

Importantly, the collaboration was not happenstance. It was conducted under the umbrella of the Science and Technology Agreement, the first bilateral treaty signed between America and China upon reestablishing diplomatic relations in 1979. This treaty facilitated the exchange of scientists and students, scientific and technological information, joint projects and courses, as well as collaborations on courses and conferences.

Fast forward a few decades and today it would be a lot harder for such collaborative research projects. In 2021 and 2022, papers jointly written by American and Chinese researchers fell for the first time in nearly 20 years and the number of visas issued by the US to Chinese students and academics declined dramatically from the peak in 2015.[26]

---

[25] Folic Acid Use in China Reduces Neural Tube Birth Defects by 85 Percent. Centers for Disease Control and Prevention, November 10, 1999. Available at: https://archive.cdc.gov/www_cdc_gov/media/pressrel/r991122.htm.

[26] American and Chinese Scientists Are Decoupling, Too. *The Economist*, October 11, 2023. Available at: www.economist.com/science-and-technology/2023/10/11/american-and-chinese-scientists-are-decoupling-too

The US CHIPS and Science Act that provided government subsidies and funding for semiconductor R&D, production, and workforce development has strict "guardrails" to limit recipients of US funding from engaging in joint research or technology licensing efforts with foreign entities of concern.[27] In 2020, the US blacklisted several educational institutions, including the Harbin Institute of Technology, the "MIT of China." This limits joint research projects, exchange programs with US universities, and even access to US made simulation and research software such as MATLAB.[28]

At the same time, Chinese rules made the export of many different types of data more challenging and foreign social science researchers found it harder to access economic and social surveys in the country. Employment by Chinese firms in the US declined by more than 60 percent between 2017 and 2021, and Chinese foreign direct investment in the US cratered to $2.49 billion in 2022, the smallest since 2009.[29]

The decline in joint research is not limited to US–China cooperation. Scientific collaboration between Russia and the West also dropped dramatically with the Ukraine war.[30]

What are the consequences of technology decoupling for innovation and firm performance? On the one hand, it is possible that decoupling can hurt firm performance by limiting access to foreign state-of-the-art technology. This is indeed one rationale for de-risking and decoupling. At the same time, it is also possible that decoupling can improve a company's performance by allowing it to develop its

---

[27] US Finalizes Rules to Prevent China from Benefiting from $52 billion in Chip Funding. *Reuters*, September 23, 2023. Available at: www.reuters.com/technology/us-finalizes-rules-prevent-china-benefiting-52-bln-chips-funding-2023-09-22/

[28] US Blacklists "China's MIT" as Tech War Enters New Phase. *Nikkei Asia*, June 17, 2020. Available at: https://asia.nikkei.com/Business/Technology/US-blacklists-China-s-MIT-as-tech-war-enters-new-phase

[29] China Shows Signs of Decoupling from US as FDI, Trade Falls. Bloomberg.com, September 7, 2023.

[30] Russia-West Scientific Collaboration a Casualty of Ukraine War. Phys.org, March 26, 2022. Available at: https://phys.org/news/2022-03-russia-west-scientific-collaboration-casualty-ukraine.html

own technologies while being sheltered from competition. Which of these effects will dominate, on average?

In one study, researchers looked at how publicly listed companies in the US and China cited domestic vis-à-vis foreign patents.[31] Firms that increased citations to domestic patents relative to foreign ones can be understood to be pursuing their own technological trajectory, and hence decoupled from the technology ecosystem of the other country.

While there was a short-term bump in indigenous innovation for Chinese firms, their productivity and valuation suffered over two to three years. This suggests indigenous innovation is associated with costs of "reinventing-the-wheel."

American firms also experienced a significant drop in firm valuation. Researchers projected that a hypothetical increase in US–China technology decoupling of 7.4% – which was the overall rate of technology integration between 2000 and 2019 – was associated with a 13.1% increase in China's firm patenting activity one year later, followed by a 2.1% drop in firm productivity and 5.2% decrease in firm valuation after two or three years. The decline in firm valuation for US firms was roughly half as large.

Contrast this with attempts to increase the cooperation between US and Taiwanese companies on drones. Executives from US drone companies visited Taiwan along with officials from the US Commerce Department, the Pentagon's Innovation Unit, and the Defense Department.[32] Their goal was to build a supply chain that did not rely on China. Both the Americans and Taiwanese saw opportunities for greater cross-border integration in the sector.

---

[31] How Does Decoupling Affect Firm Performance and Innovation in China and the U.S.? Stanford Center on China's Economy and Institutions Brief, May 15, 2023. Available at: https://sccei.fsi.stanford.edu/china-briefs/how-does-decoupling-affect-firm-performance-and-innovation-china-and-us

[32] US and Taiwan Seek to Strengthen Drone Supply Chain to Keep China Out. *Financial Times*, September 20, 2024. Available at: www.ft.com/content/ce851c48-6aa5-48d2-b28a-6c806cc10518

Competing Standards

When you use your smartphone today, you probably have dozens of apps at your fingertips. And many thousands more that you can easily download and pay for in the app store. This includes a top-rated loan app in Kenya, a post office app in Bangladesh, a photo enhancer app in Canada, a sports betting app in Ghana, a digital payment app in India, a news app in Japan, a shopping app in Portugal, and a social media app in the US. This broad access didn't just happen. Google's Android and Play Store as well as Apple's App Store methodically and deliberately offered a standardized set of technologies that developers around the world could use to build and customize apps in hundreds of domains and millions of use cases.

Technology standards play an important role in fostering innovation. They are nonproprietary but create a technological base in an industry upon which more advanced and complex products can be developed. They can increase efficiency of technology development and commercialization. One study of UK manufacturing firms found that the use of technology standards significantly enables a firm's incremental innovation (although reducing its incentive to deliver radical innovation).[33] When there are collaborative arrangements across firms to promote the adoption of technology standards, the rate of follow-on innovation based on those shared standards increases by about 14 percent.[34]

But technological standards are increasingly getting front row seats in geopolitical contestation. It is possible that in areas where US–China rivalry is high – such as the technology enabling the "internet of things," semiconductors, and artificial intelligence – technology standards may end up divided into two competing and

---

[33] Foucart, R., & Li, Q. C. (2021). The role of technology standards in product innovation: Theory and evidence from UK manufacturing firms. *Research Policy, 50*(2), 104157.

[34] Vakili, K. (2016). Collaborative promotion of technology standards and the impact on innovation, industry structure, and organizational capabilities: Evidence from modern patent pools. *Organization Science, 27*(6), 1504–1524.

incompatible stacks. Users may find themselves stuck in one system, unable to build on or use features of the other system without incurring high costs.

Take, for example, the smart city projects that the Chinese government has been actively promoting in many developing countries. These projects aim to automate municipal functions by incorporating many emerging technologies such as big data analysis, telecommunication systems, facial recognition, and AI cameras. When cities rely on purchases of Chinese products and deals with Chinese firms, they may end up being locked-in to Chinese standards. In the same way, cities relying on American products and American firms may end up being locked-in to US standards. The key issue is that switching becomes costly after a point, leading to lower innovation and less efficient systems.

Championing "native" standards is a stated objective in some instances. The Chinese have adopted the Standards 2035 Project to develop technical standards in a variety of domains and export these standards by strategically using its high-level officials and leaders at global standard setting organizations.

India has built a collection of digital platforms involving identity, payments, and data management – often referred to as the "India Stack" or "Digital Public Infrastructure" – that it would like to offer for free to other developing countries, and in the process build its economy and increase its influence. Indian IT firms may get lucrative development and maintenance contracts while the country's regulatory power will grow if many countries adopt the Indian-made system as an alternative to Western or Chinese systems.[35]

Another area where standards competition is evident is space exploration. In 2024, China successfully landed a probe on the far side of the moon to collect the first lunar samples from there. It was a moment of pride for the China National Space

---

[35] How India Is Using Digital Technology to Project Power. *The Economist*, June 4, 2023. Available at: www.economist.com/asia/2023/06/04/how-india-is-using-digital-technology-to-project-power

Administration, with the state news agency Xinhua calling the Chang'e-6 lander "the first endeavor of its kind in the history of human lunar exploration."³⁶ This mission is part of an increasingly ambitious lunar strategy for China, as China and the US are competing to establish the governing framework for lunar exploration. This is important because setting the rules for how the moon's resources can be mined and used in space will shape who has leadership in space.

CONSEQUENCES FOR CORPORATE INNOVATION

Many companies have set up foreign R&D labs to access diverse knowledge bases and human capital. The foreign R&D expenditure of US multinational corporations grew approximately seven-fold between 1989 and 2013.³⁷ The locations are also more diverse. While just five countries – the United Kingdom, Germany, Japan, France, and Canada – dominated US foreign R&D, their share fell nearly 30 percentage points since the 1990s. A host of new hubs emerged, including in China, India, and Israel.

There was especially fast growth in emerging markets. Global R&D units were not just interested in adapting products developed in the rich world for the large markets of China and India, but also in original product development and sophisticated basic research. In China alone, there were over 716,000 researchers working for foreign firms by 2021, who spent about $52 billion annually on R&D.³⁸ Even in the midst of harsh COVID-19 lockdowns, Shanghai saw the opening of twenty-five new foreign R&D centers in 2022. Foreign companies were especially attracted by the large pool of talented (but cheaper to

---

[36] China's Chang'e-6 Lands on Moon's Far Side to Collect Samples. *Xinhua*, June 2, 2024. Available at: https://english.www.gov.cn/news/202406/02/content_WS665bc29ec6d0868f4e8e7c54.html

[37] For an overview of US corporate R&D's globalization, see Branstetter, L. G., Glennon, B., & Jensen, J. B. (2019). The IT revolution and the globalization of R&D. *Innovation Policy and the Economy*, 19(1), 1–37.

[38] China Is the West's Corporate R&D Lab. Can It Remain So? *The Economist*, July 18, 2024. Available at: www.economist.com/business/2024/07/18/china-is-the-wests-corporate-r-and-d-lab-can-it-remain-so

employ) researchers as well as a regulatory regime that allowed for the testing and development of new-fangled technologies at breakneck speed.

What will be the impact of geopolitics on foreign R&D labs and corporate innovation? Geopolitical tensions can disrupt the flow of ideas, talent, and resources that are crucial for driving technological progress and economic growth. The increased uncertainty and risk will result in lower innovation, and more incremental rather than breakthrough innovation.

One concern is the greater difficulty in moving intellectual property across borders. China, for example, introduced restrictions on the international transfer of intellectual property and required assessment of national security considerations in some cases.[39] Exports of some AI, including TikTok's recommendation algorithm, need government permission to be shared with foreign entities.[40] US export controls include restrictions on quantum computers and components, advanced chipmaking tools, semiconductor technology, components related to metals and metal alloys, and some AI applications.[41] US private equity and venture capital funds also faced restrictions on their investments in some countries.[42]

For some companies, this means foreign R&D is not as attractive. They will withdraw from locations that are geopolitical rivals and redirect their foreign R&D investments to friendlier locations. IBM, the American technology company, decided the increased

---

[39] China: Introduces "Measures for the Overseas Transfer of Intellectual Property Rights," March 29, 2018. UNCTAD Investment Policy Hub. Available at: https://investmentpolicy.unctad.org/investment-policy-monitor/measures/3252/china-introduces-measures-for-the-overseas-transfers-of-intellectual-property-rights-trial-
[40] What China's New Export Rules Mean for TikTok's US Sale. *Financial Times*, August 31, 2020. Available at: www.ft.com/content/a8480c0d-7cce-4f10-88ec-6b8294e71ec4
[41] US Rolls Out New Chip-Related Export Controls as China Makes Industry Advances. *CNBC*, September 6, 2024. Available at: www.cnbc.com/2024/09/06/us-china-quantum-chip-related-export-controls.html
[42] US Investors Face Uncertain Future in China after Tech Ban. *Financial Times*, August 11, 2023. Available at: www.ft.com/content/8de1cd77-fe94-45d5-aa23-09faf7f89f15

compliance risks and higher personnel costs in China no longer warranted running R&D operations there. The company closed a cutting-edge research lab in 2021 after more than two decades of operations. A few years later, IBM shut down its entire China R&D department affecting more than 1,000 jobs.[43]

For other companies, greater restrictions can force them to innovate further. This is because they shift priorities to particular concerns and focus attention on specific problems. Take the case of Huawei, the Chinese telecommunications and technology company. Since 2012, the company witnessed ever greater restrictions on sales to Western customers and in acquiring technology and components from American companies. This initially hobbled the Chinese behemoth. Without access to the semiconductor chips it needed, Huawei was forced to sell its main smartphone business. The Chairman described the impact of sanctions as[44]: "It has caused a lot of damage to us. […] Life was not easy for us."

But the company pivoted and began to find ways to thrive again. By 2024, it reentered the smartphone business and its profits soared. It introduced new models that sold out within minutes and competed with other high-end models. The sales of its telecommunications equipment began to rise again. In 2023, the company's profits were roughly $12 billion, vastly more than its competitors such as Ericsson and Nokia. How did they manage this transformation?

The company reoriented its business toward China, as foreign sales accounted for a diminishing share. At the same time, the firm decided to address its political problems with technological fixes.[45] Its 114,000 employees who work in R&D accounted for more

---

[43] IBM Shuts China R&D Operations in Latest Retreat by US Companies. *The Wall Street Journal*, August 26, 2024. Available at: www.wsj.com/business/ibm-shuts-china-r-d-operations-in-latest-retreat-by-u-s-companies-b37cd9a0

[44] Huawei's Business Damaged by US Sanctions despite Success at Home. *BBC*, March 31, 2021. Available at: www.bbc.com/news/technology-56590001

[45] America's Assassination Attempt on Huawei Is Backfiring. *The Economist*, June 13, 2024. Available at: www.economist.com/briefing/2024/06/13/americas-assassination-attempt-on-huawei-is-backfiring

than half of the total workforce. The R&D budget was a massive $23 billion, exceeded only by American's biggest technology firms such as Alphabet, Amazon, Apple, and Microsoft.

The research efforts led to the development of in-house replacements for components and software that it could no longer access from foreign suppliers. It sourced semiconductor chips from local manufacturers and created an investment unit to support local firms working on relevant technologies. Huawei's Harmony, an operating system for electronics, was not only incorporated into its popular devices but also attracted millions of developers to write applications – setting it up as a potential rival to Google's Android and Apple's iOS. Ultimately, caught in the geopolitical crossfire, Huawei was incentivized to innovate. And innovate it did.

Huawei was not alone in addressing geopolitical problems with technological solutions. One study examined how antidumping duties imposed by the US government against Chinese exporters affected those companies' product innovations.[46] Collecting relevant data from 1985 to 2015, researchers found that a US antidumping sanction on a product from China increased the number of patents filed by Chinese exporting companies. These innovations allowed the product to become more differentiated and thus escape from the price competition inherent in lower value-added products. More differentiated products are also less at risk of triggering future antidumping sanctions. Overall, antidumping sanctions had the unintended consequence of prompting targeted firms to become more innovative.

MANAGING INNOVATION IN THE SHADOW OF GEOPOLITICS

One of the core advantages of multinational companies is their ability to identify and incorporate new knowledge and innovation from

---

[46] Huang, K. G., Jia, N., & Ge, Y. (2024). Forced to innovate? Consequences of United States' anti-dumping sanctions on innovations of Chinese exporters. *Research Policy*, 53(1), 104899.

different parts of the world. But geopolitical challenges threaten this key advantage. How can firms balance the conflicting pressures?

One answer is to carefully consider the trade-offs between greater diversity of knowledge and the increased geopolitical tensions. In the IBM example above, the company exited China. However, they planned to add engineers and researchers in other countries, including India. In a similar vein, managers can identify a range of countries to locate their R&D labs – giving them diversity – but also narrow that list to choose only those that have friendly relations with their home countries.

Another option is to keep more sensitive projects at home. This means creating a supporting organization structure where some of the company's R&D workforce do not have access to projects being carried out in other locations. Firms that have civilian and military operations already have similar structures in place, which could serve as a blueprint for other R&D functions in different countries.

Alternately, companies can distribute projects across different R&D divisions in such a way that on their own the project's value is limited. Only when combined with complementary assets that are available in another location will the real value of those innovations become evident.

Finally, companies should also consider differentiating between technologies needed in different markets. If an innovation is valuable in a foreign market but not the local one where it is developed, then geopolitical pressures may be less of a concern.

4 Corporate Strategies for Managing Geopolitics

A celebrated private-equity investor, when asked about how much he thought about geopolitical risk, reportedly once responded "Hardly at all. We look at companies, the cash flows, the investments themselves."[1] Surely, you ask yourself, if a globe-trotting, private-jet-traveling billionaire isn't worried, should you be?

Historically, market reaction to geopolitical events seem to suggest that conflicts will fall far short of the worst fears. The reaction to geopolitical events has been subdued: The benchmark US S&P 500 index barely moved in response to the 2023 attacks in the Middle East; the S&P 500 recovered all its losses following the 9/11 terror attacks in roughly five weeks; and across different geopolitical crises since World War II, the S&P 500 index recovered fully in about thirty-three days.[2] Markets seem to place greater emphasis on broader economic growth, monetary and fiscal policy, and technical market factors than geopolitical events.[3]

On the other hand, there is also growing evidence of a strong negative relationship between geopolitical risk and corporate investment. In one study, researchers constructed a geopolitical risk index using adverse events associated with wars, terrorism, and tensions among states that affect the peaceful course of international relations.[4]

---

[1] Why Investors Are Ignoring War, Terror and Turmoil. *Financial Times*, September 8, 2014. Available at: www.ft.com/content/dc245222-34de-11e4-ba5d-00144feabdc0

[2] Why Markets Are Relatively Calm in the Geopolitical Storm. *Financial Times*, October 23, 2023. Available at: www.ft.com/content/d194a8a2-60c1-4afe-83bf-44e529e16d40

[3] Are Markets Ignoring Geopolitical Risk? Madison Faller, JP Morgan Wealth Management, October 20, 2023. Available at: www.jpmorgan.com/insights/outlook/market-outlook/are-markets-ignoring-the-geopolitical-risks

[4] Caldara, D., & Iacoviello, M. (2022). Measuring geopolitical risk. *American Economic Review*, 112(4), 1194–1225.

They found this aggregate index is associated with lower investment by firms. Another set of researchers estimated that when a news-based index of geopolitical risk doubled, firms reduced their investment in the following quarter by 14 percent.[5] In their earnings calls and corporate filings, S&P 500 companies used the word "geopolitics" 12,000 times in 2023, which was about three times what they did two years prior.[6] More than nine in ten companies surveyed in 2022 reported a political risk loss (compared to 35% a few years prior) and the proportion of companies who purchased political risk insurance grew nearly three times from 25% in 2019 to 68% in 2022.[7]

Why do firms react negatively to geopolitical tensions? What is the impact of geopolitical uncertainty on companies? What are some risk mitigation strategies?

THE STRUCTURAL APPROACH

BlackRock Chairman Larry Fink declared the fragmented geopolitical landscape as a structural force shaping the firm's returns in one July 2023 earning call.[8] A popular party game helps to explain why. In this game, you are asked to build a tower of paper cups. The winner is the one who builds the tallest free-standing tower. You start by putting one cup on the table, add another one on top, and so on. You can build a taller and more stable tower if you have a wider base with multiple cups on the table. Adding each additional cup, however, increases the load on the system. At some point, the weight of an additional cup is too much for the structure to support. It will become unstable and the tower collapses. Engineers deal with structural loads all the time and carefully analyze the effect of

---

[5] Wang, X., Wu, Y., & Xu, W. (2023). Geopolitical risk and investment. *Journal of Money, Credit and Banking*.

[6] The Global Economy Enters and Era of Upheaval. *Bloomberg*, September 18, 2023. Available at: www.bloomberg.com/graphics/2023-geopolitical-investments-economic-shift/

[7] How Are Global Businesses Managing Today's Political Risk? 2023 Survey and Report. Produced for WTW, Oxford Analytica.

[8] BlackRock Q2 2023 Earnings Call Transcript. Available at: www.fool.com/earnings/call-transcripts/2023/07/14/blackrock-blk-q2-2023-earnings-call-transcript/

loads in designing safe structures. Think of roads, bridges, aircrafts, machines, space stations, and everything else in between. When the system experiences the expected load, there is usually no damage to it. A sudden spike in the load can break the system if it hasn't been accounted for in the design. But the maximum load that a system can safely carry declines with wear and tear. Without regular maintenance, the load-bearing capacity of the structure declines.

In the same way, the structures that support global interactions of companies – how they transact with one another, reach customers, provide goods and services, make and receive payments, and employ people – are subject to various loads. Design features allow them to withstand regular stresses. But unexpected loads as well as constant friction can fray the edges and make the system less robust.

Rising geopolitical tensions do exactly this. They slowly chip away at the basic structures needed to support global interactions. As discussed in Chapter 1, this includes challenges to *market access, level playing field, investment security,* and *institutional alignment*. In other words, geopolitical tensions influence the geographic and product markets where a company can compete in, how accessible markets are to one company versus its competitors, the safety and security of the firm's investments and personnel, and the standards that the company will have to comply with.

How can companies be successful in such an environment? There is clearly no one right answer.

COGNITIVE FRAMES FOR STRATEGIC DECISIONS

An important part of any top manager's job is to make strategic decisions for the company. What exactly are these? A strategic decision is one that is highly interdependent with a host of other choices a company makes.[9] First, they are shaped and influenced by other

---

[9] See generally: Leiblein, M. J., Reuer, J. J., & Zenger, T. (2018). What makes a decision strategic?. *Strategy Science*, 3(4), 558–573. Leiblein, M. J., Reuer, J. J., Larsen, M. M., & Pedersen, T. (2022). When are global decisions strategic?. *Global Strategy Journal*, 12(4), 714–737.

decisions being made by the company. Managers need to understand the fit or interdependence of one choice with other choices the company is making. For example, if a technology company decides to emphasize privacy in its marketing and customer acquisition, then it is constrained in the choices it has in generating revenues. A heavy dependence on advertising revenues may not fit with its choice regarding privacy. Second, strategic decisions are also interdependent with decisions of other actors outside the company. Managers need to take into account the choices of competitors, suppliers, buyers, and complementors. In other words, a firm's choices shape its relative position in the ecosystem where it competes. Finally, strategic decisions are intertemporally interdependent. Today's decisions are a function of organizational choices made in the past and will shape and guide decisions potentially far into the future. Why is this the case? It is because strategic decisions involve irreversible commitments or demand path-dependent investments. Today's decision can open up or shut down future decision opportunities for the firm.

Consider a scenario where a company is trying to determine if they should give a project the green light. For example, should a new AI-supported search model be implemented? One could begin with an approach such as the net present value (NPV) to make an investment decision. This will commit the decision-maker to a fixed course of action and highlight clear trade-offs between costs and benefits. But this decision-making rule does not reflect other issues that may be relevant and important. A strategic approach, on the other hand, would make the investment decision within a broader context. For instance, even if there is no significant improvement in performance, is there a risk that competitors would preemptively adopt the model and leverage it for hard-to-claw-back first mover reputational advantages among clients? By contrast, is the demand uncertainty large enough that it makes sense to delay or stage the investment in the project? In some cases, there may be a strategic imperative to wait (or not) even if there are (or no) immediate financial benefits to making that decision.

All this means strategic decisions are complex; companies and managers can't use simple rules or optimization calculations to determine the best course of action. Searching through a strategy space with numerous elements can be exceedingly difficult. Even when managers have a clear understanding of the set of interdependent activities they desire, complementarities among these individual activity choices imply that managing the transition to the newly targeted alignment will be difficult.

Managers making strategic decisions under geopolitical tensions face a double whammy. Not only do they have to face a complex and highly interdependent decision space but also have to take into account how the decision space itself is shifting because of geopolitical tensions. It is not sufficient to evaluate how competitors may react in a given market, but you also need to account for the fact that your company's market access itself may be under question. Determining how the company's choices today will constrain their future actions gets a lot more complicated if the nature of the playing field changes. Interdependent decisions about resource allocation are not as valuable when some of those resources are not secured. Does it make sense for the company to invest in markers of quality if those standards are going to be different in the future? Geopolitical tensions constitute an overarching cloud that governs, facilitates, and constrains the decisions a company can make, but it is a fast-moving cloud whose shape and structure changes.

In such a challenging decision-making environment, how can managers make strategic decisions? As with other demanding decision-making, they need intuition, imagination, representations, theories, or judgments to cognitively model interrelationships and shape their thinking. They need to have an imagined future where geopolitical tensions reshape the company's operations and the industry's structure. But with so much uncertainty, it is hard to do this. Any attempt to build different scenarios will necessarily be incomplete. And many companies can be stuck, unsure about what to do next or unable to choose among different ways to deal with challenges their firm may (or may not) face. One way to break through is to rely on heuristics, or simple decision-making rules. Heuristics can be biased or lead to colored decision-making; but they also serve as important tools to enable, rather than limit, decision-making in a dynamic and uncertain environment. They allow decision-makers to ignore most information and focus attention on specific decisions. Heuristics are not good or bad, but they vary in the extent to which they trade off frugality (or limiting the volume of information) against predictive accuracy. To limit biases, it is helpful to have multiple views.

In one study of an inexperienced Australian mining company, researchers found that senior managers relied on cognitive efforts based on heuristics to assess a potential acquisition of a mine in a politically risky African market.[10] Managers in this company had no experience of investing abroad, let alone in a country that was politically unstable, violent, and corrupt. While the company's geologists may have been excited about the mining prospects, the non-geologists were immediately more concerned about the political challenges. In their study, the researchers reported that different managers tried to estimate the probability of hazardous events and identify the key actors, interactions, and interrelationships. Interestingly, individuals with different roles highlighted different concerns and devoted cognitive resources to different aspects of the issue. While the Chief Executive Officer asked broadly about the country's rule of law, the Chief Financial Officer was worried about repatriating earnings. The general manager of community relations focused on the labor market and quality of government services, while the General Counsel examined legislative clauses that could become roadblocks. Their recommendations varied, but managers with greater experience in hazardous countries created richer representations of the political environment, identifying more actors, events, and structural relationships that may be relevant.

[10] Maitland, E., & Sammartino, A. (2015). Decision making and uncertainty: The role of heuristics and experience in assessing a politically hazardous environment. *Strategic Management Journal*, 36(10), 1554–1578.

In the context of geopolitical tensions as well, different individuals can come up with scenarios that reflect their own experiences and heuristics and vary significantly from each other. Two very experienced and astute followers of the Indian economy projected different views of how global geopolitical tensions will shape the Indian economy.[11] Arvind Subramanian, an economist and former Chief Economic Advisor to the Indian Government, was optimistic, arguing that geopolitical headwinds suggest a decline in China's exports, creating a big opportunity for India in manufacturing. On the other hand, Raghuram Rajan, an economist and former chief of India's Central Bank, was less sanguine, arguing India's opportunity in spillover manufacturing was going to be limited because only few jobs – and only in some strategic sectors – will move out of China. These are two different worldviews based on heuristics and experiences of the decision-maker. How, then, will organizations decide which one should be acted upon?

One study suggests how it is often (but not necessarily how it should be) resolved. In this study of a telecommunications firm during a challenging time, managers attempted to transform their own cognitive frames into the dominant ones of the organization.[12] Like in previous studies, managers had different views about the direction of the market and about the kinds of solutions that would be appropriate. When these clashed, managers engaged in a highly political contest to make their frames resonate and to mobilize action in their favor. Those who could skillfully engage in these practices shaped the frame that prevailed.

STRATEGIES FOR MANAGING GEOPOLITICAL RISKS

In this section, we explore how managers can make strategic decisions to actively manage geopolitical risks. Broadly, these are decisions about resources (who gets what), competitive advantage (how to win), and firm organization (who does what).

---

[11] Comments at the Tamil Nadu Global Investors Meet, January 7–8, 2024.
[12] Kaplan, S. (2008). Framing contests: Strategy making under uncertainty. *Organization Science*, 19(5), 729–752.

Resources (Who Gets What)

Accessing Government Resources

At some level, every manager is worried about exactly the same thing: inflow of resources and the reallocation of resources within the organization. Rising geopolitical tensions means many firms now can turn to the state for resources.

Spurred by geopolitical competition, industrial policy is back in vogue. Governments around the world offer resources, subsidies, tax breaks, and other incentives to strengthen their own companies or lure important firms from friendly partner countries to contribute to and strengthen the domestic ecosystem. There are many examples of governments offering financial and other support to "their" companies. They include the European Green Deal, the US Inflation Reduction Act (IRA) and the CHIPS and Science Act, Chinese Belt and Road Initiative and the Made in China 2025 policy, and Japan's support package for green technology.

While it is easy to understand why governments do so, it is also important to acknowledge the competition for companies and investments. For some companies, at least, this means they can afford to go on a shopping spree around the world and look for the best deals.[13] Intel, the American chip company, was offered $11 billion in subsidies by the German government to build two semiconductor plants there. And in a strange reversal, the German carmaker BMW, lured by American subsidies, announced a new battery plant in the US. Similarly, the UK electric vehicle start-up Arrival, planned to manufacture in the US instead of its home country thanks to tax breaks it would receive there.

Micron Technologies, a US memory chip company, announced in 2023 that they would invest in a new $2.75 billion chip assembly and test facility in Gujarat, India. Of this headline grabbing figure, however, Micron Technologies only committed to $825 million,

---

[13] The Economic Losers in the New World Order. *The Wall Street Journal*, August 14, 2023. Available at: www.wsj.com/articles/global-economy-economic-losers-fba30b53

with the rest coming from the Indian central and state governments.[14] But, as *The Economist* noted, while the plant was expected to create 5,000 jobs directly and 15,000 indirectly, "each job cost $100,000 – nearly 40 times India's average income per person."[15] In addition, for the company's unit to become operational, Micron would need access to advanced equipment, processing and grinding tools, and ultra-high purity gases provided by its supply chain partners such as South Korea's Simmtech, Japan's Disco Corp., Singapore Kulicke & Soffa, and France's Air Liquide. These supply chain partners also sought incentives from the government, including financial support, access to land, water, and electricity, as well as support in finding the talent for semiconductors.[16] At the time of writing, at least one of these companies received additional subsidies to invest in the country.[17]

When a company depends on the state for significant resources, it becomes constrained in other ways. This idea was codified in one of the most impactful theories of organizations and strategic management. In 1978, Jeffrey Pfeffer and Jerry Salancik wrote the influential book *The External Control of Organizations: A Resource Dependence Perspective*.[18] They argued that companies are not autonomous but depend on a network of external actors for various types of resources for their functioning. However, the actions of

---

[14] Micron Confirms up to $825 Million Investment in India Chip Factory. *Reuters*, June 22, 2023. Available at: www.reuters.com/technology/micron-confirms-up-825-mln-investment-india-chip-facility-2023-06-22/

[15] How to Put Boosters under India's Economy. *The Economist*, December 14, 2023. Available at: www.economist.com/finance-and-economics/2023/12/14/how-to-put-boosters-under-indias-economy

[16] Micron Suppliers Too Seek Government Incentives, As Company All Set to Produce Chips in India by 2024 End. *Financial Express*, July 31, 2023. Available at: www.financialexpress.com/business/industry-micron-suppliers-seek-government-incentives-too-3192996/

[17] Simmtech to Invest Rs 1,250 cr for Chip Components Plant in Gujarat, *Deccan Herald*, January 12, 2024. Available at: www.deccanherald.com/business/simmtech-to-invest-rs-1-250-cr-for-chip-components-plant-in-gujarat-2845238

[18] Pfeffer, J., & Salancik, G. R. (1978). *The external control of organizations: A resource dependence perspective*. New York: Harper & Row.

the external actors are uncertain, so the company's continued access to the needed resources and hence their success and survival are also uncertain. As a result, according to the Resource Dependence Theory, actors controlling the resources end up with power, which they use to shape the firm's choices.

In the context of industrial policy, governments may argue that dependence is exactly the point. They want to be able to influence the actions of firms in their jurisdictions so that can leverage those actors toward national security goals and generate positive externalities domestically. But companies that would like to avoid such dependencies develop strategies to enhance their bargaining power. This could include taking political action, increasing production, diversifying, or developing links to other resource providers.

Take the case of Panasonic. The Japanese conglomerate and Tesla battery supplier has found the US market a stable and profitable one. The company invested about $8 billion in two US plants and considered additional investments.[19] The US market helped boost the group's profits to $2.59 billion in 2023[20] despite slowdown in Asian demand for consumer electronics and Chinese factory automation. However, its record profits came on the back of a large subsidy from the US government. Should a new US administration be less enthusiastic about electric vehicles, it would be a threat to Panasonic's business. How should Panasonic adapt to higher costs and lower revenues in the absence of subsidies? Should they pivot away from the US despite their investments there? Should they diversify further away from batteries and electric vehicles? What will be the impact of American or other foreign competitors? What will be the company's core capabilities and differentiators if they switch? How will conflicting goals or expectations shape the company's workforce?

---

[19] Panasonic Plans Second $4 Billion US EV Battery Plant. *PV Magazine*, August 29, 2022. Available at: https://pv-magazine-usa.com/2022/08/29/panasonic-plans-second-4-billion-u-s-ev-battery-plant/

[20] Panasonic Sees Record Profit on Robust Battery Demand, US Tax Credit. *Reuters*, May 10, 2023. Available at: www.reuters.com/technology/panasonic-q4-profit-falls-35-misses-market-expectations-2023-05-10/

In evaluating these questions, the company's choices will be dependent on their American operations and the investments they have already made. In other words, their decision will be path dependent. Their past actions (in this case accepting US subsidies) will constrain and shape the choices they have in the future.

Listen to Scott White, the cofounder of Pragmatic Semiconductor, a British company developing small, low-cost plants for its ultra-thin semiconductor chips. Founded in 2010, the company was headquartered in Cambridge, UK, with two fabrication plants in the North East of England. Evaluating whether the company should continue in the UK, he said,[21]

> We can comfortably be profitable without <government> incentives but if everyone is offering them elsewhere, that makes the cost of production higher here.

Moving production and manufacturing to the US and choosing that country as the base of operations seemed to be on the cards. And if that came to be, the company was likely to consider American markets for their public listing. Here's Pragmatic's Scott White again, discussing a potential listing on the London Stock Exchange[22]:

> If all of our manufacturing ends up being overseas and all of our customers are overseas, it just wouldn't make any sense <to list in the UK>.

Thus, the firm's decisions today about accepting government subsidies will be linked to location choice, financing, and competitors. And this decision will shape the company's choices in the future.

At the same time, accessing the geopolitically induced state resources is itself resource intensive for companies. Don't discount the time and resources your company will need to spend in order to

---

[21] Rishi Sunak to Unveil Semiconductor Partnership with Japan. *Financial Times*, May 18, 2023. Available at: www.ft.com/content/28ee0dc6-aad9-4509-8c7f-25e5fba1711b

[22] Pragmatic Founder Suggests US Move over Lack of Government Support. UKTN, April 26, 2023. Available at: www.uktech.news/deep-tech/pragmatic-semiconductor-us-move-20230426

get a better deal or access those subsidies. US semiconductor suppliers and customers came together as a unified front in lobbying and pushing Congress to approve the CHIPS Act. But even before the ink on the $52 billion deal dried, companies were jostling to get a bigger share of those subsidies.

Securing Resources

Another consequence of geopolitical tensions is that companies will be looking to secure their existing resources and move them away from markets that could be affected by the tensions. As geopolitical tensions increased, many Western multinational companies began moving some of their existing or planned investments out of China. Between July and September 2023, for example, foreign direct investment into China was *minus* $11.8 billion, the first negative figure since 1998.[23] In other words, there were more withdrawals and downsizing than new investments in the country. The semiconductor sector was particularly striking: China's share of foreign investment shrunk from 48% in 2018 to 1% in 2022.

According to the US Department of State, de-risking is the "phenomenon of financial institutions terminating or restricting business relationships with clients or categories of clients to avoid, rather than manage, risk."[24] For many companies, however, completely terminating any business activity in countries where they face geopolitical risk is unlikely and unrealistic. Instead, they look for alternative approaches. One strategy common for among Western companies worried about rising geopolitical tensions with China is the "China+1" strategy. Companies avoided concentrating their investments in China while channeling investment into other promising economies that were friendlier to the West, such

---

[23] Foreign Investment in China Turns Negative for the First Time. *Nikkei Asia*, November 4, 2023. Available at: https://asia.nikkei.com/Economy/Foreign-investment-in-China-turns-negative-for-first-time

[24] De-risking. U.S. Department of State. Available at: www.state.gov/de-risking/#:~:text=De%2Drisking%20refers%20to%20the,%2C%20rather%20than%20manage%2C%20risk

as Vietnam, India, or Thailand. The American technology company Apple, for example, announced that it would make one in four iPhones in India by 2025.[25] Similarly HP, an American personal computer maker, planned to shift the production of some commercial notebook computers to Mexico and a portion of its consumer laptop production to Thailand.[26]

Chinese companies also see geographic location as key to managing geopolitical tensions and securing resources. Man Wah was one of China's largest furniture companies, and the United States was one of their main markets. With geopolitical tensions between the US and China rising, and shipping prices surging, the company decided to set up operations in Mexico to take advantage of the country's membership in the North American trading bloc. In 2022, the company acquired land and began constructing a factory in Mexico.[27] But there was no time to waste. Even as the factory was being constructed, they began producing sofas at a small, leased plant in Mexico.

Competitive Advantage (How to Win)

Managers and scholars of international businesses have long argued that a foreign company is often viewed as an outsider. Foreign firms face a "liability of foreignness," or additional costs when doing business abroad. These are costs over and above the normal costs of doing business in a market, that is, costs that local or domestic firms do not face. Some are additional costs from managing spatial distance such as the cost of travel, transportation, and coordination over distance and time zones. Other costs stem from the

---

[25] Apple Aims to Make a Quarter of the World's iPhones in India. *The Wall Street Journal*, December 8, 2023. Available at: www.wsj.com/tech/apple-aims-to-make-a-quarter-of-the-worlds-iphones-in-india-ab7f6342

[26] HP to Move Production of Millions of PCs to Thailand, Mexico. *Nikkei Asia*, July 18, 2023. Available at: https://asia.nikkei.com/Spotlight/Supply-Chain/HP-to-move-production-of-millions-of-PCs-to-Thailand-Mexico

[27] Why Chinese Companies Are Investing Billions in Mexico. *The New York Times*, February 3, 2023. Available at: www.nytimes.com/2023/02/03/business/china-mexico-trade.html

foreign firm's unfamiliarity with the local business practices, customer preferences, and disadvantage in labor markets. Yet others are because of government policies either in the foreign country or in the firm's own country of origin. This last category is especially relevant under heightened geopolitical tensions, when firms from a rival country are likely to face greater government scrutiny, intervention, and restrictions. In the context of geopolitical competition, however, a firm's disadvantage depends not just on its foreignness but also on the type of foreignness. Some foreign firms – that is, those from friendly countries – experience a relatively small disadvantage. But the liabilities are magnified for a firm from a rival country as they are seen as particularly threatening to the country's national security. Simply being from a country that is considered to be a geopolitical rival or adversary is enough to engender mistrust, lower customers' willingness to buy, and initiate government restrictions on the firm. In other words, and as discussed in Chapters 1 and 2, geopolitics influences how firms compete by highlighting their nationality or country of origin.

To compete, firms may decide to localize their operations and de-emphasize their foreign status. If a firm faces a disadvantage because of its foreign status, it can take actions to decrease its "outsiderness." Companies can alter their products, supply chains, marketing, and even ownership to meet the needs of a specific local market. The idea is to signal that they are insiders or locals and should be treated as such.

Such a strategy can be effective. One study found that when foreign firms change their behavior to imitate local firms, their performance improves.[28] The researchers examined 80 foreign banks with 170 subsidiaries from 25 countries operating in the US from 1978 to 2006. What they were interested in was how similar the foreign

[28] Wu, Z., & Salomon, R. (2016). Does imitation reduce the liability of foreignness? Linking distance, isomorphism, and performance. *Strategic Management Journal*, 37(12), 2441–2462.

bank's asset strategy – or how a bank allocates its assets across various products such as commercial loans, residential loans, and securities – was to the average asset strategy of all US commercial banks in the same local metropolitan area. The more similar the asset strategies, the better off foreign firms were. When foreign firms, especially from countries that were dissimilar to the US, mimicked the behavior of US firms, they improved their initial performance.

For firms caught in geopolitical tensions, a similar localization strategy can help to reduce their outsiderness. They can embrace practices rooted in the local economy and move control of the company to the host country. Such moves can help them to also de-emphasize their foreign origin, especially if they are from a rival country.

One example is MG Motor, a legacy British auto company owned by the Shanghai-based Chinese state-owned automobile company, SAIC. The company entered the Indian market in 2017 and also acquired a manufacturing facility there. However, following border clashes between India and China in 2020, the Indian government became more cautious about Chinese investment in the country. As a result, financial support for the firm's Indian subsidiary from the Chinese parent company became more challenging. The company's answer to this challenge was to localize its operations further and become more "Indian." They set in motion a plan to dilute ownership such that it will become a majority Indian-owned company. They also planned to increase manufacturing of vehicle components in the country and integrate further with local supply chains. Explaining their approach, the CEO Emeritus of MG Motor India was thus quoted[29]:

> MG India's unwavering dedication to India is deeply ingrained in our ethos. Our growth strategy is centred around strengthening localisation (and) aligning more closely with the government's "Make in India" initiative.

---

[29] MG Motor to Dilute Chinese Holding, Become Majority Indian Owned. *The Week*, May 10, 2023. Available at: www.theweek.in/news/biz-tech/2023/05/10/mg-motor-to-dilute-chinese-holding-become-majority-indian-owned.html

Another example of localization comes from Alibaba's expansion in Europe. The Chinese e-commerce platform aimed to target customers in Europe by positioning itself as an insider. The President of the company summarized the approach as[30]:

> What we will focus more for the future is to build local businesses, so you will see something called Tmall which we have in China become Tmall in Europe, which means we will serve local brands and local customers in local markets.

But simply emphasizing their localness may not be sufficient if the firm is controlled – either directly or indirectly – by a hostile foreign government. Even if a foreign government has only legal or regulatory authority over the firm's operations, it can make the foreign firm appear as a threat. The problem is that the company or its managers cannot credibly distance themselves from their own governments or commit that they will not act to support their government's geopolitical objectives when operating in another country. With this baggage, how can they compete in international markets?

As highlighted in Chapters 1 and 2, and in research with my collaborators, the answer may be to actively and purposefully de-link from their country of origin.[31] For example, companies could relocate their headquarters to more "neutral" location to shield against geopolitical risk. Domiciling in a new country can allow firms to dilute their identity or change perceptions of corporate nationality. To compete in Western markets, PDD Holdings, the parent company of discount ecommerce site Pinduoduo and online marketplace Temu, shifted its headquarters from Shanghai to Ireland.[32] The idea was to

---

[30] Alibaba Aims to Expand Local Business in Europe, President Says. *Reuters*, June 15, 2023. Available at: www.reuters.com/business/retail-consumer/alibaba-president-jack-ma-remains-biggest-shareholder-still-cares-about-company-2023-06-15/

[31] Blake, D., Jandhyala, S., Beazer, Q., & Cunha, R. (2024). Managing Geopolitics in the Digital Age. Working Paper.

[32] Pinduoduo Owner Moves Headquarters to Ireland amid US-China Tensions. *Financial Times*, May 4, 2023. Available at: www.ft.com/content/801ac5c4-9863-444e-986a-1e40280ea07f

signal that corporate decision-making came under the jurisdiction of a different, and more friendly, country. Major decisions that affect the company's operations, customer data, and hiring would take place away from the influence of the Chinese stakeholders.

Singapore emerged as a popular hub for Chinese companies looking to move their headquarters or reincorporating in a neutral location. So popular that the move that it was dubbed "Singapore washing."[33] China's Shunwei Capital was one company that took advantage of this location to overcome geopolitical tensions. The venture capital firm was established by Lei Jun, the founder of smartphone maker Xiaomi. They scouted attractive deals in India but faced challenges. The Indian government was cautious about investments from China after border clashes raised tensions between the two countries. Several regulatory measures targeted Chinese companies specifically. But Shunwei Capital found a way to invest in an Indian market automation platform WebEngage and dairy brand Country Delight. The deals were done through SWC Global and entity that described itself as the Singapore affiliate of a leading multibillion venture capital firm based in Asia.[34] As one manager of a Singapore-based Chinese technology company was quoted by the *Financial Times*:

> Setting up in Singapore has a whole range of benefits for a Chinese company. [...] If we do business from China, we hit a wall of tariffs and suspicion over everything we want to do in the US market. From Singapore, there are no tariffs and the suspicion is much less.

Firm Organization (Who Does What)

The third pillar is determining who does what. When competing in global markets, companies have to configure their assets – human,

---

[33] Chinese Companies Set Up in Singapore to Hedge against Geopolitical Risk. *Financial Times*, November 30, 2022. Available at: www.ft.com/content/a0c11e3e-ab72-4b4b-a55c-557191e53938

[34] China's New Back Doors into Western Markets. *Financial Times*, September 5, 2024. Available at: www.ft.com/content/5583db36-5141-413f-9687-2c3f4968ff07

physical, intellectual, and organizational – in the service of specific goals. They have to identify workflows, procedures, and systems in order to fit current business goals and implement changes to support new plans. What should each part of the organization do to deliver the final objective? Where should decision-making authority be concentrated? Who in the organization controls budgets and directs resources? Where should production be based? These are important questions for all companies but come with a special relevance for firms competing in global markets under geopolitical tensions.

The general premise of a global company is that under some conditions, it is more efficient for the multinational firm to keep operations in foreign markets internal, that is, within the same company. If it is difficult to rely on outside actors and/or partners to execute the firm's operations (or more expensive to do so), it makes sense for the company to undertake those activities across the world. In the world with geopolitical tensions, multinational firms are asking themselves if the one firm approach is still the best option if different parts of the firm cannot complement each other and work together to create efficiencies.

Take the case of Sequoia Capital, the American venture capital firm. In its global expansion, the company created dedicated funds for different countries and regions, with different levels of independence for the subsidiaries. At the same time, there was knowledge sharing across funds, with best practices being transmitted across Sequoia offices and investment decisions. Fund managers' ability to generate above average returns was aided by an integrated, worldwide hive. Similarly, centralized back-office functions provided a cost advantage. The company raised funds from one market and invested in start-ups in another. Some of the profits of the global arms were shared among the global group. Armed with such advantages, Sequoia Capital backed high tech companies in the US such as Apple, Zoom, Instagram, and DoorDash; invested in over 1,000 firms in China including JD.com and Alibaba; and had over $9 billion under management in India and Southeast Asia.³⁵ But geopolitical tensions raised questions about the continued viability of such a structure. In China, deploying the billions of dollars raised from US investors into China's priority sectors such as semiconductors and artificial intelligence became more challenging. At the same time, increased US controls on exporting sensitive technologies to China meant a delicate balancing act for the company. When the US government introduced new restrictions on US venture capital and private equity firms preventing them from investing in artificial investing, quantum computing, and semiconductors, US firms were asking themselves whether being a global firm continued to make sense. For Sequoia Capital, the answer was a clear no. The company announced it would split into three entities, Sequoia Capital in the US and Europe, Peak XV Partners in India and Southeast Asia, and HongShan in China.³⁶ A few months later, their rival Silicon Valley venture firm GGV Capital also announced they would split into two independent businesses focused on Asia and the US, respectively.³⁷

A slightly different approach is to create a local-for-local operation, but house it within the same company. This means there is a devolution of decision-making, supply chains, coordination, and control to operations in different countries. The company's top managers still play an advisory or coordinating role across subsidiaries but leave a lot of the decisions to be made by local managers in a way that best suits the local conditions. Since policies are decided and enacted locally, this approach is considered by some companies as an answer to rising geopolitical tensions.

---

[35] Sequoia Breakup Will Expose Go-Local Consequences. *Reuters*, June 7, 2023. Available at: www.reuters.com/breakingviews/sequoia-breakup-will-expose-go-local-consequences-2023-06-06/

[36] Sequoia Splits China and India Arms from US Mothership to Avoid "Portfolio Conflict" and "Market Confusion," *TechCrunch*, June 6, 2023. Available at: https://techcrunch.com/2023/06/06/sequoia-rebrands-china-india-and-southeast-asia-units/

[37] Venture Firm GGV Capital to Split Off China Business after US Pressure. *Financial Times*, September 22, 2023. Available at: www.ft.com/content/4052e549-4d1e-49a9-adcc-ca66731a427e

One example is Astra Zeneca, the British–Swedish pharmaceutical company. The company viewed China as an essential element of its growth strategy. China was one of the company's largest markets, where an aging population that was increasingly affected by chronic diseases drove demand for pharmaceutical products. At the same time, Astra Zeneca also saw an opportunity in the country's scientists. As more Chinese biotech companies invested in innovation and developed new drugs, Astra Zeneca believed they were in a good spot to deliver those new medicines to the world.

But as geopolitical tensions between China and the West increased, Astra Zeneca had to find a way to balance its interests. They initially considered spinning off the China operations into a separate company to protect the parent firm but didn't go through with it. Instead, they decided to separate drug production along the China–US fault lines. Their goal was to make the same medicines in different facilities to serve markets separately and independently. Here is the CEO describing the company's plans[38]:

> We have a very large supply chain, and we are organizing ourselves so that we can actually supply the United States and Europe independently. [...] And we also are building our presence here in China, so we can actually supply Chinese patients independently.

Their German rival, Merck, also had a similar take. Their goal was to create "a China-for-China approach so that also the vast majority of products we are going to produce in China is actually supposed to be for the Chinese market."

Even if firms do not spin out or divide the firm into multiple entities, they can still modify the organizational to have better control over distant operations. Firms generally tend to have more control over projects that are closer to the headquarters or top

---

[38] Astra Zeneca Plans Independent Drug Supply Chains for US and China, CEO Says. *Fierce Pharma*, March 27, 2024. Available at: www.fiercepharma.com/manufacturing/astrazeneca-builds-separate-drug-supply-chains-us-and-china-ceo-says

managers. But when projects are taken over by teams in more distant locations, the firm not only has to worry about risks in that market but also its own ability to control actions of teams that are far away. A rational response, then, is to keep more sensitive projects in the home country. One example is R&D and intellectual property. US multinational companies increased their investment in foreign R&D from approximately $14 billion in 1997 to over $55 billion in 2015. But what is really telling is that they still kept most of their R&D at home in the United States: about 83 percent of R&D in 2015, only slightly lower than the 92 percent in 1989.[39]

One challenge is protecting their R&D in foreign markets with relatively weak intellectual property rights, despite the availability of low-cost and high skilled scientific talent there. To balance these opposing pressures, firms think carefully about how to distribute projects across different R&D divisions. One way is to limit their exposure in countries with weak intellectual property protection by choosing the technologies that teams in those countries would work on. In particular, if these technologies needed other complementary technologies or assets to be really valuable, and those complementary assets were only available in other locations of the firm, then potential downside of IP loss is also limited. This is exactly what a study of over 1,500 US headquartered firms with global R&D efforts found: Technologies developed by teams in countries with weak intellectual property protection had strong internal linkages and depended on other technologies the firm already had.[40] Another option is to differentiate between technologies that will be used in the foreign country versus what will be used in the home market. If a technology developed by a team is valuable in a foreign market

---

[39] Branstetter, L. G., Glennon, B., & Jensen, J. B. (2019). The New Global Invention Machine: A Look inside the R&D Networks of US Multinationals. Working Paper. Available at: www.brookings.edu/wp-content/uploads/2019/12/Branstetter-et-al._The-New-Global-Invention-Machine_Brookings_v6.pdf

[40] Zhao, M. (2006). Conducting R&D in countries with weak intellectual property rights protection. *Management Science*, 52(8), 1185–1199.

(but not the local one where it is developed), then weak intellectual property protection is less of a concern.[41]

Firms are taking a similar approach to geopolitical tensions as well. By carefully choosing projects for locations, and people for projects, they aim to balance geopolitical tensions with access to talent. The case of Microsoft's AI lab in China is particularly interesting. Microsoft opened an advanced research lab in Beijing in 1998. Referring to the availability of highly skilled talent there, the then Chairman Bill Gates, wrote[42]:

> ...we are making large investments there, because we believe in its future – not only as a place for Microsoft to business but also as a fertile source of new ideas about how technology can improve people's lives.
>
> ... We chose Beijing as the site for this lab – one of only two international research facilities operated by Microsoft – because it offers an opportunity to tap into the deep pool of intellectual talent in China, as well as providing a test bed for addressing some of the unique challenges the Chinese marketplace presents.

By 2018, Microsoft had invested over $1 billion in R&D efforts in China, with some major scientific breakthroughs that turned into transformative products and services. *MIT Technology Review* described Microsoft's Chinese research labs as "the world's hottest computer lab" and a "powerhouse of infotech R&D."[43] Many of the researchers who worked there were at the top of their fields. They made big early strides in natural language processing. They were among the first researchers to develop artificial intelligence models

---

[41] Nandkumar, A., & Srikanth, K. (2016). Right person in the right place: How the host country IPR influences the distribution of inventors in offshore R&D projects of multinational enterprises. *Strategic Management Journal*, 37(8), 1715–1733.

[42] Yes, More Trade with China. Bill Gates in the *Washington Post*, May 23, 2000. Available at: www.washingtonpost.com/archive/opinions/2000/05/23/yes-more-trade-with-china/80438c20-4fdb-4895-99a6-61776068a636/

[43] The World's Hottest Computer Lab. Huang, G.T., *MIT Technology Review*, June 1, 2004. Available at: www.technologyreview.com/2004/06/01/232827/the-worlds-hottest-computer-lab/

that could read and answer questions about a document about as well as humans could.[44] They had early success with machine translation systems, which achieved the quality and accuracy of a bilingual person.[45] The Lab also served as a springboard for researchers' careers with many leaving for key positions at other Chinese technology companies or founding their own companies.

But nearly a quarter century after Bill Gates' push into China, a different CEO had to grapple with very different issues. As tensions between the US and China grew, the company took a long and hard look at what to do with the prized lab. National security concerns were being raised by the US. One risk was that Chinese authorities could hack or infiltrate the lab. Another was researchers leaving the lab to work with the government. Microsoft took a two-pronged organizational design approach to addressing this problem.[46] First, they limited what projects researchers in China could work on. Researchers from China, for instance, were not allowed to join the small team at Microsoft that had early access to an advanced AI system, GPT-4. There were also restrictions on the technologies the lab could work on. Work on sensitive technologies such as quantum computing, facial recognition, and synthetic media was limited. The second part of Microsoft's approach dealt with the researchers themselves. Hiring was under scrutiny. The company blocked hiring or working with students and researchers from universities affiliated with China's military. Individual researchers were also moved out of the China Lab and relocated to a newly opened outpost of the lab in Vancouver, Canada. With these organizational safeguards, Microsoft planned to continue operating the lab in China.

---

[44] Microsoft Create AI That Can Read a Document and Answer Questions about It As Well As a Person. Microsoft Blog, January 15, 2018.
[45] Microsoft Reaches a Historic Milestone, Using AI to Match Human Performance in Translating News from Chinese to English. Microsoft Blog, March 14, 2018.
[46] Microsoft Debates What to Do with AI Lab in China. *New York Times*, January 10, 2024. Available at: www.nytimes.com/2024/01/10/technology/microsoft-china-ai-lab.html

Table 4.1 *Managing geopolitical challenges*

	Resources	Competitive advantage	Organization
Impact of geopolitical tensions on global companies	• Resource access is controlled by government • Restrictions on use of resources • Competitors may have resource advantage	• Outsiderness as a liability • Perception of state control hurts foreign businesses, especially if company is from adversarial countries	• Supply chain risks • Restrictions on sharing resources and knowledge across subsidiaries within the company
Strategies to manage geopolitically driven challenges	• Identify resource munificent locations, including foreign countries • Evaluate path dependency in use of specific resources • Secure resources (including investments) through geographic diversification	• Embrace localization and local embeddedness • Evaluate if control rights can be moved to more neutral locations • Manage perceptions of corporate nationality	• Local-for-local approach giving local subsidiaries greater independence • Spin out businesses to operate independently across geopolitical fault lines • Keep sensitive projects (and employees working on those projects) close to home

Summarizing Strategies

The previous sections laid out how a company's strategic decisions are impacted by geopolitics, and how managers can respond. These are summarized in Table 4.1. Broadly, managers can focus on three critical pillars of strategy making to assess their risks and identify approaches to minimize or overcome these challenges. These decisions involve resources (who gets what), competitive advantage (how to win), and firm organization (who does what).

ONLY FOR STRATEGIC SECTORS, RIGHT?

Traditional thinking on geopolitics often focused on what might be considered as strategic sectors, that is, areas of the economy that hold critical importance for a country's security and interest. These sectors often have a direct impact on a country's competitiveness especially vis-à-vis rival countries, their defense capabilities, and their long-term development. But what exactly is a strategic sector? This remains elusive. New technologies related to artificial intelligence were treated as central to national interest, even though they were in very early stages of development and their potential was untested. Back in 2008, national security industries in the US included sectors such as advanced materials and processing, chemicals, information technology, telecommunications, aerospace, and energy. But the US expanded this list substantially in 2022, including microelectronics, artificial intelligence, biotechnology and biomanufacturing, quantum computing, advanced clean energy, climate adaptation technologies, critical materials such as lithium and rare earth elements, and elements of the agricultural industrial base.[47] The point is that it is not always clear what is, or could become, a strategic sector.

---

[47] Executive Order on Ensuring Robust Consideration of Evolving National Security Risks by the Committee on Foreign Investment in the United States. The White House, September 15, 2022. Available at: www.whitehouse.gov/briefing-room/presidential-actions/2022/09/15/executive-order-on-ensuring-robust-consideration-of-evolving-national-security-risks-by-the-committee-on-foreign-investment-in-the-united-states/

But in some ways, it doesn't really matter what counts as a strategic sector. The structural approach to assessing the impact of geopolitical tensions applies to firms in all industries, whether a government body classifies it as a national security industry or not. When faced with rising tensions, governments and firms tend to become risk averse and see potential challenges where none existed before. Governments become more cautious about interactions with rival countries along any number of dimensions. Firms in many different industries can be impacted by geopolitical tensions, even if the extent of the impact varies.

Take the case of the toy industry. It is hard to see how brightly colored blocks for toddlers, dolls in all shapes and sizes, or board games of varying difficulty could be of strategic national interest. The relatively low concern regarding national security is reflected in the fact that about 80 percent of all toys sold in the US and Europe are manufactured in China. Despite rising labor costs, China has a firm hold on this sector. It is challenging to reshore away from the country, as many potential alternative locations lack sufficiently large labor pool or high-quality infrastructure. But this industry also came under scrutiny and toys were caught in the geopolitical crossfire. Tariffs on manufactured goods increased from the US–China trade war, adding to costs for producers. And although tariffs on toys are still relatively low, this could change if China's "permanent normal trade relations" status is withdrawn as some lawmakers have demanded.[48] What is the strategic implication? Toy manufacturers have to take a close look at their company's organization and determine where activities will take place.

One alternative is India, whose competitiveness in the toy industry is increasing. The country's share of imports from China declined from 94% in 2013 to 64% in 2024. The Indian government

---

[48] Toy Manufacturers' Shift from China Is No Child's Play. *Reuters*, January 16, 2024. Available at: www.reuters.com/business/retail-consumer/toy-manufacturers-shift-china-is-no-childs-play-2024-01-15/

put in place a number of measures, including a focused National Action Plan for Toys that included an increase in basic customs duty on toys, sample testing to curb substandard imports, and support through cluster-based approaches.[49] As a result, the number of manufacturing units doubled, gross sale value increased, and labor productivity rose. Finally, Indian's rise as a toy exporting nation was supported by its greater integration into the toy value chain and zero-duty market access for domestically manufactured toys in critical markets such as Australia and the UAE.

So, whether toys are strategic or not, the industry was impacted by geopolitical tensions.

Take another example: Hollywood. For decades, American filmmakers relied on expertise from the US Defense Department in making movies. The Pentagon allowed shooting on military bases, Navy ships, and other locations. They weighed in on the filmmaking process to ensure authentic settings and accurate technical information. Think of a movie such as Top Gun. In 1986, audiences flocked to theatres to see Tom Cruise star as Pete "Maverick" Mitchell engage in risky missions and daring maneuvers. But according to the producer, the movie would not have been made without the military's assistance which included significant input on various aspects from locations and equipment to personnel.[50]

As it turns out, several Hollywood films had successful runs in China. But to get to Chinese screens, filmmakers had to cut or modify scenes that Chinese censors objected to. With growing geopolitical tensions, Chinese censorship raised the cost for Hollywood filmmakers. The US Defense Department updated its rules to "prohibit assistance to any directors who plan to comply or will likely comply with censorship demands from the Chinese government in

---

[49] See the Economic Survey 2023–2024. Government of India, Ministry of Finance, July 2024. Available at: www.indiabudget.gov.in/economicsurvey/

[50] The Long, Long, Twisty Affair between the US Military and Hollywood. *Vox*, May 27, 2022. Available at: www.vox.com/23141487/top-gun-maverick-us-military-hollywood-oscar-winner-best-sound

order to distribute their movie there."⁵¹ At the same time, China has advanced ambitions to become a cultural influence. They have supported efforts by local filmmakers to create films in line with China's global aspirations.⁵² This means Hollywood is caught in the middle of trade and diplomatic tensions between China and the US, with significant strategic implications. What kind of products (movies) should American filmmakers focus on? What government resources do they depend on? Do they have a plan for what to do if those resources are withdrawn? Thus, geopolitical tensions are reshaping many industries, even those not traditionally considered as being relevant for national security.

ONLY FOR LARGE MULTINATIONAL FIRMS, RIGHT?

It is easy to be lulled into the idea that geopolitics is only relevant for large multinational firms. You might rightly wonder why small and medium-sized enterprises that have no exports or foreign operations should pay attention to geopolitics when they have to make payroll, focus on sales, invest in technology, and keep employee turnover low. But in some ways, size does not matter.

Take the case of start-ups. The US National Counterintelligence and Security Center has warned technology start-ups that they may be intricately tied to global geopolitics. The US government alerted companies that "foreign threat actors" may use private investment including venture capital and private equity to not only exploit start-ups but also threaten economic and national security.⁵³ They cautioned that by investing in early-stage US start-ups, foreign actors could potentially take advantage of their need for cash and gain access

---

[51] Pentagon to Filmmakers: We Won't Help You If You Kowtow to China. *Politico*, June 30, 2023. Available at: www.politico.com/news/2023/06/30/pentagon-to-filmmakers-we-wont-help-you-if-you-kowtow-to-china-00104315

[52] Why China Has Lost Interest in Hollywood Movies. *New York Times*, January 23, 2024. Available at: www.nytimes.com/2024/01/23/business/china-box-office-hollywood.html

[53] US Warns Tech Start-Ups on Security Threats from Foreign Investors. *Financial Times*, July 25, 2024. Available at: www.ft.com/content/cedfc2cf-209e-4af6-97f5-56fca6ebdb56

to intellectual property under the guise of due diligence. The government's warning mentioned a UK company that faced bankruptcy after sharing its intellectual property with a potential Chinese acquiror – one that ultimately abandoned the deal.

At the same time, large venture capital firms that back dozens of start-ups encouraged portfolio companies to tighten staff vetting. As one former counterintelligence officer noted, there are human-driven risks for companies[54]:

> Some employers have realised that when they are hiring people, they have to understand if they have any vulnerabilities they should be aware of. [...] Simply maintaining ties to certain countries means [an individual] could be vulnerable to being exploited, even if they do not want to cause the company harm.

Or consider companies such as Océinde, a family-owned French paint producer and Teknos, a fourth-generation family-owned firm in Finland. Both companies found themselves caught up in the geopolitics of the paint industry.[55]

A key ingredient in paints and coatings is titanium dioxide. The same compound is also used in the aerospace industry to produce titanium metal used in aircrafts, making a strategic ingredient.

The production of titanium dioxide was dominated by Chinese producers, who controlled about 83% of the global market, up from 29% in 2008. The rise in China's production and market share was accompanied by the closure of non-Chinese production, including an estimated five producers in the European Union. Following an anti-dumping investigation, the European Union proposed tariffs of up to 39.7 percent on Chinese exports of titanium dioxide.

---

[54] Silicon Valley Steps Up Staff Screening over Chinese Espionage Threat. *Financial Times*, June 19, 2024. Available at: www.ft.com/content/c5594136-55f7-43c3-8914-d1c4290f6670

[55] Paint Makers Say EU Tariffs on Chinese Imports Risk Bankrupting Them. *Financial Times*, September 29, 2024. Available at: www.ft.com/content/f606f907-32f7-4c43-963d-84e723eb55cd

For Océinde and Teknos, this meant being caught in the middle. If prices of titanium dioxide went up in the European Union, they would have to pass on higher costs to customers risking a downturn in the industry. On the other hand, if Chinese supply was diverted elsewhere, there would be a shortage of raw materials, which would result in production disruptions. What could they do? They joined other paint makers in pushing the European Union to rethink their tariffs. Another option they considered was evaluating locations outside the European Union block for future investments.

NAVIGATING COMPLEXITY

Geopolitical tensions can have far reaching consequences and increase stress on the structures supporting global interactions of multinational companies. To operate in this world, a whack-a-mole approach of addressing issues when and where they crop up is not sufficient. Companies need to make some core strategic decisions to actively manage these tensions. For many, this means changing the way they undertake global operations through resource allocation, reshaping their competitive advantage, and reorganizing the global firm. Getting to those decisions can be hard since it relies on the (often competing) cognitive frames of decision-makers.

5 Managing Geopolitics
Whose Job Is It?

Every strategy needs the right implementation. Without it, even the best laid plans often fail. As companies increasingly acknowledge the need to actively manage the impact of rising geopolitical tensions, they are looking for trained and professional staff to carry out these critical functions. They need a team that is forward looking, has a global orientation, and takes a balanced approach to managing geopolitics. Too few, however, have such a team.

SKILLS FOR MANAGING GEOPOLITICS

Even as companies hunt for geopolitical advice, it is worth taking a step back to assess what skills are needed. Broadly, this is about: **S**canning, **P**ersonalizing, **P**lanning, and **P**ivoting (**S-PPP**) (Figure 5.1).

Scanning

Companies need to understand the global landscape and assess where friction may arise. To be one step ahead of the adverse consequences of limited market access, unequal playing field, poor investment security, and institutional misalignment, they need to have good access to some baseline information. What are the trends in important markets? What are the relevant events and policy actions that have consequences for the future of the business? What opportunities might exist during times of flux?

To collate such information, firms mostly rely on two types of sources. The first is former diplomats, senior civil servants, and politicians, whose rolodexes and political antenna are both useful to companies. Government officials are well versed in the informal norms around enacting, discarding, or enforcing rules and regulations. They are also aware of procedures for changing or enforcing

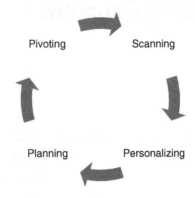

FIGURE 5.1 Skills for managing geopolitics

policies and experience the discussions or bargaining processes around policy adoption and change. These individuals draw on prior experience or networks to open doors for companies. They are able to make introductions and get the right people in the room. They are also able to leverage their expertise to gauge which way the policy winds are shifting in a market. One Japanese diplomat was quoted by the *Financial Times* as saying[1]:

> [Companies] are desperate for a more granular understanding of risk and basically using the foreign ministry as a source of expertise, and they figure they can give themselves what they don't have by offering [diplomats they are trying to hire] money.

Lee Feinstein, a former American ambassador, similarly noted that many companies valued advice from those who have been "in the room where it happens."[2] A pharmaceutical company in Demark explained that[3] "[w]e recently hired two people from the Danish

---

[1] Companies on the Hunt for Geopolitical Advice. *Financial Times*, October 17, 2023. Available at: www.ft.com/content/608a43e2-710c-4918-84d6-e0d75511918e

[2] Inside the Secretive Business of Geopolitical Advice. *The Economist*, October 5, 2023. Available at: www.economist.com/business/2023/10/05/inside-the-secretive-business-of-geopolitical-advice

[3] Quoted in Sofka, W., Grimpe, C., & Kaiser, U. (2021). Understanding the unwritten rules of the game: Government work experience and salary premiums in foreign MNC subsidiaries. *Journal of International Business Studies*, 1–23.

Medicines Agency. They help us to understand issues related to regulation and safety concerns. It is critically important for us to have experienced people in this area."

And companies are willing to pay for this expertise. In one study, researchers found foreign multinational companies paid salary premiums when hiring former government officials because of their superior procedural knowledge about policy making and their political connections to decision-makers.[4] In their study, the researchers quoted the HR consultant of a German multinational firm saying:

> When I screen CVs and compare applicants, such a [government work] position looks valuable to me. It is not only about the contacts that this person may have. He or she has knowledge about processes and what actions may be acceptable.

The researchers also found that foreign companies in Denmark valued such information more than local domestic companies – who may already have a better feel for their local economies. How much more? On average, former government employees joining subsidiaries of foreign multinational companies were paid about 3.25 percent more than similar employees joining domestic companies.

The second source is professional analysts. They rely less on individuals' personal contacts or experience, and more on data gathered from different sources. Typically, this includes several associates with knowledge of the history, politics, economics, and social factors of a particular region. Complementing this group is data gathered from other publicly available sources. Official government statements can offer insight into the country's positioning. Press reports can provide real-time on-the-ground data. For instance, the Global Database of Events, Language and Tone (GDELT) Project (www.gdeltproject.org) monitors "the world's broadcast, print, and web news from nearly every

---

[4] Sofka, W., Grimpe, C., & Kaiser, U. (2021). Understanding the unwritten rules of the game: Government work experience and salary premiums in foreign MNC subsidiaries. *Journal of International Business Studies*, 1–23.

corner of every country in over 100 languages and identifies the people, locations, organizations, themes, sources, emotions, counts, quotes, images and events driving our global society every second of every day." Documents put out by multilateral agencies like the United Nations, the World Bank, and the International Monetary Fund provide insights into macro trends like global development, trade, and economic indicators. Company filings, annual reports, and press releases also remain important data sources. Finally, alternative data sources such as blogs, forums, social media, e-commerce platforms, and satellite images generate nontraditional, big, and unstructured data from digital environments. Once data from multiple sources are collected, analysts use their data and analytical skills to make forecasts about how geopolitical factors will influence the global landscape. This includes, but is not limited to, trend analysis, pattern recognition, econometric modeling, and increasingly machine learning models. Advances in artificial intelligence allow for greater data processing power, automated data extraction, and faster machine learning algorithms.

A note of caution. In today's information age, it is easy to access lots of data. A manager is more likely to have too much information rather than too little. But not all of this information will be relevant or accurate. The key is to separate the signal from the noise. A good analyst will take into account the quality of the data and its relevance to the issue while ensuring that it is timely. This means collecting data from a variety of sources and paying attention to different levels of the problem.

Personalizing

Not every geopolitical event will have the same impact on all companies. While geopolitical analysis and forecasting provides the starting point, the next step is to determine which aspects are relevant for your particular business, and how. This step requires domain expertise, familiarity with the firm's operations, and strong internal ties – none of which are skills those undertaking the scanning step are necessarily best equipped with.

One aspect is customization of the analytical insights – either from former government officials or professional analysts – to the specific business case. For example, like many mining companies, Anglo American is interested in understanding a country's rule of law before committing to a 30 or 40 year mining project there. As Richard Price, the company's General Counsel, commented[5]:

> An erosion of the rule of law, perhaps through greater political interference, potentially gives rise to less regulatory certainty, less security of tenure – which is hugely important to us – less certainty around legal outcomes, a potentially deteriorating security situation, heightened criminality, and corruption.

To assess a country's rule of law, one could rely on a number of secondary sources that gather and report data on aspects such as the constraints on government powers, absence of corruption, open government, fundamental rights, and security. For instance, the World Justice Project index collates information from multiple data sources to rank more than 100 countries and jurisdictions annually. However, these data will be much more useful to Anglo American when they refer to the specific locations where the company has projects. Importantly, when specific leading and lagging indicators of potential volatility that matter for Anglo American's mining projects are included, these data can be used to preemptively manage hot spots. This requires domain expertise – specifically understanding the pain points of the business – which is different from the knowledge former political operatives and professional analysts provide. So, Anglo American developed their own dashboard that would be customized for its needs.

A second aspect is gathering and monitoring data that is relevant to the firm's specific operational challenges. Often, this means collecting relevant data from within the firm rather than relying on external primary or secondary sources. In other words, casting a wide

---

[5] Geopolitical Upheaval Recasts Chief Legal Officer Role. *Financial Times*, April 20, 2023. Available at: www.ft.com/content/edcdfa3e-577e-4ef3-a0a0-861e92e883bb

net in terms of data gathering is useful for geopolitical analysts to report on general global trends, or even specific trends in a given market or industry, but it does not always align with the challenges that a particular company faces. For AB InBev, the Belgium-based multinational brewer, one important issue was potential corruption linked to its global sales force. To address this, the company constructed a tool that could continuously audit their record-keeping practices across the company and alert them to real-time concerns.[6]

Planning

Once companies have data and information about the most relevant geopolitical indicators, they need to evaluate how shifts in the geopolitical environment will affect **their** business. This is arguably the harder part of geopolitical analysis. It combines existing data/trends with imagination and domain knowledge to explore the potential future states of the world as relevant for the business.

A common method advocated in this step is scenario planning. A formal planning approach allows decision-makers to simplify a large volume of data into a limited number of possible future states. The methodology is helpful as it examines the joint impact of various uncertainties, rather than looking at a single trend in isolation. Broadly, it is to identify different story lines that capture how various elements might interact under certain conditions. It is, however, more than just the outcome of a complex machine learning simulation as it includes aspects that are not (or cannot) be modeled. In this way, it calls for some degree of subjectivity.

Scenario planning became popular in the corporate world in the 1960s and 1970s and was most famously used by Shell to address uncertainty during the oil crisis of the 1970s. Since then, a number of companies have used it under various conditions.[7]

---

[6] Ibid.
[7] For more examples, see Ramirez, R., Churchhouse, S., Palermo, A., & Hoffmann, J. (2017). Using scenario planning to reshape strategy. *MIT Sloan Management Review*, 58(4).

Geopolitical scenario planning is hard because there are many variables one might wish to consider. However, the goal is to produce a small number of good enough final scenarios that can capture important distinctions. As Paul Schoemaker, one of the leading experts in strategic decision-making highlighted, good scenarios share a few criteria.[8] First, they are relevant to the company, that is, they connect with the mental models of senior executives and middle managers. Second, each scenario is internally consistent and does not have assumptions that are incompatible with each other. Third, every scenario tells a different story. Each describes a generically different future rather than variations of the same theme. Finally, scenarios should describe a state that is expected to last for a long time. There is little point in preparing for a highly uncertain eventuality that is going to be short-lived.

Here is one example that takes into account these criteria. Stephen Kobrin, a professor at the Wharton School, provided one illustration of archetypical scenarios that multinational companies might face due to growing geopolitical tensions.[9] He argued that notwithstanding the globalization backlash, we are unlikely to return to completely independent national markets. Instead, we are "likely to be stuck with an international economy from which we can neither withdraw nor manage effectively, a prolonged period of angst and uncertainty." He calls the first possible scenario "Muddle Through." In this scenario, the US and China manage geopolitical tensions and a degree of multilateral cooperation continues to exist. This means that while there may be backlash against globalization, government responses focus primarily on immigration and sociocultural issues. Anti-trade and anti-investment measures will have little effect and are mostly symbolic. Trade and investment will not sharply increase or decrease. The second possible scenario in his analysis is "Irrational

---

[8] Schoemaker, P. J. (1995). Scenario planning: A tool for strategic thinking. *MIT Sloan Management Review*, 36(2).

[9] Kobrin, S. J. (2017). Bricks and mortar in a borderless world: Globalization, the backlash, and the multinational enterprise. *Global Strategy Journal*, 7(2), 159–171.

Exuberance" where geopolitical tensions increase. There is constant risk of conflict among major powers and the rules-based international economic order collapses. The US withdraws from its international role while China imposes its own leadership. There is a spiraling increase in anti-trade and investment measures with a steep decline in the cross-border flow of goods and capital. In the third scenario – the "Billiard Table World" – we swing between a relatively open and relatively closed world. Rising geopolitical tensions are contained but national security concerns continue to persist. The US withdraws globally, but minilateralism emerges with multiple powers taking lead roles in their own regions or spheres of influence. Bowing to nationalism countries impose more restrictions on international flows of capital and goods but find that this increases costs for their own citizens. Those restrictions may be rescinded, but the lessons are only short lived as populists will impose restrictions again in an apparently never-ending cycle. The future of the international economy is more uncertain and less dependable.

Another example is from the Center for Strategic and International Studies. They highlight four potential scenarios of geopolitical order in 2025–30[10]: (1) Skull & Bones (weak United States, weak China); (2) Hammer & Sickle (weak United States, strong China); (3) Stars & Stripes (strong United States, weak China); and (4) Yin & Yang (strong United States, strong China). In the first scenario (Skull & Bones), the world order fragments, there is sustained low growth, supply chains are fragmented, and there is an increase in protectionism and nationalism. In the second scenario (Hammer & Sickle), China doubles down on military and technology advancement, while the US retreats from international leadership. Global trade is largely controlled by Chinese coercive practices, while a weak US economy drags down trade partners. In the third scenario

---

[10] 'Four Scenarios for Geopolitical Order in 2025–2030: What Will Great Power Competition Look Like?', Center for Strategic and International Studies, September 16, 2020.

(Stars & Stripes), the United States renews commitment to leading the international system, while the Chinese economy contracts and growth slows. The world economy is generally strong although Chinese trade partners will be adversely impacted. In the final scenario (Yin & Yang), the United States and China are both strong and assertive but cooperate on selected issues. There may be technology decoupling, but world trade remains largely intact. The world economy is stable with a strong recovery.

After identifying scenarios, companies should ask themselves how their organization will be impacted in each case. Indeed, more time has to be spent exploring how the different scenarios will reshape the firm's business and what actions the company could possibly take. For this, individuals participating in the scenario planning exercise should be able to articulate their sense of the future as well as the main building blocks of the company's current strategy. It should be collaborative and involve groups at different levels and functional backgrounds. Any strategic initiative should then be explored in the context of the possible scenarios. In practice, this might mean asking how the proposed strategy would be affected by each of the scenarios identified. In addition, what should be done to mitigate or exploit those scenarios. Thus, the scenarios act as guiding principles in strategy formation.

In Chapter 1, we discussed how geopolitical tensions influence companies. This offers a framework for planning. Managers can better understand how their businesses will be impacted by directing attention to the key issues of (1) market access, (2) level playing field, (3) investment security, and (4) institutional alignment. During periods of high geopolitical contestation, government policies – despite their varied forms – tend to cluster around these issue areas. These dimensions allow governments to reshape the basic market structure and influence how global companies can operate internationally.

As a result, companies can begin to ask themselves how each element of their value chain may be impacted by these factors. If there are indicators, for instance, that continued market access is going to be challenging, managers may focus on how their sales and revenues may be impacted. If the playing field is not level, what are the implications for competition, marketing, and product pricing in global markets? Alternatively, when companies are sensitized to potential risks of investment security, they may choose to forego a potential opportunity or scale down investment in a location. Finally, if there are leading indicators that institutional misalignment is likely, firms may evaluate the efficiency of global supply chains and the cost of adapting their products to different markets.

Pivoting

What if all your analysis tells you that your business is facing serious headwinds? Or that the current products and services may not meet the changing needs of the market? One option is to pivot, or to reorient strategic direction through reallocation or restructuring of resources, attention, or activities. In other words, change the direction of your strategy to survive in a new world. Pivots must be aligned with long-term expectations or trends. They should also reflect the company's existing capabilities and not undermine strategic intent. Ultimately, pivots must offer a path to a sustainable future that is profitable.

A good illustration is of a global technology company that witnessed troubling trends in many key markets related to its cloud storage business.[11] There was growing anxiety among policymakers and customers, who worried that if their data were stored on servers in other countries, then local governments could access their confidential information. Faced with this challenge, one option was to focus on assuring governments and customers that there was really no reason for concern and that the data security issues were overblown. But the company pivoted by aggressively opening more data

---

[11] Described in "Turing Geopolitical Risk into Strategic Advantage," *BCG*, March 30, 2021. Available at: www.bcg.com/publications/2021/advantages-of-geopolitical-risk-management-organizations-and-processes

centers in customers' home countries. This allowed the company to significantly expand its cloud business.

Researchers examining companies that pivot find that, on average, pivoting is a slow and incremental process.[12] Firms rarely completely reorient the company's strategic direction with one decision. Rather, they take multiple incremental steps that accumulate into strategic reorientation over time.

For successful pivots, companies must not only identify opportunities and strategies that are well suited to the changing landscape but also communicate this to all relevant stakeholders. They need to do this skillfully so that they can continue to draw on the resources and support of customers, investors, regulators, and the public. As a result, a successful pivot needs not only skilled strategists but also professional communicators.

WHOSE JOB IS IT?

One question for many companies is who should be responsible for managing geopolitics. A major distinction is relying on external versus internal expertise.

External Expertise

Geopolitical advisors have existed for decades, but the previously niche business is now drawing a torrent of bankers, lawyers, consultants, and analysts. Geopolitical advisory services are now among the mainstream professional services offered by large and small companies. Specialist organizations such as the Eurasia Group and Control Risks have long played in this space. But as demand for services has skyrocketed, divisions of companies such as Lazard, Goldman Sachs, PwC, McKinsey, and Teneo are all pitching for geopolitical advisory and/or risk evaluation services.

---

[12] Kirtley, J., & O'Mahony, S. (2023). What is a pivot? Explaining when and how entrepreneurial firms decide to make strategic change and pivot. *Strategic Management Journal*, 44(1), 197–230.

External expertise is especially helpful in the scanning stage. They house former diplomats, senior civil servants, and politicians as well as a growing number of analysts and data professionals. Combining the expertise of people and data, they are in a unique position to scan the environment and offer leading indicators of geopolitical change.

However, their expertise – as noted above – is more limited in the personalizing, planning, and pivoting phases. For these steps to be effective, external expertise must be combined with internal strengths, knowledge, and awareness.

Internal Expertise

Much of the hard work of managing geopolitical tensions lies within the company, but there is little guidance on how to do so. From board members to junior employees, companies are looking at different sources of skills and expertise to manage tensions.

Board of directors: This group is in a unique position to deal with external geopolitical threats. A company's board members are often the highest level in the company responsible for strategic decision-making. In general, the job of the board is to set strategic objectives in partnership with the company's managers and ensure the firm has sufficient resources to meet its objectives. The board outlines a risk management framework to monitor and manage risks and is accountable to key stakeholder groups.

To the extent that geopolitical tensions shape the companies' opportunities and threats, boards have to prioritize it in their decision-making. Many companies have put geopolitics on the agenda of their board of directors.[13] But for the board to be able to do its job well, it should have the relevant skills and expertise. A good starting point is having a diverse board with individuals who are forward-looking and have exposure to key markets. This could include individuals with experience in scanning, analyzing,

---

[13] Geopolitical Resilience: The New Board Imperative. McKinsey & Company, August 8, 2023. Available at: www.mckinsey.com/capabilities/risk-and-resilience/our-insights/geopolitical-resilience-the-new-board-imperative

and managing geopolitical tensions. Such directors can also play a role in conducting business diplomacy and engaging relevant stakeholders when necessary.

Boards also have another important task: Since they are not involved in the daily management of the company, they are well positioned to take the long view and really assess the assumptions underlying the company's opportunities and risks. They can take the time to develop and assess different scenarios and evaluate their implications for the company, which managers who are closely involved in daily operations may be more constrained in doing.

Top management: CEOs of global companies are increasingly putting geopolitics at the front and center of what they do. They are commenting on this publicly, a far cry from the days when politics was not their concern[14]: Jamie Dimon, the chief executive officer of JP Morgan Chase & Co. noted that "This may be the most dangerous time the world has seen in decades"; Ajay Banga, the President of the World Bank, highlighted the "dangerous juncture" for the global economy; Larry Fink, the CEO of BlackRock Inc. discussed a future with "less hope and a lot more fear." More importantly, they are looking at integrating geopolitics into their strategic decision-making.

Some companies define roles such as the "chief geopolitical officer" in a sign of how seriously the topic is taken.[15] For Mitsubishi, the Japanese conglomerate, a global intelligence committee headed by the president is a way to gather information and inform top managers on "geopolitical risk, economic conditions, new technologies, policy trends."

Other companies are calling on their general counsel or chief legal officers to outline a strategy for managing geopolitical risks. In-house lawyers are expected to understand and manage risk for

---

[14] Nothing Worries CEOs Right Now as Much as Geopolitics. *Bloomberg BusinessWeek*, November 2, 2023. Available at: www.bloomberg.com/news/articles/2023-11-02/tumultuous-times-for-global-politics-scare-wall-street-business-leaders

[15] Companies on the Hunt for Geopolitical Advice as Tensions Rise. *Financial Times*, October 17, 2023. Available at: www.ft.com/content/608a43e2-710c-4918-84d6-e0d75511918e

the company. They are trained to deal with issues such as contractual terms, intellectual property, regulatory issues, and compliance. Law schools haven't prepared them for fast-moving geopolitical challenges, but advising senior management on these issues and informing the company's strategy is increasingly an important part of their job. As the chief legal officer at an international consumer goods company reportedly commented[16]: "My role now is primarily as a C-suite strategic adviser. Giving technical legal advice is only 15 per cent of my job."

Government affairs teams: Many companies have a division (or some individuals) to form and maintain connections with external stakeholders. When dealing with policy issues, their main functions typically include (a) supplying information on actions taken or contemplated by governments, (b) assisting in obtaining government contracts, and (c) providing some form of representation before regulatory or legislative bodies. These teams play an important role in managing geopolitics because they can translate external information into internal relevance. Their sensemaking role and work background makes them uniquely positioned to do so. For instance, one study of companies in the European Union found that companies delegate government affairs functions to in-house managers with specific competencies, who stay in place for long periods, and possess detailed knowledge of the core competencies of the firm.[17]

One company that has epitomized this function is Microsoft. They have built an army of over 2,000 corporate diplomats working in legal, corporate, and government affairs divisions and on issues as diverse as regulation of artificial intelligence, protecting elections, tackling cyberwarfare against states, and identifying misinformation campaigns. Running on more than $1 billion a year, this unit

---

[16] Wanted: In-House Legal Leaders Who Can Interpret World Events. *Financial Times*, May 25, 2023. Available at: www.ft.com/content/100af542-9dec-4433-8a60-9f35e26753fa

[17] Coen, D., & Vannoni, M. (2020). The strategic management of government affairs in Brussels. *Business & Society*, 59(4), 612–641.

has even set up a representative office at the United Nations.[18] All of this works because this division reports directly to the president of the company and works with the top management. This means that the work of the division is integrated into the strategic thinking of the top management team. It is not a standalone function that is far removed from the rest of the organization.

Cross-functional teams: If geopolitical tensions play out in different markets and affect various value chain activities, a company will want several people in the organization to be engaged in strategic decision-making. This includes line managers who are focused on their own functions or businesses. For example, a marketing manager in one subsidiary may recognize that sales to government departments are declining as governments emphasize local procurement. This manager could come up with tactics at the local level to address this challenge, for example, creating partnerships with local firms or changing their supply chain to enable the company to meet local procurement guidelines. At the same time, top managers also need to be engaged so that they can coordinate the company's actions across different markets. The company may discover, for instance, that changing their supply chain to meet local procurement in one country disadvantages them in their home country where their government would like to have greater domestic control of supply chains. To pull off this balancing act, the company's country managers, functional managers, and top managers all have to share information and enable joint decision-making. This can be facilitated via cross-functional teams where different parts of the organization are represented.

FOCUSING ATTENTION

If companies are to proactively manage geopolitical factors – either to take advantage of opportunities or to buffer against risk – they need

---

[18] How Brad Smith Used Microsoft's $1bn Law and Lobbying Machine to Win Activision Battle. *Financial Times*, October 14, 2023. Available at: www.ft.com/content/07c507bd-2ce7-4345-85bd-0c27f408afbe

to pay attention to them. This may seem trivial, but it is anything but. Just as the squeaky wheel gets the grease, a company's resources can only be diverted to issues that managers recognize as one.

As it turns out, the difference between a company's success and its failure can come down to how much attention managers are paying to their external environment.

Researchers in one study examined the issues that were getting attention in failed versus successful companies. They compared fifty-seven companies that eventually went bankrupt with fifty-seven similar companies that were thriving.[19] To identify the specific issues these companies were paying attention to, the researchers examined senior managers' letters to shareholders in the five years prior. During normal circumstances, senior managers of surviving and failed companies paid equal attention to internal and external issues. But the big difference was what they did during crisis time. Failed firms paid a lot of attention to internal issues and the firm's resource constraints but not a lot to the changes taking place in the external environment. By contrast, managers in successful firms paid more attention to the critical aspects of the external environment. They didn't deny changes that were occurring and picked up on critical aspects of their external environment.

So, are geopolitical issues recognized as ones that deserve managers' attention? After all, there is only so much attention to go around. What managers focus on, and what they do, depends on the specific context. If geopolitical tensions are high and there are daily reminders of how these forces shape market competition, these issues will get a lot of attention. But when the situation is largely consistent and stable, there will not be much attention. But at another level, diverting attention to specific issues is not about an objective state of the world. It is about how individuals perceive the possibilities and

---

[19] D'Aveni, R. A., & MacMillan, I. C. (1990). Crisis and the content of managerial communications: A study of the focus of attention of top managers in surviving and failing firms. *Administrative Science Quarterly*, 634–657.

restrictions that they confront. Their own mental image of the issue colors their interpretation of events, actions, and context.

Ultimately, whether managers focus their attention on geopolitical issues and allow those issues to guide their strategic decision-making depends on their world view.

LOOKING AHEAD TO ARCHITECTURAL CHANGES

It would be reasonable to assume that some companies and managers are skeptical of deep, long-lasting changes that require systemic changes in their organizations because they assess geopolitical tensions as transient. Or they believe that specific events in far-away locations will not immediately impact their businesses. However, as I have argued in this book, the biggest impact of geopolitics will come from structural changes: that geopolitical tensions are reshaping the structural factors underpinning thirty (or more) years of global competition. Each factor in isolation may not have significant consequences, but together they can fundamentally alter how a global business operates or the environment in which it competes.

A useful parallel is technological change. Not all technological advancements are of the major kind. But occasionally, there is a series of seemingly small advances that together can torpedo a business. Consider Xerox, the company that created and popularized paper copiers. By the mid 1970s, the company faced growing competition from companies that offered smaller and more reliable models. The new models didn't need a whole lot of new engineering or technological advancements. But Xerox, the company that invented the core technologies and had significant experience making successful copiers, struggled to match its new competitors' products. After eight years of missteps and false starts, Xerox finally introduced a competitive model. But by this time, it had already lost half of its market share and faced significant financial problems.

Why did Xerox struggle? The company was faced with what researchers Rebecca Henderson and Kim Clark called "architectural innovations."[20] These are innovations that change the way in which the different components of a product are linked together but the fundamental design concepts don't change. As they explain, consider a company that makes large, ceiling-mounted fans. For this company, the introduction of a portable fan is an architectural innovation. The primary components such as the blade, motor, and control system are largely the same, but how those components interact with each other changes. The smaller size and colocation of the motor and the blade mean that the interaction between motor size, blade dimensions, and air circulation become more complicated than just shrinking each component.

But this is challenging for our large ceiling mounted fan manufacturer. Much of what the ceiling fan firm knows is indeed useful in the new product, but some of what it knows becomes a disadvantage and actually harms it. Recognizing what is useful and what is not, and obtaining new knowledge when necessary is hard for the established firm because of how it is organized and managed. One reason is because of embedded communication channels within the established firm. A ceiling fan company may have created a division for fan blades and another for motors. Engineers within those divisions build specialized knowledge about what works and what doesn't. And they are incentivized to become better in their specific siloed roles. They only interact with other engineers occasionally. This is the architecture of the firm.

When faced with a new challenge – such as the portable fan – the company may at first believe it has the right structure to solve the problem. After all, the components haven't changed, and the ceiling fan company has engineers who have excellent expertise on fan blades and motors. These divisions will continue to talk with each other to come up with new designs within their old framework.

---

[20] Henderson, R. M., & Clark, K. B. (1990). Architectural innovation: The reconfiguration of existing product technologies and the failure of established firms. *Administrative Science Quarterly*, 9–30.

However, they will eventually realize that they may have been talking about the wrong things or that they can't address the problem without considering the blades and the motor together. But how do they move forward? Do they simply modify the channels of communication, perhaps going from monthly meetings between engineers in different departments to weekly check-ins? Or do they have to gut the entire structure and organize the company differently? Should they attempt to modify the old product or build a new product? Ultimately, to be successful, the company will need to experiment, build, and apply new architectural knowledge effectively, which is time consuming.

Some of the same challenges apply to firms trying to navigate geopolitical tensions. While some established companies will see challenges, new ones may emerge to take advantage of the opportunities. Established companies may see some of their markets disappear or find that they are at a competitive disadvantage. They may decide, at first, that their existing architecture only needs some tweaks to respond to geopolitical risks. Perhaps more information, data, reporting, or risk analysis could be incorporated into their decision-making. But if the fundamental landscape for global businesses is being reshaped by structural factors as I have argued, then architectural changes would most certainly be needed.

6 Geopolitics and the Future of Work

Imagine working from the poolside with your laptop, sipping a drink, and watching the magnificent sunset on a tropical island. A short hop away are sun-kissed sandy beaches caressed by gentle waves. Or rugged coastlines where towering cliffs meet the crashing embrace of the sea. Other perks include spiritual retreats, sanctuaries of tranquility amid nature's grandeur, and warm hospitality. For some people, this was the reality during the COVID-19 pandemic. Escaping lockdowns in cities across the world, they moved to places such as Bali, Chiang Mai, and Hawaii. So long as they had good Wi-Fi connectivity, the freedom to work from anywhere, and flexible schedules, it seemed that digital nomads did, in fact, have it all. And for some, there was even an economic upside as they earned incomes in high-wage economies while living in relatively low-cost locations. Governments of countries such as Indonesia, Estonia, Portugal, Barbados, Costa Rica, and Malaysia got into the act and offered special visas to attract digital nomads.

That was the promise. A global landscape where people have the freedom to work from anywhere. Geographical boundaries dissolve as advanced technologies seamlessly connect professionals across continents and pave the way for a truly borderless workforce. The concept of a traditional office becomes an antiquated notion. Innovative companies recognize the immense talent that transcends physical borders, offering competitive compensation and opportunities for growth. Individuals are empowered to craft lifestyles that nurture their well-being while making a lasting impact on society, unhindered by the limitations of location.

But geopolitical tensions seem to throw a spanner in the works. The once-borderless world envisioned by digital nomads is facing new boundaries and constraints imposed by the realities of rising geopolitical tensions. As countries emphasize sovereignty, data security, and the protection of strategic interests, questions about how a global company coordinates its distributed workforce are increasingly fraught. The escalating competition between global powers for technological dominance has led to a fragmentation of the digital landscape, with countries increasingly imposing restrictions on the use of certain online tools, platforms, and services. Maintaining a secure digital footprint becomes challenging. Concerns about privacy and the potential for censorship or monitoring of online activities is changing the way workers interact with their jobs in both big and small ways.

How are geopolitical tensions shaping the future of work? While the allure of a borderless world remains strong, it is crucial to recognize the complexities and potential pitfalls that lie ahead. The workforce of the future may look different from the traditional one, but not in the ways you might have thought. We will look at how the landscape of work is being transformed, focusing on the who, where, and how of work.

"WHO" WORKS?

Rising geopolitical tensions means one of the biggest challenges for global companies is to address who can work on different types of projects. This is especially relevant in sensitive sectors and rapidly evolving technologies.

Work by Foreign Nationals

In sensitive sectors such as defense and critical infrastructure, there have always been nationality restrictions on who works on specific projects. For example, Lockheed Martin, an American aerospace and defense manufacturer, routinely hires for certain roles from only among American citizens with some form of security clearance. A job advertisement for a Logistics Engineering Associate Manager at this company clearly indicated that the role required government security clearance, and the job candidate must be a US citizen to be considered.[1] However, many other organizations are increasingly restricting who works on leading, or on the most cutting-edge technologies internally. Amid growing US–China tensions, some states have explicitly initiated limitations on who works on research projects. In May 2023, the State of Florida in the US squashed the recruitment of graduate students and staff members from China, Russia, and other countries labeled as of concern.[2] While researchers at the state's flagship universities were concerned about how their research competitiveness will be affected by the new rules, talented Chinese students would consider graduate schools and research opportunities elsewhere.

As early as 2019, US semiconductor companies such as Intel, Qualcomm, and GlobalFoundries witnessed increased challenges in hiring new Chinese employees or moving existing employees to key projects in the United States.[3] The US government sharply slowed approvals for semiconductor companies to hire Chinese nationals for advanced engineering jobs, even as talent supply domestically was rather scarce.

At the same time, Chinese companies have also faced challenges in attracting and hiring foreign workers. At Huawei, the giant networking company, hiring Chinese nationals has been the priority, although they are attempting to target non-Chinese hires from overseas as well.[4]

---

[1] Logistics Engineering Asc Mgr – Material Control – Secret (June 7, 2024). Job listed on Lockheed Martin website. Available at: www.lockheedmartinjobs.com/job/lexington/logistics-engineering-asc-mgr-material-control-secret/694/66125533136 (accessed on June 10, 2024).

[2] Florida Law Chills Chinese Student Recruitment. *New York Times*, December 15, 2023. Available at: www.nytimes.com/2023/12/15/us/florida-law-chills-chinese-student-recruitment.html

[3] U.S. Slows Hiring of Chinese Nationals by Chip Makers. *The Wall Street Journal*, May 21, 2019. Available at: www.wsj.com/articles/u-s-slows-hiring-of-chinese-nationals-by-chip-makers-11558431000

[4] China's Talent Strapped Multinationals Cast Their Line Internationally to Reel Back Overseas Chinese. *South China Morning Post*, July 11, 2023. Available at: www.scmp.com/economy/china-economy/article/3227264/chinas-talent-strapped-multinationals-cast-their-line-internationally-reel-back-ethnic-chinese

This has been challenging, even as the Chinese government has made visas simpler and cheaper to acquire, and increased tax incentives to make life for foreign residents more appealing. As one supply chain consultant was quoted in *The Wall Street Journal*,

> If you're a foreigner with a family and looking to grow your career, you no longer need to be in China, now that destination is Southeast Asia, India, or the Middle East.[5]

Another lawyer similarly noted that while back in the day upwardly mobile executives were fighting to come to China – the place where things happened – that allure was fading and "people don't see that there's an upside." At the same time, most multinational firms actually benefit from maintaining a diverse international workforce and facilitating cross-border movement of employees.[6] This helps to bridge communication gaps and instill a consistent global corporate culture. Firms can leverage local expertise and drive innovation through a diverse talent pool. But the lack of cross-pollination can lead to missed opportunities and misalignment with local market dynamics, as was evident in how many foreign automakers were caught off-guard by the sudden rise of China's electric vehicles during the pandemic when international travel was restricted. Indeed, research shows that having expatriate managers in local role can increase knowledge transfer between a firm's headquarters and its subsidiaries.[7]

The question of who works can lead all the way to the top of the firm. Consider the California-based space transportation start-up Momentus. The start-up was founded by Mikhail Kokorich and

---

[5] China Turns on the Charm for Foreigners but Its Allure Has Faded, *The Wall Street Journal*, March 18, 2024. Available at: www.wsj.com/world/china/china-turns-on-the-charm-for-foreigners-but-its-allure-has-faded-90f0df1f

[6] Leahy, Joe. (2024). China's Expat Gap Problem, Opinion Column in the *Financial Times*. Available at: www.ft.com/content/dfd5c399-976f-4f0b-8a1b-fbac495100b6

[7] Harzing, A. W., Pudelko, M., & Reiche, S. B. (2016). The bridging role of expatriates and inpatriates in knowledge transfer in multinational corporations. *Human Resource Management*, 55(4), 679–695.

was valued at $1.2 billion. The company then struck a deal to merge with Stable Road Acquisition Corporation. The goal was to turn the combined entity into a publicly traded company with a further cash infusion. For a start-up, and a founder, this is the dream scenario. But just prior to the merger, the chief executive resigned. As it turns out, being a Russian citizen meant Kokorich would not be able to review technical information about his own company's projects due to the US government's export control regulations.[8]

Notwithstanding these challenges, some have argued that the ongoing technological rivalry between the United States and China is really a battle for skilled scientists and engineers. One report argues that at the heart of this competition is talent that can drive technological innovation and economic supremacy.[9] China's leadership has called talent as the "first resource" in the quest for technological independence, and views the shortage of high-skilled labor as a significant hurdle in advancing fields such as artificial intelligence and biotechnology. This perspective is also echoed by industry leaders like Huawei's founder, who emphasized the importance of attracting talent as a key lesson from America's success. At the same time, while America has long been an attractive location for global talent, China's sheer scale allows it to produce vast numbers of science, technology, engineering and mathematics (STEM) graduates annually. China is projected to produce 77,000 STEM PhD graduates by 2025, compared to 40,000 in the US (and only 23,000 domestic graduates).[10]

---

[8] Momentus CEO Resigns amid US Government Concerns. *Space News*, January 26, 2021. Available at: https://spacenews.com/momentus-ceo-resigns-amid-u-s-government-concerns/

[9] Zwetsloot, R. (2021). Winning the Tech Talent Competition, Center for Strategic and International Studies, October 2021. Available at: www.wita.org/wp-content/uploads/2021/11/211028_Zwetsloot_Talent_Competition.pdf

[10] Zwetsloot, R., Corrigan, J., Weinstein, E., Peterson, D., Gehlhaus, D., & Fedasiuk, R. (2021). China Is Fast Outpacing US STEM PhD Growth. Center for Security and Emerging Technology, August 2021. Washington, DC. Available at: https://cset.georgetown.edu/publication/china-is-fast-outpacing-u-s-stem-phd-growth/

Other countries took a different approach. Ever since OpenAI launched ChatGPT, several attempts to create AI national champions have taken hold. For some countries in the Gulf, this meant leveraging foreign talent.[11] AI programs at richly endowed universities such as the King Abdullah University of Science and Technology in Saudi Arabia and the Mohamed bin Zayed University of Artificial Intelligence in Abu Dhabi actively sought out and recruited star researchers, professors, and administrators from leading Western institutions. At the same time, many of their students came from China. Together, they collaborated on creating leading AI capabilities in the region, working with local companies and firms.[12]

Work of Experts

For decades, the Chinese military has grappled with the formidable challenge of deploying a fleet of aircraft carriers capable of projecting power across the vast expanses of the world's oceans. The critical obstacle is mastering the intricate skills needed for carrier-based aviation operations – taking off from and landing on the confined, pitching decks of aircraft carriers at sea is hard. To accelerate the training of its aviators in the highly specialized tactics and techniques essential for conducting sophisticated carrier operations, the Chinese decided to tap the expertise of veteran American pilots. They purportedly set up a series of shell companies, including some operating in South Africa, to recruit former F-18 pilots as instructors for Chinese pilots. Lucrative contracts that offer hundreds of thousands of dollars and the opportunity to fly exotic aircraft could attract some former US naval aviators to sign up as instructors. The

---

[11] Welcome to the Era of AI Nationalism. *The Economist*, January 1, 2024. Available at: www.economist.com/business/2024/01/01/welcome-to-the-era-of-ai-nationalism

[12] Such efforts raised concerns in the US about whether the partnership would work against their interests. But to ensure that American firms continued to have a seat at the table, the US government brokered a deal for Microsoft to invest in an AI company there. See: Microsoft Makes High-Stakes Play in Tech Cold War with Emirati AI Deal. *New York Times*, April 16, 2024. Available at: www.nytimes.com/2024/04/16/technology/microsoft-g42-uae-ai.html

problem: This violates American export control laws and regulations that prohibit the dissemination of not just sensitive military technologies but also expertise to foreign adversaries without proper oversight. The US and its partners released a bulletin to deter current or former service members from training foreign nationals.[13]

Similar restrictions on technical experts sharing their work are also evident in the case of processing rare earth metals. While Western rare earth companies have struggled to master the technical complexities of processing rare earth metals, Chinese experts have a keen grasp of solvent extraction processes to refine strategic minerals. To ensure that these experts do not share their knowledge widely, China – using national security grounds – banned the export of technology to make rare earth magnets and technology to extract and separate critical materials.[14]

Growing export controls also impact the job prospects of foreign national experts. In the United States, for example, firms face uncertainty as export controls burden their talent acquisition. While many immigrants and foreign nationals come from countries that are subject to US export controls, they make significant contributions to the country's innovation ecosystem. At the same time, small and medium-sized companies who lack the scale and sophistication to navigate the complex regulations would be hesitant to hire them. For some companies it is a double-edged sword. While they may be extra cautious about hiring foreigners in order to play it safe, the same decision could also get them into trouble. Take the case of the law firm Arnold & Porter and the legal staffing company Law Resources. They were investigated by the Department of Justice for hiring discrimination based on

---

[13] Allies Warn Former Fighter Pilots Not to Train Chinese Military Members. *New York Times*, June 5, 2024. Available at: www.nytimes.com/2024/06/05/us/politics/us-china-pilots-allies.html

[14] China Bans Exports of Rare Earth Processing Tech over National Security. *Reuters*, December 22, 2023. Available at: www.reuters.com/markets/commodities/china-bans-export-rare-earths-processing-technologies-2023-12-21/

citizenship status. The parties settled claims that the companies violated the antidiscrimination provision of the Immigration and Nationality Act by screening out US citizens with dual citizenships and US citizens with work authorization from a document review project because of their citizenship status. The firms had to pay civil penalties and back pay while being publicly rebuked by the Department of Justice.[15]

Increasing restrictions on experts can also throttle corporate innovation. In one study, researchers focused on high-skilled workers in the United States.[16] The authors traced the patents filed by 707 US-based multinational companies to examine how new rules introduced in 2004 to limit the number of skilled foreign workers shaped innovation outcomes. They found that when the new rules came into effect, US multinational corporations increased the geographic dispersion of their research and development (R&D) workforce. However, this also likely led to increased coordination challenges. Consequently, innovation performance of the affected firms declined.

Domestic Employment

Geopolitics can shape the domestic employment landscape as well. One consequence of restrictions on foreign sales and export restrictions is that firms take a hit to their bottom line, which results in lower local employment. Consider the case of Lam Research, a California-based wafer fabrication equipment supplier. Approximately a third of the company's revenues in early 2022 came from China, but that share was expected to decline significantly. Lam executives estimated that their revenues in 2023 would be about $2 billion to $2.5 billion lower (constituting about 13 percent of their FY 2022 revenues), which they directly attributed to the US government's restrictions on shipping

---

[15] Justice Department Settles Immigration-Related Discrimination Claims against Law Firm and Legal Staffing Agency, Office of Public Affairs – U.S. Department of Justice, July 23, 2020. Available at: www.justice.gov/opa/pr/justice-department-settles-immigration-related-discrimination-claims-against-law-firm-and

[16] Nayak, D., Moreira, S., & Mudambi, R. (2025). Restrictive immigration policies and MNE innovation. Journal of International Business Studies, 56(1), 84–104.

chip technologies to China.[17] To reduce expenses in a further declining memory market, the company cut about 1,300 jobs, or 7 percent of their workforce.[18]

On the other side of the world, Chinese firms' ability to generate local employment has also been more muted. As trade tensions and stringent export controls kicked in, Chinese firms found accessing the more lucrative markets in the United States and Europe more arduous. They diverted attention to toward emerging economies of Southeast Asia and other countries aligned with China's Belt and Road Initiative. But these markets have lower purchasing power. As firms' revenue generation and growth prospects dim, their ability to generate jobs at home is also lower.[19]

But geopolitics is also associated with increased employment in other ways. The most striking example is hiring by defense companies. Companies such as Raytheon Technologies, BAE Systems, and Northrop Grumman witnessed an increase in orders from around the world as geopolitical threats increased and governments boosted defense spending. To keep up, these companies looked to recruit workers at the fastest rate since the end of the Cold War. When the *Financial Times* ran a survey of large defense companies in 2024, they found that 10 companies were looking to add 37,000 positions in all.[20] Most firms planned to increase their headcount by about 10–15 percent in a short period. The new positions were across the board, from apprentices to experienced career executives. In demand were engineers, software developers, and cybersecurity analysts as well as welders and mechanics.

---

[17] US Ban on China Chip Exports Rebounds, Causes 2700 Job Losses. *The Register*, January 27, 2023. Available at: www.theregister.com/2023/01/27/lam_research_layoffs_q2_2023/

[18] Lam Research to Cut 7% of Workforce after Weak Forecast. Bloomberg.com, January 26, 2023. Available at: www.bloomberg.com/news/articles/2023-01-25/lam-research-to-cut-7-of-workforce-after-forecast-disappoints

[19] China Employment Pressure "Worsening" This Year in Absence of Solutions to Shore Up Jobs. *South China Morning Post*, February 1, 2024.

[20] Global Defense Groups Hiring at Fastest Rate in Decades amid Record Orders. *Financial Times*, June 17, 2024. Available at: www.ft.com/content/9625dbaa-5d36-4bee-8610-f16ab7ad6b1d

Job Characteristics

In 2019, Pew Research undertook a series of focus groups in the United States and the United Kingdom. The two countries had, in 2016, participated in divisive votes on issues of globalization and immigration and time was ripe for a comparison between the two.[21] The study reiterated the narrative of being "left behind" as common in both countries. Respondents emphasized how globalization's impact left them disoriented, resulted in industrial closures, forced migration from their communities, and brought about significant economic hardship. These forces left many feeling adrift and struggling to adapt to new realities. At the same time, participants also talked about being "swept up" by globalization. The influx of investment and new job creation sometimes overshadowed and replaced traditional occupations. Simultaneously, it drove up property values, potentially displacing some people from their homes and communities. In both cases, participants experienced feelings of alienation and loss.

These stories align with the idea that the backlash to globalization is rooted in the mass public, and a growing share of losers of globalization increasingly lash out against it. A new study, however, brings much more color to this idea.[22] At the center of their analysis is an individual's job. For some individuals, the authors argue, the competition from products/services that are imported into the country poses more of a challenge to their future job prospects. Among individuals who recognize the threat of free trade to their jobs and perceive the costs of finding a new job to be high, the sentiments of not just protectionism but also xenophobia and isolationism are high.

---

[21] In the U.S. and UK, Globalization Leaves Some Feeling "Left Behind" or "Swept Up." Pew Research, October 5, 2020. Available at: www.pewresearch.org/global/2020/10/05/in-u-s-and-uk-globalization-leaves-some-feeling-left-behind-or-swept-up/

[22] Bisbee, J., & Rosendorff, B. P. (2024). Antiglobalization sentiment: Exposure and immobility. *American Journal of Political Science*, 1–18. https://doi.org/10.1111/ajps.12872

"WHERE" CAN WORK BE DONE?

Transformation of Work Location

In the late 1990s and early 2000s, India experienced a dramatic expansion in IT employment and outsourcing. While the Y2K problem created a huge demand for skilled IT workers, government policies that opened up the sector and the availability of a large pool of low-cost English-speaking engineering talent meant that India was a sought-after destination for foreign multinational firms looking for significant cost savings. Much of this, however, was restricted to back-office functions such as call centers, IT infrastructure management, data entry, and accounting. The work itself was limited to routine, repetitive tasks with little value addition or innovation involved.

Twenty years on, India's talent pool remained attractive for many multinational corporations. But the nature of work has been transformed. Rather than outsourcing to IT consultants, international companies focused on setting up their own integrated offices in the country to drive strategic value creation and innovation. Referred to as global capability centers, these operations cut across diverse functions and domains and formed an integrated part of the parent company's global operations. Because they keep things in-house, core work – which was never outsourced before – can be offshored to the company's own operations in India.[23] This includes sensitive projects related to intellectual property and customer data and in cutting-edge areas such as cybersecurity systems and artificial intelligence.

Take the example of Pratt & Whitney, an aerospace subsidiary of the American defense company RTX.[24] In January 2023, the company opened its India Engineering Center with an initial pool

---

[23] India's Back Office Boom Sparks "War" for IT Service Workers, *Financial Times*, November 20, 2023.
[24] Joining a Journey: Pratt & Whitney India Engineering Center Will Help Drive the Future of Commercial Flight. Pratt & Whitney news brief, January 27, 2023. Available at: www.prattwhitney.com/en/newsroom/news/2023/01/27/joining-a-journey-pw-india-engineering-center

of about 50 employees and a plan to add 450 more within 5 years. Engineers at Pratt & Whitney's new center focus on world-class technologies for aero, mechanical, and control systems in commercial engines. Using common tools and methods, their work is fully integrated with similar Pratt & Whitney centers in the United States, Canada, Puerto Rico, and Poland.

In contrast, the company's operations in China appear to emphasize after-market services and support. Although the company had a customer training center in China since the early 2000s, the focus has been on in-country product support ecosystem for Chinese customers.[25]

More generally, the type of work carried out in Chinese subsidiaries of foreign multinational firms has undergone a discernable shift. Where China was previously an attractive destination for high-end R&D labs, the shine appears to have dulled considerably amid the steady rise in geopolitical tensions between China and the West. Multinational corporations have grown increasingly wary of the risks associated with conducting sensitive, core R&D activities within China's borders. Concerns around intellectual property theft, forced technology transfers, and the push for self-reliance in strategic industries have prompted many firms to reevaluate they type of work that is carried out in their Chinese subsidiaries. In a survey published by the European Union Chamber of Commerce in China, several respondents noted that regional R&D centers in China were being reassessed.[26] Singapore was viewed as an attractive alternative location for some. Others debated about whether a growing R&D footprint in Southeast Asia should be led by their regional R&D headquarters in China or the one in India.

---

[25] Pratt & Whitney Enginewise Solutions Strengthen Foothold in China. Pratt & Whitney news brief, September 27, 2021. Available at: www.prattwhitney.com/en/newsroom/news/2021/09/27/pw-enginewise-solutions-strengthen-foothold-in-china

[26] China's Innovation System: The Localization Dilemma. 2023. Report by the European Union Chamber of Commerce in China. Available at: https://merics.org/sites/default/files/2023-04/2023%20China%27s%20innovation%20ecosystem%20the%20localisation%20dilemma.pdf

Data Sovereignty and Data Localization

Between 2005 and 2017, the share of internet traffic crossing national borders rose from roughly 10% to 26%.[27] Approximately 15% of e-commerce was international in 2016, about 15% of friendships on Facebook were across countries, 20% of trending videos on YouTube ranked among the top ten videos in more than a single country, and about 25% of Twitter followers were located in different countries than from the people they followed. Since 2019, the amount of data crossing national borders has tripled.[28]

The dream of a unified, global, borderless internet, however, is increasingly colliding with the geopolitical realities of data sovereignty. As countries exert greater control over digital resources within their sovereign boundaries, the confidentiality, integrity, and availability of data in cross-border transactions are challenged. As one McKinsey and World Economic Forum study found, the cross-border share of data flows fell 2 percent in 2022 after having grown substantially in the decade prior.[29]

This means the premise of the digital nomad is under question. Those who would like the ability of working remotely from various locations around the world using technology tools have to question its feasibility. One challenge comes from restricted access to cloud services and/or sensitive data. American business travelers to China, for example, may not have access to their work email. In other cases, one may not be able to access or process sensitive data from a client based in a country with strict data localization laws if the user is in another country; resulting in potential disruptions to work and productivity.

At the same time, there is a balkanization of data regulations across the world. A company's remote workers – or even workers

---

[27] DHL Globalization Index 2019, Figure 1.11 (pp. 24–25).
[28] DHL Global Connectedness Report, 2024, p. 41.
[29] The Global Cooperation Barometer Insight Report, January 2024. World Economic Forum in collaboration with McKinsey & Company. Available at: www3.weforum.org/docs/WEF_The_Global_Cooperation_Barometer_2024.pdf

in local subsidiaries of multinational corporations – have to be aware of and adhere to specific data protection laws and requirements in each location they work from. With potential legal consequences, the complexity and risks of distributed work becomes more challenging.

In turn, global companies are more cautious about engaging remote workers or distributing work across countries as they are fearful of security breaches or theft of trade secrets. For Latham & Watkins, one of the world's largest law firms, this meant cutting off automatic access to its international databases for its lawyers in Hong Kong. Their access was also restricted from other Asian centers such as Singapore, Seoul, and Tokyo.[30] In other words, while employees had default access to China documents, they needed explicit permission to see other content in the firm's international databases.

Overall, such restrictions could limit job opportunities and wage growth, especially in emerging or developing countries. Indeed, foreign direct investment is one the largest sources of external financing to developing countries, often higher than the contributions of remittances, private debt and portfolio equity, or official development assistance. As one World Bank study summarized, foreign direct investment contributes directly to job growth and wages in the country.[31] In 2018, for example, greenfield foreign direct investment projects created approximately 2.3 million new jobs. If global companies demonstrate hesitancy or apprehension toward implementing remote or distributed work models, there will be limited job opportunities in those countries that need them the most.

Finally, remote or globally distributed work could also have some additional costs that are not always visible at first brush. This

---

[30] Latham & Watkins Cuts Off Its Hong Kong Lawyers from International Databases. *Financial Times*, February 13, 2024. Available at: www.ft.com/content/9c0dc8aa-0418-4a0e-9629-699b77656234

[31] Saurav, A., Liu, Y., & Sinha, A. (2020). Foreign Direct Investment and Employment Outcomes in Developing Countries – A Literature Review of the Effects of FDI on Job Creation and Wages. In Focus – Investment Climate: Finance, Competitiveness and Innovation. World Bank Group.

includes costs associated with virtual private networks, secure cloud storage, and encrypted communication tools.

Reconfiguration of Supply Chains

It used to be the case that global supply chains were built to maximize efficiency and minimize costs. Rising geopolitical tensions, however, are prodding companies to shift from "just-in-time" to "just-in-case." In other words, companies are moving away from globally dispersed, lean, cost-optimized supply chains toward more resilient regional ones, even if it means higher costs. They are diversifying their suppliers across multiple countries, "reshoring" or "nearshoring" production closer to their end markets and decreasing dependence on suppliers from rival countries. These moves are expected to buffer them from delays or hold-ups, forced technology transfers, and the potential for economic coercion.

A company like Apple had nearly 200 direct suppliers, accounting for about 98 percent of their procurement spending. Since 2020, Chinese suppliers have been the largest camp, but number of suppliers from other countries such as Vietnam, Thailand, and India have been increasing.[32] HP announced that they would move the production of millions of PCs to Thailand and Mexico.[33]

At the same time, there is quite a bit of duplication in how companies are looking to buffer their value chains. For Astra Zeneca, a company with the world's largest sales of pharmaceutical products in China, the goal is to hit a revenue target of $80 billion by 2030. To do so, however, the company needs to circumvent increased US–China tensions. Even though pharmaceutical drugs are not impacted by tariffs, the company is evaluating different ways to buffer its Chinese business. As their chief executive

---

[32] Apple Moves Closer to China Despite Supply Chain Shifts. *Nikkei Asia*, April 26, 2024. Available at: https://asia.nikkei.com/Business/Business-Spotlight/Apple-moves-closer-to-China-despite-supply-chain-shifts

[33] HP to Move Production of Millions of PCs to Thailand, Mexico. *Nikkei Asia*, July 18, 2023. Available at: https://asia.nikkei.com/Spotlight/Supply-Chain/HP-to-move-production-of-millions-of-PCs-to-Thailand-Mexico

was quoted in the *Financial Times*,³⁴ "[w]e hope for the best and plan for the worst. [...] Planning for the worst means you have to consider there might be tensions in the supply chain."

Their approach is to duplicate operations in different regions – a clear deviation from the prior efficiency-focused approach. They plan to manufacture the same medicine in different facilities to serve various markets separately. As the CEO explained on the sidelines of the Bo'ao Forum for Asia,³⁵

> We are organizing ourselves so we can supply the US and Europe independently. We also are building a presence here in China so we can actually supply Chinese patients independently.

In contrast, Tesla, the American manufacturer of electric vehicles, is in the middle of an industry witnessing rising tensions, Chinese competition, and tariffs. The majority of vital electronic parts and components including displays, printed circuit boards, camera lenses, and semiconductors are produced in China and Taiwan. To buffer against potential supply chain disruptions, the Tesla's goal is to have alternative supply sources for non-China markets. This includes putting pressure on their existing suppliers to start building components and parts outside of China and Taiwan.³⁶ For many suppliers, this is hard to do as the mature supply chain is China and Taiwan. However, it again highlights the trade-off related to efficiency and costs versus control of supply chains.

One study examined the complicated effects on supply chains.³⁷ They examined the transaction value between Chinese suppliers

---

³⁴ AstraZeneca to Build Chinese Supply Chain as US-Sino Tensions Increase. *Financial Times*, May 22, 2024. Available at: www.ft.com/content/e54ac617-9869-4ba2-8933-8cc91942044e

³⁵ Astra to Split Drug Production along China-US Fault Lines. *Bloomberg*, March 27, 2024. Available at: www.bloomberg.com/news/articles/2024-03-27/astra-splits-up-drug-production-as-us-seeks-to-cut-china-ties

³⁶ Tesla Pushes Suppliers to Produce Parts Outside China and Taiwan. *Financial Times*, May 29, 2024. Available at: www.ft.com/content/6623fbc7-6a67-403d-89b0-0c117b8d2b6b

³⁷ Fan, D., Ma, P., Cui, L., & Yiu, D. W. (2024). Locking in overseas buyers amid geopolitical conflicts. *Journal of Operations Management*, 70(5), 756–792.

and US buyers by comparing two groups. One group consisted of 343 Chinese suppliers of US buyers whose products were impacted by increased US tariffs. The comparison group was another set of similar Chinese suppliers of US buyers whose products were not affected by changes in US tariffs. The researchers found that when new US tariff hikes were implemented, the transaction value in the first group declined by approximately 18 percent. But this decline was not uniform across Chinese suppliers. Innovative and socially responsible Chinese suppliers showed more resilience, effectively retaining US buyers amid the trade war. However, Chinese suppliers who were seen as having ties with local politicians were less attractive to US buyers.

RESHAPING "HOW" WORK IS DONE

Escalating geopolitical tensions have cast a long shadow over how work is done in both multinational corporations and domestic firms.

Revising the Job Description

Top managers are generally a harried lot. They must manage a range of issues, stretching from short-term demands to long-term strategic thinking. They must have a finger on the pulse of their customers as well as their competitors. The workforce at their companies is diverse, with geographic, national, cultural, and time-zone differences. They must also engage with multiple stakeholders whose agendas may not be aligned. They face environmental, social, and technological challenges. With so much on their plate, it is not surprising that they largely ignored geopolitics while they could still do so. According to a consultant, Fortune 500 CEOs had been taking a "geopolitical nap." As he described it:[38]

---

[38] War in Europe Is Waking CEOs Up from Their "Geopolitical Nap." *Fortune*, June 20, 2024. Available at: https://fortune.com/2024/06/20/war-in-europe-ceos-bcg-center-for-geopolitics-nikolaus-lang/

> Most people who are in leadership positions today always operated in an environment where geopolitics didn't play a role. ... [Those] who are in their 40s or 50s today have not known inflation for 20 years, or conflict for 60 to 70 years. But in the past five years, [they] experienced a series of exogenous shocks they were simply not prepared for... It puts a lot of pressure on leaders.

Focusing purely on the financial and operational fundamentals of the business is a luxury few top managers can afford today. They need to have the skills to build and maintain relationships with multiple governmental and nongovernmental stakeholders. Managers have to consider how their company's actions are aligned (or not) with the objectives of different stakeholders but also deliver value at the same time.

Meet Christophe Fouquet,[39] a father of six, an opera fan, a veteran of the semiconductor industry, and a physics graduate. He is technically sophisticated, wary of politics, and prefers to keep a low profile. He is also the CEO of the Dutch company ASML, which makes highly complex machinery needed to produce semiconductor chips.

When an opportunity to lead a company that holds a monopoly over the world's most advanced chipmaking came knocking, Fouquet believed his technical background and relationship with customers would be critical in the role. But he was soon to learn that his job might be something different after all.

The company's unique position in the chip industry put it squarely in the midst of geopolitical tensions. The Dutch government imposed restrictions on selling the company's more advanced

---

[39] This section drew on the following articles – (1) The New CEO Trapped in the US-China Chip Battle. *The Wall Street Journal*, June 5, 2024. Available at: www.wsj.com/tech/the-ceo-trapped-in-the-u-s-china-chip-battle-7340c949. (2) New CEO of Dutch Chips Champ Enters US-China Fray. *Politico*, April 24, 2024. Available at: www.politico.eu/article/christophe-fouquet-asml-dutch-chips-us-china-microchips-trade-war/ (3) Semiconductor Giant ASML Has a New Boss, and a Big Problem. *Wired*, April 22, 2024. Available at: www.wired.com/story/asml-ceo-chip-war-christophe-fouquet/

machines to China. The US had instituted additional guardrails to prevent ASML from selling certain machines containing American made components to specific Chinese chip factories. They also wanted to prevent the servicing of some of ASML's tools in China.

Fouquet was drawn squarely into addressing political concerns. He noted that his company's role was not to decide "what is right and what is wrong" but to educate officials about the company's technology and the possible repercussions of restrictions. He had to highlight to relevant policymakers the possibility of unintended consequences. For instance, stopping ASML from servicing certain machines in China would not prevent those machines from making chips but would put ASML at a disadvantage. The company would no longer know where all of its tools were or what was being done with them. In other words, they would lose control over their product. Such a step would also encourage Chinese competitors to build their own lithography systems that might eventually compete with ASML's.

But political wrangling is new at ASML. Anything diverting attention from technology was previously considered unnecessary fuss and summarily dismissed. So, to support Fouquet's public facing role, the company needed organizational changes as well. They had to hire politically savvy lobbyists and consultants in Europe and the US. With this, managing government affairs teams is another task for the top manager.

As if this wasn't challenging enough, Fouquet had additional problems on his plate. As tensions increased, he had to decide if the Netherlands was the most strategic place for ASML to be based in. The company had previously threatened to leave the country over concerns about adequate workforce, anti-immigration rhetoric, and the political rise of the far right. As a Frenchman leading a Dutch company, he faced greater scrutiny over choices addressing these topics.

Foreign-born CEOs of multinational companies are increasingly common, but their foreignness can be a critical issue when performance is poor. In one study, researchers examined the likelihood of foreign-born versus native-born CEOs being dismissed.[40] When a company's performance dipped, the likelihood of native-born CEOs being dismissed was roughly 4% but that of foreign-born CEOs was nearly four times higher at 16%.

Work, Life, and the Commute

Meet Geeta, a fictional twenty-two-year-old woman in India. Geeta graduated with a bachelor's degree in commerce from a regional college in South India, where she lived with her family. As she was completing her education, she learnt about the possibility of working at a large multinational company making and assembling phones. She was interviewed for the job and liked what she heard. The pay seemed good and work relatively easy. She accepted the role, which entailed assembling iPhones for Foxconn, a Taiwanese company that is a large supplier for Apple and the world's largest contract manufacturer of electronics.

But there was one issue that had to be resolved before she could start her new job. The job was hundreds of kilometers from her home. Where would she live and how would she get to work?

As an executive at another iPhone supplier noted,[41] "Generally, people in India expect to commute to work from their homes and, when their shift is over, go home and have dinner with their family." For other electronic companies in India, this meant bussing workers to-and-fro. But this limits the scale of any single factory to a few tens of thousands.

Foxconn – Geeta's employer – had other ideas. Importing the idea of worker dormitories from their operations in China where they had up to 300,00 employees working at a single plant, they made

---

[40] Thams, Y., & Rickley, M. (2024). Are foreign-born CEOs held to a higher performance standard? The role of national origin in CEO dismissals. *Global Strategy Journal*, 14(3), 578–603.

[41] India Bets on Worker Dormitories as Apple Leads Tech Pivot from China. *Financial Times*, December 12, 2023. Available at: www.ft.com/content/d3977a01-6c74-4ff8-8b3b-c6884d886350

plans to house workers in hostels nearby. The hostels provided food and accommodation. With transportation arranged by the company, it offered one potentially safe and efficient option for workers. For the company as well, there was greater flexibility in rearranging work hours to meet fluctuating demands. Plans for dormitories accommodating tens of thousands of beds were underway in states such as Tamil Nadu, Karnataka, and Telangana.

But there are big challenges to this model. Women workers housed in hostels found their movement restricted and lives isolated.[42] There were complaints and protests about the quality of dormitories and dining rooms.[43]

By 2024, the companies took a slightly different approach. Apple's contract manufacturers were planning homes for their employees built as part of a public–private partnership. In Tamil Nadu, the state with the largest Foxconn operations, about 58,000 houses were being built by the State Industries Promotion Corporation of Tamil Nadu with funding from government and private sources.[44] The massive employee housing program was aimed at improving efficiency and providing security to migrant women in the age group of 19–24 years, who made up almost 80 percent of the workforce in this industry. Contrast this with the housing challenges that a single woman face around the country.[45]

But Geeta's job itself is a byproduct of geopolitics. In 2021, Apple produced about 1 percent of its flagship iPhones in India.

---

[42] India's iPhone Factory Is Keeping Women Workers Isolated. Scroll.in, March 6, 2024. Available at: https://scroll.in/article/1064027/indias-iphone-factory-is-keeping-women-workers-isolated

[43] Apple Puts Supplier Foxconn's India Plant on Notice after Protests. *Reuters*, December 29, 2021. Available at: www.reuters.com/business/foxconn-apple-say-worker-dorms-india-iphone-plant-dont-meet-required-standards-2021-12-29/

[44] Apple to Provide Houses to Employees in India; Construction of 78,000 Units Underway: Report. *CNBC TV 18*, April 8, 2024. Available at: www.cnbctv18.com/business/apple-to-provide-houses-to-employees-in-india-construction-of-78000-units-underway-report-19393789.htm

[45] No Single Women: Chennai's Rental Problem. *The Times of India*, August 3, 2023. Available at: https://timesofindia.indiatimes.com/city/chennai/no-single-women-chennais-rental-problem/articleshow/102374108.cms

By 2025, that number was expected to be 25 percent.[46] Looking to diversify its supply chain away from China, Apple identified India as a country with potential. Apple's move, along with that of its suppliers, created 100,000 jobs in India. The most striking aspect is that nearly three-quarters of the newly created jobs were staffed by young women, who were just starting their careers and beginning to support their families financially. This was a significant shift away from the extremely low labor force participation of women in the country.

But while geopolitics made it possible for Geeta to find a relatively good job, it also changed her expectations about the relationship with an employer. Where to live, how to commute, and even the way of life was changing.

Workplace Culture

At some point, most global companies have to figure out how to manage global teams. Navigating cultural, time zones, and organizational differences is challenging in the best of times. Creating a unified workforce, where team members feel like they belong to an organization equally, no matter where they are geographically located, is one of the enduring challenges of managing multinational enterprises.[47] Done right, global teams can link the world together, tap into a diverse talent pool, exploit local expertise, unite far-flung groups, and make the company more efficient. However, when global teams struggle to collaborate effectively, they can create discord, lead to misunderstandings, and potentially derail entire projects. Indeed, research on international human resource management indicates

---

[46] Apple to Move 25% of iPhone Production to India by 2025, 20% iPad and Apple Watch to Vietnam, Analysts Say. *TechCrunch*, September 21, 2022. Available at: https://techcrunch.com/2022/09/21/apple-to-move-25-iphone-production-to-india-by-2025-20-ipad-and-apple-watch-to-vietnam/

[47] "Locals," "Cosmopolitans," and Other Keys to Creating Successful Global Teams. Knowledge@Wharton, September 12, 2009. Available at: https://knowledge.wharton.upenn.edu/article/locals-cosmopolitans-and-other-keys-to-creating-successful-global-teams/

that when there are cultural differences in the workplace, they generate significant social frictions.[48]

Yet rising geopolitical tensions have forced many global companies to implement organizational changes that tilt the balance toward discord rather than harmony. Increasing government regulations and oversight mean that multinational corporations have to institute structural changes that segment regions and teams, create distinctions among employees undertaking similar roles but are based in different geographies, create communication firewalls, and update travel and staffing policies. The sense of inclusivity and connection within the firm is being eroded.

As one researcher at the Beijing-based Microsoft Research Asia team who was planning to relocate to the office in Vancouver put it,[49]

> Previously, being a Chinese national working in an American institution meant having access to great resources from both countries. The space for communication is narrowing.

In a study by McKinsey, the authors highlighted how global teams can address these challenges.[50] To prevent stirring internal sentiment, firms may opt to restrict discussions on geopolitically sensitive issues to senior leaders at headquarters and top in-country executives. They also have to sensitively continue to create a sense of global connectivity. In their study, McKinsey pointed to a leading US firm that aimed to increase cultural cohesion by purposefully

---

[48] See, for example: Neeley, T. B. (2013). Language matters: Status loss and achieved status distinctions in global organizations. *Organization Science*, 24(2), 476–497.; Reiche, B. S., Harzing, A. W., & Pudelko, M. (2017). Why and how does shared language affect subsidiary knowledge inflows? A social identity perspective. In *Language in International Business: Developing a Field* (pp. 209–253). Cham: Springer International Publishing.

[49] Microsoft to Move Top AI Experts from China to New Lab in Canada. *Financial Times*, June 10, 2023. Available at: www.ft.com/content/d21d2f85-7531-4536-bcce-8ca38620fe55

[50] Can Your Company Remain Global and if So, How? *McKinsey Quarterly*, May 17, 2024. Available at: www.mckinsey.com/capabilities/strategy-and-corporate-finance/our-insights/can-your-company-remain-global-and-if-so-how

bringing the entire incoming class of employees from a geopolitically distant market to its global headquarters to enhance shared learning and connectivity.

Notwithstanding such measures, managers have to be aware that multinational corporations can be sites of national identify politics which emphasize the "us vs. them" narrative.[51]

Business Travel

When Lina stepped off the plane in one of the world's largest and busiest airports, she couldn't shake the eldritch feeling that she was being watched. Not just the usual curious glances at a foreigner, but something more intense and purposeful. Her burner phone buzzed – an abrupt reminder from headquarters. "Trust no one. Rely only on yourself" the message read, before self-deleting. She held her nondescript bag closer, acutely aware of her mission. The dummy laptop in her bag was loaded with innocuous data, while real information was encrypted in a series of random photos on her phone. Lina smiled wryly. Three years ago, she had been a simple tech executive – a top graduate of her class at business school, a fast-rising talent in her company, and a tech-enthusiast who believed at least some of the world's problems could be solved by new advances in her fast-growing industry. Today, she felt more like a character from a Le Carre novel. One misstep during her three-day business trip, and the entire operation could unravel. This would be the first of many challenges. Welcome to the new world of international business, where every trip is a high-stakes game.

While Lina and her trip are fictional, her challenges are not unfamiliar to managers around the world. One *Wall Street Journal* article pointed to experts advising business travelers to China to assume that anything on a phone, laptop, or other digital device can

---

[51] Vaara, E., Tienari, J., & Koveshnikov, A. (2021). From cultural differences to identity politics: A critical discursive approach to national identity in multinational corporations. *Journal of Management Studies*, 58(8), 2052–2081.

be viewed by authorities.[52] They recommended leaving your everyday phone and computer at home and traveling with only "burner" devices – a smartphone or laptop that has been wiped of data or apps and has only a small number of must-have contacts, encrypted communication apps, and a VPN. They also recommended always keeping your device on your person. Notwithstanding these recommendations, assume that your communications are not totally secure. So, executives need to be careful about the messages they send and/or receive.

Many global companies have adopted similar guidelines. In industries such as aerospace and semiconductors, firms have long asked US employees to take separate phones and laptops to China over security concerns. Consulting companies such as McKinsey and accounting firms such as Deloitte and KPMG have also reportedly introduced similar guidelines with respect to executive travel to Hong Kong.

At the same time, stringent data security measures in China have also forced foreign firms operating there to limit the sharing of China-based information outside the country, even of day-to-day corporate operations. Reports suggest executives based in China are also sometimes advised not to take their laptops and smartphones out of the country, even to other countries in Asia, making it difficult to manage regional operations from the country.[53]

Retooling and Reskilling

For many countries, energy security remains an enduring concern. While coal-fired power plants led China's growth for years, the country's leadership turned to an ambitious plan to limit its

---

[52] The New Rules for Business Travel to China. *The Wall Street Journal*, May 27, 2023. Available at: www.wsj.com/world/the-new-rules-for-business-travel-to-china-f476f7b7

[53] Burner Laptops and Smaller Profits: Firms Portray Their China Challenges. *The New York Times*, September 19, 2023. Available at: www.nytimes.com/2023/09/19/business/american-european-chamber-commerce-china.html

reliance on imported fossil fuels and phase-out polluting coal-based plants. While heavily investing in renewable sources such as wind and solar, they have also significantly expanded their nuclear power capacity. In the ten years leading to 2024, China constructed thirty-seven new nuclear reactors, bringing the total to fifty-five. This rapid expansion contrasts sharply with the United States, which remains the global leader with ninety-three reactors but only added two during the same period. With nearly dozen new ones under development, China is poised to become the world's largest nuclear power producer in the near future. In contrast to the early days of its nuclear program, when the country imported much of its nuclear technology, most of the new and planned reactors are based on Chinese designs.[54]

Following its success at home, the Chinese nuclear power sector looked outward, to reshape global energy markets.[55] Karachi's Paradise Point nuclear power stations that use the Chinese-designed Hualong One reactors offer a promising start for an export push.[56] With domestic suppliers providing more than 90 percent of the equipment, the power station was billed as a successful collaborative innovation effort. Over the next decade, Chinese plans for international expansion lie across Asia, the Middle East, and Africa. However, Chinese attempts at exporting nuclear technology have faced resistance in other markets.

Nonetheless, as concerns grow about energy security and the threat of gas supplies following Russia's invasion of Ukraine, countries such as India, the US, France, Britain, and Poland are planning to revive

---

[54] China Is Building Nuclear Reactors Faster than Any Other Country. *The Economist*, November 30, 2023. Available at: www.economist.com/china/2023/11/30/china-is-building-nuclear-reactors-faster-than-any-other-country

[55] Xi's Climate Goals Boost China's Nuclear Industry. *Financial Times*, June 21, 2024. Available at: www.ft.com/content/af88f874-69b2-478e-9d33-ad3b31468258

[56] US$2.7 Billion China-Designed Nuclear Power Plant Launched in Pakistan amid Energy Crisis. *South China Morning Post*, February 2, 2023. Available at: www.scmp.com/news/asia/south-asia/article/3208918/us27-billion-china-designed-nuclear-plant-launched-pakistan-amid-energy-crisis

older plants or start new ones. Others are also looking at nuclear power as a technology with the potential to offset climate change issues.

As the biggest wave of new projects in decades comes on board, there is an acute skills gap.[57] Tens of thousands of workers are needed to build atomic power stations, and nuclear engineers and technicians will have to be trained. In Western economies, it is retirees sustaining this effort.[58] Jean-Marc Miraucourt, a sixty-nine-year-old former engineer at the French state-owned nuclear operator EDF, continues to advice the company even after retiring in 2019. At Newcleo, a European start-up focused on developing small reactors, the chief scientific officer is aged seventy-five and a sixty-two-year-old engineer is helping to train new joiners.

LEADING FORWARD

In 2012, Anne-Marie Slaughter, an American lawyer and foreign policy analyst, wrote an influential article titled "Why Women Still Can't Have it All."[59] It called attention to the structural factors in the American labor market that prevented women from excelling at work while also managing meaningful social and family relationships outside work. In the dozen years since, remote work and job flexibility was often offered as one solution that could help some in the labor force. However, as geopolitical tensions escalate, the possibilities for remote workers are coming under increased scrutiny. The fantasy of the digital nomad promises to be just that – a fantasy.

At the same time, geopolitical tensions are reshaping the landscape of work, influencing who works, how work is performed, and where it takes place. As nations become increasingly protective of their technological advantages and intellectual property, there is a

---

[57] UK Ministers Plan Task Force to Plug Nuclear Skills Gap. *Financial Times*, August 1, 2023. Available at: www.ft.com/content/2e420836-c529-484b-a119-9f0b833acb08

[58] Nuclear Industry Brings Back "Silver Tsunami" of Retirees. *Financial Times*, May 17, 2024. Available at: www.ft.com/content/eb89cbc1-2cc3-48d4-9c8c-e2c10f2b2ce0

[59] Slaughter, A.-M. (2012). Why Women Still Can't Have It All. *The Atlantic*, July/August 2012. Available at: www.theatlantic.com/magazine/archive/2012/07/why-women-still-cant-have-it-all/309020/

shift toward more localized talent pools. While creating new opportunities in some regions, it is also limiting them in others. The nature of work itself is evolving in response to these tensions. Remote work, cybersecurity, new protocols, and organizational practices are fundamentally altering how employees interact with information and each other. Moreover, the physical location of work is being reevaluated. Companies are diversifying their operational footprints to mitigate risks associated with geopolitical hotspots, leading to the emergence of new global hubs and the decline of others.

As we look to the future, it is clear that adaptability will be the key. Workers, companies, and nations that can nimbly navigate this new geopolitical reality will thrive, while those that cling to outdated models may struggle.

What can you do?

Managers can proactively address the challenges posed by an increasingly complex geopolitical landscape, ensuring their organizations remain agile, secure, and culturally adept.

Build geopolitical competence: Companies should put in place organizational structures and expertise to incorporate geopolitical considerations at the highest level of strategic decision-making. Board, top managers, specialized teams, outside consultants, line managers, and local teams should work together to provide strategic thinking on geopolitics for the company.

Balancing a global workforce: Managers could develop comprehensive remote work policies that acknowledge and adapt to the nuances of a globally distributed team. State-of-the-art collaboration tools that ensure seamless communication are only the first step. There needs to be ongoing attempts to create and maintain company culture in an environment of lowered trust.

Fortify cybersecurity defenses: With rising threats, firms have to invest in regular security audits. Implement robust authentication systems across all systems to prevent unauthorized access. Develop and deliver periodic cybersecurity training programs that keep all employees up-to-date on the latest threats and best practices.

Workforce resilience through diversification: In some sectors, who works, and on which projects, is an aspect that companies have to actively monitor. Even if a company is not in a security sector, they need to keep a keen one on workforce development. Create a comprehensive talent acquisition strategy that targets multiple global regions, reducing dependence on any single talent pool. Develop strategic partnerships with educational institutions in diverse locations to cultivate a pipeline of future talent. Establish redundant supply chains across different geopolitical zones to mitigate the risk of disruptions. Implement a sophisticated risk assessment matrix for evaluating suppliers and talent sources.

Cultivate cross-cultural competence: Take an active approach to integrating a globally distributed team. Institute mandatory cross-cultural training programs for managers, focusing on practical skills for leading diverse teams. Establish a global mentorship program that pairs employees from different backgrounds, fostering mutual understanding and knowledge exchange. Encourage open dialogue, when possible, and share diverse perspectives.

7   Computational Geopolitics

> I often say that when you can measure what you are speaking about and express it in numbers you know something about it; but when you cannot measure it, when you cannot express it in numbers, your knowledge is of a meagre and unsatisfactory kind: it may be the beginning of knowledge, but you have scarcely, in your thoughts, advanced to the stage of *science*, whatever the matter may be.
>
> —Lord Kelvin[1]

In this chapter, we will address how one could quantify and explore the impact of geopolitics on global businesses. Broadly, computational geopolitics is an attempt to integrate quantitative methods and geopolitical analysis to understand and predict trends. It equips researchers, analysts, managers, and their companies with analytical capabilities to anticipate and respond appropriately to geopolitical challenges. It enables strategic decision-making by identifying and quantifying risks and opportunities. It also allows companies to assess the attractiveness of different markets and adapt to varying regulatory approaches.

WHY NOW? THE RELEVANCE OF A COMPUTATIONAL APPROACH

There is a confluence of factors that have led to the proliferation of computational methods to analyze geopolitics and its impact on firms. One is the exponential growth in data. The digital revolution has given rise to an unprecedented volume of data from a variety of sources. Data vendors offer a dizzying range of information, including

---

[1] Kelvin, W. T. B. (1891). *Popular Lectures and Addresses: Constitution of matter. 2d ed. 1891.-v. 2. Geology and general physics. 1894.-v. 3. Navigational affairs. 1891* (Vol. 1). Macmillan and Company.

on consumer behavior, financial analytics, and health-care data. Companies, in turn, are seeking external data to complement their internal, proprietary datasets. Together, these data allow researchers and analysts to capture different aspects of the global political, economic, and social trends worldwide.

Accompanying the growth in data are major improvements in computing power. Modern high-performance computing systems can process and analyze huge datasets at speeds unimaginable only a decade ago. But to analyze large datasets, you need to store them somewhere first. Enter, the cloud.

With the growth of cloud computing, access to powerful computing and storage capabilities has been democratized. Even start-ups and small companies can access vast computational resources without the need for upfront investment in hardware. The cloud therefore not only provides scalable compute on demand and massive volumes of storage but also ubiquitous data access, all while supporting extremely high availability and reliability. Could services from Google and Amazon, for example, have durability rated at an impressive 11 9s, or reliable 99.99999999999 percent of the time. What does that mean? If you stored 1 billion objects, you would likely go a hundred years without losing a single one.[2]

Finally, increasingly sophisticated algorithms in machine learning and artificial intelligence offer companies a way to detect patterns that would have been missed previously. They allow firms to make better predictions or generate insights from complex data in a way that may surpass human capabilities.

Thanks to this confluence of massive and ever-increasing data, more powerful computing, reliable, and accessible storage, and innovations in algorithms, understanding the complex geopolitical world – a computationally intensive project – becomes a feasible, and indeed, essential undertaking for an increasing number of companies.

---

[2] How Cloud Storage Delivers 11 Nines of Durability – and How You Can Help. *Google Cloud Blog*, January 29, 2021. Available at: https://cloud.google.com/blog/products/storage-data-transfer/understanding-cloud-storage-11-9s-durability-target

METHODOLOGICAL APPROACHES

As with other types of quantitative analyses, the methodological approaches in computational geopolitics are varied. Some call for careful construction of surveys and experiments. Others use advanced technologies such as machine learning, big data analytics, and simulation or statistical models. Regardless of the method used, researchers and analysts should be circumspect about three aspects:

- Research question
- Research design
- Appropriate data

First, be clear about the question you are trying to address. Are you asking the right question to address your concern? Does the scope of the question allow you to answer it in a meaningful way? Do you have a clear hypothesis that can be tested?

A good research question is focused, feasible, specific, and relevant. It is also ethical. In other words, the question is important enough to justify asking people to take on some risk or inconvenience for the sake of others.

Second, your research design should allow you to answer your question. A well-constructed research design serves as a blueprint for the study. It will ensure that the process of answering the research question is systematic and coherent, while allowing the analyst to achieve (statistically) valid and reliable conclusions at the desired confidence levels. This calls for careful attention to potential biases in the analysis, sampling considerations, data collection methods, and data analysis procedures.

Finally, ask yourself if you can have the right data, or the right data with enough volume, to answer your questions. As advanced methods such as machine learning and big data analytics rapidly become more commonplace, they require large troves of appropriate data to build and train models. This can be primary (collected firsthand by the analyst) or secondary data (obtained from disparate data sources and put together into one cohesive whole). High-quality data are accurate, complete, and reliable. They capture the construct that the analyst is interested in. The data sources are credible, and there is enough data to support the research conclusions. But high-quality data are also hard to come by. Data collection is an art form, and data cleaning and cohesive dataset construction before one embarks on a data science project takes upwards of 70 percent of the total project time.

TOOLS AND TECHNIQUES IN COMPUTATIONAL GEOPOLITICS

Let us delve into the arsenal of tools and techniques that empower analysts to understand the complexities of geopolitical tensions and anticipate future developments. While there have been several methodological advances in the field of international relations to understand, measure, and predict geopolitical changes, I will emphasize approaches that enable researchers, analysts, and managers understand the implications of broader geopolitical changes for specific companies or economic outcomes such as international trade and investment.

I discuss some examples to highlight different approaches. These are not by any means exhaustive but were chosen to highlight the diversity of approaches that could be used to address specific research questions. By integrating these diverse methodologies together, organizations can better position themselves to navigate the complexities of the global environment.

Measuring Geopolitical Tensions Using Big Data

Managers, analysts, bankers, actuaries, and others have long had to assess geopolitical tensions. A central question for these researchers is estimating the magnitude and severity of geopolitical tensions, and to determine whether they are significant or minor. Historically, their assessments relied primarily on qualitative studies or using rough proxies. Analysts studied particular historical contexts, countries, and geographies to estimate patterns and trends of evolving geopolitical tensions. Before digital archives, analysts and researchers pored over newspaper articles to manually gauge public sentiment and categorize events that could indicate relevance for geopolitical analysis. There was a lot of emphasis on expert opinion and on using diplomatic reports. Insights from political scientists, historians, and diplomats who could provide context and predictions based on their expertise allowed managers, analysts, and researchers to build proxies for quantifying geopolitical tensions.

More recently, however, expert opinions and manual coding are being replaced by more sophisticated methodologies, as well as machine coding of finer-grained and more comprehensive data sources.

Broadly, these approaches fall into three categories: events-based, textual, and empirical.

Events-based approach: This approach leverages historical and real-time events to assess and quantify geopolitical risks. Generally, such measures aim to capture cooperative and conflictual interactions between actors across a pair of countries. A useful source to construct such a measure is the Global Database on Events, Language, and Tone (GDELT) – a global database that records events, themes, and behavior across the world based on news reporting in over 100 languages. It covers events from 1979 to the present, with data from 2017 onwards accessible conveniently in your web browser through a comprehensive API.

Each news event identifies the actors involved (their location, ethnic, religious, and group attributes) and the actions they performed. The events are also tagged with attributes that help to assess the tone involved. In particular, every event is mapped to a conflict–cooperation scale developed by the political scientist Joshua Goldstein.[3] Events that are conflictual in nature are given negative scores; more important or significant the event, the more negative the score. For instance, a threat without specific negative

---

[3] Goldstein, J. S. (1992). A conflict-cooperation scale for WEIS events data. *Journal of Conflict Resolution*, 36(2), 369–385.

sanctions stated has a score of –4.4, while a threat with force specified is scored –7.0, and a military attack, clash, or assault has the lowest score of –10.0. On the other hand, if events between two countries are cooperative in nature, they receive a positive score. Again, the more cooperative the event, the more positive the score: Endorsing the other's policy or position is scored +3.6 while extending military assistance is scored +8.3.

Using this database, my coauthors and I constructed one measure of geopolitical tensions.[4] We first separately identified conflict events and cooperative events based on the Goldstein score. We then constructed a conflict score between country-pairs based on the frequency and salience of negative events between them. Similarly, the cooperation score reflects the frequency and salience of positive events between the country pair.

With these measures, and data pertaining to over 5,800 cross-border acquisitions, we found that conflictual relationships between the home and host country hinder the likelihood of acquisitions by Sovereign Wealth Funds more than private firms. On the other hand, cooperative relations helped Sovereign Wealth Funds more than private firms. Thus, state ownership shapes the extent to which investors are sensitive to geopolitical relations.

One potential pitfall in identifying events through news reporting is that the news media itself may be affected by political interference. To overcome potential biases, alternate data sources can be used to supplement these data, or the data scientist using the data may apply a "correction" onto the conclusions obtained from analyzing data from such sources or geographies.

Google Trends offers one such data source to examine issue salience in societies.[5] By providing data on search volumes for specific

---

[4] Wang, D., Weiner, R. J., Li, Q., & Jandhyala, S. (2021). Leviathan as foreign investor: Geopolitics and sovereign wealth funds. *Journal of International Business Studies*, 52(7), 1238–1255.

[5] Puhr, H., & Kupfer, A. (2023). Media in the geopolitical crossfire: Identification and novel data sources for IB research. *AIB Insights*, 23(1), 1–6.

topics, this data source provides an alternate approximation of issue salience that is demand driven (by users looking for information) rather than information supplied by the news media. When search volume for a topic is greater, we can infer that the demand for information on that topic is higher in a country and correspondingly the greater the issue salience. This is especially useful during periods of abrupt geopolitical transitions.

Textual approaches: The textual approach analyzes newspaper articles, online searches, and other sources of communication to capture issues that are frequently highlighted. Although the construction of specific measures may vary, they generally calculate the relative frequency of published articles and topics devoted to geopolitical events.

One example is the machine learning-based geopolitical risk index created by the economists Dario Caldara and Matteo Iacoviello.[6] They examined about 25 million news articles through automated searches of the electronic archives leading English-language newspapers in the US, UK, and Canada: the *Chicago Tribune, The Daily Telegraph,* the *Financial Times, The Globe and Mail, The Guardian,* the *Los Angeles Times, The New York Times, USA Today, The Wall Street Journal,* and *The Washinton Post.* Their geopolitical index was then constructed by counting, in each month, the share of total published articles discussing adverse geopolitical events and associated threats.

However, to construct their measure, they first needed to identify articles that covered geopolitical events. This was achieved through a dictionary-based approach, where they selected words and phrases associated with geopolitical events and threats. These words/phrases were identified from their definition of geopolitical risk, a corpus of words likely to be used in conjunction with war-related words, and high-frequency words that appear in newspapers

---

[6] Caldara, D., & Iacoviello, M. (2022). Measuring geopolitical risk. *American Economic Review, 112*(4), 1194–1225.

on days of high geopolitical tensions (e.g., "crisis" has a relative term frequency of 0.25 percent on days of high geopolitical tensions compared to 0.04 percent on an average day).

This process resulted in a set of topics and threats (e.g., war, peace, military, nuclear war, terrorism, disruption, threat, buildup, and attack). Using this dictionary of words and phrases, they calculate the share of total articles that include adverse geopolitical events over a specific time period.

In recent years (1985–2020), the index spikes around several key adverse geopolitical events: the 1990 Gulf War, the 9/11 events and the 2003 invasion of Iraq, the 2011 military intervention in Libya, and around the 2014 Russian annexation of the Crimea peninsula. In a larger historical sample (1900–2020), the biggest spikes were around World War I and World War II.

Using this measure, the authors demonstrate that geopolitical risk is associated with lower investment and larger downside risks to GDP growth. The adverse consequences are stronger for firms in more exposed industries and firms that face high levels of geopolitical risk are also likely to have lower investments.

Empirical approaches: In this approach, analysts use empirical data from financial markets, including asset prices and market volatility, to assess geopolitical tensions on a global scale. It relies on the idea that significant geopolitical shocks can drive large unexpected financial outcomes that are common to a wide range of financial asset prices. By analyzing the volatility, or the degree of variation in asset prices across global markets, a measure can be constructed to estimate how much markets are collectively impacted by geopolitical events.

In their work, Robert Engle and Susana Campos-Martins proposed such a statistical measure.[7] They argue that some events can impact volatilities of most asset classes, sectors and countries, caus-

---

[7] Engle, R. F., & Campos-Martins, S. (2023). What are the events that shake our world? Measuring and hedging global COVOL. *Journal of Financial Economics*, 147(1), 221–242.

ing damage to investment portfolios. They capture the magnitude of such shocks – which they refer to as the global common volatility or COVOL – as a broad measure of all types of global financial risk. Because this measure relies on a more dynamic and immediate assessment of geopolitical risks, investors and policymakers can quickly understand and react to these factors.

Quantify Impact of Geopolitics on Trade and FDI

What is the economic implication of rising geopolitical tensions? One area of interest is to examine how specific geopolitical events such as wars, conflicts, tensions, and bilateral issues influence macro flows such as trade and foreign direct investment (FDI).

Let us illustrate this with an example. In one study of FDI flows, Quan Li and Tatiana Vashchilko were interested in identifying how the quality of interstate security relations between two countries shapes the attractiveness of the location as an investment destination for foreign multinational corporations.[8] Thus, they examined how FDI flows were affected by two central features of interstate security relations – military conflict and security alliances. Their underlying expectation was that military conflicts will reduce bilateral investment, while security alliances (and particularly defense pacts) would increase it.

To address their research question, they first clearly delineated their sample: fifty-eight countries, which included twenty-nine OECD (e.g., France, Spain, and USA) and twenty-nine non-OECD countries (e.g., Argentina, China, and India). They then collected data on bilateral FDI flows among pairs of countries. This included outward FDI from one OECD country (origin) to each of the other fifty-seven countries (destinations) or from one of the twenty-nine non-OECD countries (origin) to OECD country (destination). However, they did not have data on FDI flows between two non-OECD countries; thus, their conclusions cannot be generalized to this subsample.

---

[8] Li, Q., & Vashchilko, T. (2010). Dyadic military conflict, security alliances, and bilateral FDI flows. *Journal of International Business Studies, 41,* 765–782.

To measure interstate security relations between countries, they collected data on militarized disputes and alliances between pairs of countries. A militarized dispute referred to a militarized event that one state explicitly initiates against the government, official representatives, official forces, property, or territory of another state. An alliance between two countries was the presence or absence of defense, neutrality, or entente pacts between them.

Their main goal was to examine the empirical relationship between dyadic FDI flows and interstate security relations in their sample. But this relationship could also be affected by other aspects of the countries in question. To ensure that any findings are not an artifact of other potential explanations, they collected additional data on the most plausible alternate factors, including previous FDI and trade flows between the pairs, presence of other types of treaties, population, and per capita GDP of the origin and destination countries, as well as the geographic distance between them.

They used a dynamic panel data estimator to analyze the FDI flows among pairs of countries. They found that, all else equal, a military conflict reduced bilateral foreign investment by approximately 133 to 137 million of constant dollars. On the other hand, the presence of security alliances increased bilateral investment by 69 to 96 million of constant dollars. Their analysis offered a further interesting conclusion. While military conflict and security alliances affected bilateral investment flows in the high-income/low-income dyads (as expected), there was no effect among high-income/high-income dyads.

A similar approach can be used to examine whether the global economy is decoupling. A group of researchers at the International Monetary Fund set out to explore whether global trade and investment flows fragmented along geopolitical lines since Russia's invasion of Ukraine.[9]

---

[9] Gopinath, G., Gourinchas, P. O., Presbitero, A., & Topalova, P. B. (2024). Changing Global Linkages: A New Cold War? IMF Working Paper. WP/24/76.

They first collected quarterly data on trade for 115 countries (2017:q1 to 2023:q3) and FDI for 183 countries (2010:q1 to 2023:q4). They then divided countries into different geopolitical blocks based on each country's voting record in the United Nations. Countries that voted very similarly to the United States belonged to the US leaning bloc. Countries that voted very similarly to China were in the China leaning bloc. Countries that did not vote similarly to either the US or China were classified as a set of nonaligned countries.

The researchers then estimated a gravity model which is a conventional framework to determine trade and investment flows. Essentially, this statistical model allowed them to empirically examine how the value of trade between a source and destination country (or the number of announced FDI projects from source to destination country) changed after Russia's invasion of Ukraine in the first quarter of 2022 depending on whether the source and destination countries were (a) in the same US/Chinese blocs, (b) in different blocs (e.g., source in the US bloc and destination in the Chinese bloc), or (c) in the nonaligned bloc.

After accounting for other potential factors that may shape the outcome, they found that trade flows and the number of announced FDI projects between a US centered and a China centered bloc declined by 12% and 20% more than trade and investment between countries within the same bloc since the onset of the war in Ukraine. This was not driven solely by Chinese and/or US firms. When these two countries were excluded from the analysis, the researchers found very similar patterns.

Then, they focused on trade between the US and China. Their analysis confirmed the adverse effects of US tariffs on Chinese imports, and the precipitous decline of China as a source of US imports. At the same time, there appears to a greater role for a set of connector or nonaligned countries, which increased exports to the US while also increasing imports from China.

Overall, they found that fragmentation in trade and investment flows is becoming a reality. But as can be seen from the above description, setting up and running an effective experiment or set of experiments to extract insight from data requires a deep understanding of statistical methods, no small amount of skill, and serious work.

Assessing Corporate Responses Using Experimental Methods

In navigating the complexities of geopolitical risks, companies have at their disposal a variety of strategic options, each with its own set of potential advantages. Which ones should they choose? How does a manager assess, ex ante, whether a preferred strategy is desirable or will be effective?

This task is far from straightforward. The business environment can shift unpredictably, and the nature of geopolitical risks often involve multiple dimensions that complicate assessment. Furthermore, one could argue that a business strategy's desirability or effectiveness will only be evident in the long run, as the real measure of a strategy's success is long-term performance.

Despite these hurdles, it is critical that managers and strategists rigorously assess their proposed approaches before endorsing significant organizational or strategic changes. One way to assess a potential strategy against a path not taken is through carefully designed experiments. This approach complements intuition and guesswork with evidence-based insights. Many technology companies already embrace A/B testing, a form of experimentation, to decide on important changes. Google, for instance, runs more than 10,000 experiments each year; a typical one might be something designed to help the advertising team determine if a blue or a yellow background works better for ads.[10]

An experiment generally begins with identifying a clear hypothesis or question that needs to be answered. Then, the experiment has to be designed to isolate the variables of interest while keeping other things that could influence the outcome constant. In

---

[10] Luca, M., & Bazerman, M. H. (2020). Want to make better decisions? Start experimenting. *MIT Sloan Management Review*, 61(4), 67–73.

the Google example, for instance, two different ad interfaces could be designed and presented to separate groups. However, you have to make sure that the ad interfaces are similar in every other way except for the background color (blue in option A and yellow in option B).

Next, among the group of users, who is presented the interface with option A versus option B should be randomly determined. Random assignment is the cornerstone of experimental design. Randomly allocating participants or users to different experimental groups makes the two groups more comparable at the start of the experiment and eliminates selection bias. The next step involves collecting data on the outcomes of interest and analyzing those data using statistical tools to determine which approaches are more effective.

Clearly, an experimental approach is not well suited to answer all types of questions. It may be impossible to design a good experimental study to evaluate some of the hypotheses that companies may come up with. And at first brush, analyzing a company's strategic options during heightened geopolitical tensions may be one of those situations where the appropriateness of experimental methods could be questioned. However, in some instances, it may be the right one to provide some robust conclusions.

Let's take an example of whether a company should end its business in Russia. In response to the war in Ukraine, hundreds of multinational corporations voluntarily withdrew from Russia even as their governments were still debating about imposing sanctions and/or restrictions on companies operating there. At the same time, many other companies decided to stay put. What factors shaped managers' decisions to stay or leave?

In an interesting study, Christina Davis, Jialu Li, and Sayumi Miyano addressed this question using an experimental approach.[11]

---

[11] Davis, C. L., Li, J., & Miyano, S. (2024). Peer conformity and competition shape how business managers evaluate withdrawals from Russia amid the Ukraine War. *Proceedings of the National Academy of Sciences, 121*(37), e2406471121.

They focused on Japanese firms who faced quite a bit of uncertainty at the start of the conflict. The Japanese government quickly sided with other G7 governments in condemning Russian actions. But distance from the conflict and a general reluctance to connect aid and trade to political relations meant that Japanese businesses were uncertain about how strongly the Japanese government would use economic tools to punish Russia.

Shortly after the start of the conflict, the researchers surveyed managers in medium and large Japanese companies. All respondents were provided with general information about the conflict. However, some groups of respondents received additional information about the behavior of other companies – as it is a common practice among managers to examine what their peers are doing during periods of uncertainty. One group was informed that some US firms stopped selling their products in Russia. Another group was told that in addition to some US firms, companies from other countries such as South Korea, Sweden, Japan, and Germany were also withdrawing their businesses from Russia. A third group was informed that Chinese companies continued their sales and production activities in Russia.

The researchers then asked managers to assess whether Japanese firms should withdraw business from Russia. When they analyzed the responses, they found that Japanese managers who were informed about US and other Western country firms' withdrawal from Russia were more likely to suggest Japanese firms do the same. However, those provided with information about Chinese firms had an opposite view. In this case, support for withdrawal decreased, as market competition induced caution. This effect was large; news about Chinese firms ongoing business offset the withdrawal effect from hearing about other companies leaving.

While the Japanese study focused on managers in medium and large corporations, another study used a similar experimental approach to determine whether public opinion on an active geopolitical issue influences the foreign policy preferences of a country's leaders.[12] Using a survey experiment, researchers asked British Members of Parliament for their views about the UK military presence in the South China Sea.

Some randomly selected Members of Parliament were presented with polling information reflecting public opinion on this issue while others did not have the polling information. The researchers found that Members of Parliament who received polling information voiced opinions closer to those of the public. Thus, political leaders respond to public opinion even on geopolitical issues.

These opinions are important, since some of these may drive policy decisions with implications for trade and business across country borders.

Using Large Language Models to Understand Impact of Geopolitical Tensions

(This section was written with assistance from LLMs)

Large language models (LLMs) offer another tool to examine the impact of geopolitical tensions on companies. Their primary advantage lies in their ability to process and analyze vast amounts of textual data, and they are rapidly improving. Some potential applications include:

a. Sentiment analysis: While the tone of a geopolitical event is typically mapped along the conflict–cooperation scale (as discussed earlier in this chapter), LLMs provide an alternate approach to gauge the tone and content of public sentiment and perceptions of geopolitical events. They can analyze alternate data sources such as social media posts, financial reports, and companies' earnings calls. This would provide insights into how geopolitical tensions might, for example, affect a firm's reputation, investor confidence, or market dynamics.
b. Spotting trends: LLMs can be a useful tool in identifying geopolitical trends. By processing large datasets from various sources, LLMs can help

---

[12] Chu, J. A., & Recchia, S. (2022). Does public opinion affect the preferences of foreign policy leaders? Experimental evidence from the UK parliament. *The Journal of Politics, 84*(3), 1874–1877.

in spotting emerging trends. They can detect shifts in trade policies, sanctions, or political instability, which would in turn influence supply chains, market access, and operational costs.

c. Scenario building: One of the challenges in analyzing geopolitical tensions is identifying potential future scenarios. Large language models can assist in generating and evaluating hypothetical scenarios based on historical data and current geopolitical trends. This would then help companies anticipate potential impacts and devise appropriate responses. For example, firms could simulate the effects of different trade policies on supply chains and financial performance.

d. Risk assessment: By analyzing historical data and current trends, LLMs can also help assess the likelihood and potential impact of specific geopolitical risks. They can provide predictive insights into how these risks might evolve and affect different industries or regions.

e. Strategic recommendations: LLMs can serve as a handy tool in the first stage of strategy formulation. They can generate strategic recommendations by synthesizing insights from diverse sources, including market reports, expert analyses, and geopolitical forecasts. Managers, analysts, and consultants can choose the relevant ones to develop further as appropriate for their companies.

I highlight two examples below. Both use LLMs as a first step in understanding how geopolitics influences specific industries and firms. A note of caution is, however, necessary. Large language models generate output based on patterns learned from vast datasets, rather than factual understanding of this information. As a result, they can "hallucinate" – or produce factually incorrect or nonsensical output. This means at the current stage of development, output from large language models should be treated as the first stage of analysis – something to aid brainstorming and idea generation but not a definitive answer to the questions you are seeking to address. Any output generated by the LLM needs to be carefully screened to establish factual accuracy before it is used.

Let us say we wanted to know how issues such as trade deals, sanctions, and geopolitics have reshaped the global value chain in the smartphone industry. In particular, we want to analyze how the geographic location from which different components were sourced and the firms dominant in each component have changed between 2000 and 2024. We can use an LLM to generate this output (Example 1)[13]:

EXAMPLE 1 **Issues reshaping the global value chain in the smartphone industry**

Component	2000–2010	2010–2020	2020–2024
Processors	Qualcomm (USA) 60%	Apple (USA) 25%, Samsung (South Korea) 20%	TSMC (for Apple) (Taiwan) 30%, Samsung (South Korea) 25%
Displays	Samsung (South Korea) 40%	LG Display (South Korea) 30%	BOE Technology (China) 25%
Batteries	Sony (Japan) 35%	Samsung SDI (South Korea) 30%	CATL (China) 35%
Cameras	Sony (Japan) 40%	Sony (Japan) 45%	Samsung (South Korea) 30%
Memory	Samsung (South Korea) 35%	SK Hynix (South Korea) 30%	Micron (USA) 25%

Summary of Major Shifts

1. Processor evolution: Qualcomm's early dominance gave way to increased competition from Apple and Samsung. By 2020–24, TSMC emerged as a key player, manufacturing chips for Apple.
2. Display market changes: South Korean companies initially led, but Chinese firms like BOE Technology gained significant market share by 2020–24.
3. Battery production shift: Leadership moved from Japan (Sony) to South Korea (Samsung SDI) and then to China (CATL) in recent years.

---

[13] I used the following prompt on perplexity.ai on August 23, 2024: "Trade deals, sanctions, and geopolitics have shaped trade and FDI flows between countries. Can you take a product, e.g.: smart phones, tear it down into the most important components, and then indicate where these were predominantly sourced from decade by decade, starting with 2000 till 2024 today? For sources, indicate geography (country) and company name and any other information that might be useful. For your response, present it in a table form, with columns corresponding to year range, company, country, % of market share in each case. Provide a summary of the major shifts observed in the data." This was followed by: "Change the table to include year range values as columns."

> 4. Camera sensor consistency: Sony maintained a strong position throughout, but Samsung became a major competitor in the 2020–24 period.
> 5. Memory chip competition: South Korean companies dominated initially, but US-based Micron gained substantial market share in recent years.
> 6. Geographical trends: Overall shift from Japan and the US to South Korea, and more recently to China and Taiwan.
> 7. Vertical integration: Companies such as Apple and Samsung increasingly developed their own components, especially processors.
> 8. Rise of Chinese manufacturers: Significant growth in various component categories, particularly displays and batteries.
>
> These shifts reflect changes in technological capabilities, economic policies, and geopolitical dynamics over the past two decades. The trend toward diversification and the emergence of new players, especially from China, highlight the evolving landscape of global technology production and trade. The smartphone industry has become increasingly competitive and globally distributed, with different regions specializing in specific components and technologies.

While all LLMs can make mistakes and present inaccurate information, they nonetheless provide a first step in analysis. In the semiconductor explained in Example 1, the LLM not only produced a quick summary of how the industry was changing but also identified some trends that one might miss at first glance (for instance, the increasing vertical integration of Samsung).

Another example is using LLMs as a tool in scenario analysis. Let us say we seek the help of LLMs to identify three possible future scenarios in the semiconductor industry, with a particular focus on Intel (Example 2).[14]

---

[14] I used the following prompt on perplexity.ai on August 23, 2024: "A semiconductor company faces many geopolitical challenges. Take a company, e.g.: Intel. Generate three different scenarios that describe the market for semiconductor chips in the future. The scenarios should take into account the changing industrial policies, geopolitical rivalry, technological advances, and any other factors that are important and relevant. Also include how Intel's market position, revenues, and profits are likely to be impacted under each scenario and why."

EXAMPLE 2   Using LLMs as a tool in scenario analysis

SCENARIO 1: FRAGMENTED GLOBAL MARKET

In this scenario, geopolitical tensions escalate, leading to a fragmented global semiconductor market.

Technological Nationalism

Countries prioritize domestic chip production, implementing policies like the CHIPS Act to reduce reliance on foreign suppliers. This results in multiple regional semiconductor ecosystems rather than a single global supply chain.

Impact on Intel

- Market position: Intel leverages its strong US presence to become a key player in the American semiconductor ecosystem. However, it faces challenges in accessing other markets, particularly China.
- Revenues: Initially decrease due to lost international market share, but gradually recover as domestic demand grows.
- Profits: Margins improve due to government subsidies and reduced global competition but are offset by higher production costs in the US.

Intel benefits from increased government support but must navigate a more complex, fragmented global market.

SCENARIO 2: ACCELERATED AI-DRIVEN GROWTH

In this scenario, the rapid advancement and adoption of artificial intelligence drives unprecedented demand for high-performance chips.

Technological Leap

Breakthroughs in AI lead to a surge in demand for advanced semiconductors across various sectors, including data centers, autonomous vehicles, and consumer electronics.

Impact on Intel

- Market position: Intel's investments in AI chip development pay off, allowing it to compete effectively with specialized AI chip manufacturers.
- Revenues: Significant growth as demand for AI-capable chips skyrockets across multiple industries.

- Profits: Increase substantially due to high margins on advanced AI chips and increased production volume.

Intel's success in this scenario depends on its ability to innovate and produce cutting-edge AI-capable semiconductors.

SCENARIO 3: COLLABORATIVE GLOBAL ECOSYSTEM

In this scenario, international cooperation prevails over geopolitical rivalry, leading to a more integrated global semiconductor industry.

Global Coordination

Countries and companies collaborate to address supply chain vulnerabilities and share technological advancements. International standards and agreements facilitate smoother trade and technology transfer.

Impact on Intel

- Market position: Intel maintains its global presence but faces increased competition as the playing field levels.
- Revenues: Steady growth as the overall semiconductor market expands but with smaller market share due to increased global competition.
- Profits: Moderate growth, with pressure on margins due to global competition offset by efficiencies from a more integrated supply chain.

In this scenario, Intel benefits from a stable global market but must continuously innovate to maintain its competitive edge.

End Notes on LLMs

As noted earlier, LLM technology is rapidly evolving. There is a proliferation of models with billions of parameters that are trained on general data, and smaller models (sometimes called SLMs or small language models), with a much smaller number of parameters, that are trained on very domain-specific datasets. While some companies publish the training weights of their "Open Source" models, others keep model details secret. The price of compute power in the cloud is falling steadily, GPU chips are running these calculations faster, and algorithms are improving rapidly mostly through efforts by scientists employed in Big Tech.

CHALLENGES AND LIMITATIONS OF COMPUTATIONAL GEOPOLITICS

Understanding, modeling, analyzing, and predicting geopolitics are inherently challenging. While computational methods are getting better every day, we also need to be cautious about how to use these approaches.

Data Quality and Availability

At its core, computational approaches call for vast amounts of high-quality data from diverse sources, such as social media, news articles, government reports, and satellite images. One concern is that such data, especially from different countries, are not of the same quality.

For instance, press freedom may impact the type of information in the news media. Alternately, social media may be capturing only the voices of the most vocal, which may lead to skewed analysis. Government data may be influenced by state capacity or their own preferred political narratives, so even basic indicators such as the size of a country's economy may not always be reliable.[15]

This is evident, for example, in how data are coded in the Penn World Tables, a standard source for cross-country data on income. In this database, countries are assigned a grade corresponding to subjective data quality. A country with a grade of A has a margin of error of 10%. Countries with grades B, C, and D have margins of error of 20%, 30%, and 40%, respectively. Some countries, especially war-torn ones, may not have the ability to construct or report any data at all.[16] Yet, indicators from the very countries that

---

[15] One example is the controversy over Russia's economic statistics reported by the IMF. See: How the IMF Naively Parroted Putin's Fake Statistics – and Botched Its Economic Forecast for Russia. *Fortune*, March 6, 2023. Available at: https://fortune.com/europe/2023/03/06/imf-naively-parroted-putin-fake-statisticsand-botched-economic-forecast-russia-ukraine/

[16] Alternate approaches – such as satellite imagery-based nighttime luminosity – can offer some correction. See: Henderson, J. V., Storeygard, A., & Weil, D. N. (2012). Measuring economic growth from outer space. *American Economic Review*, 102(2),

lack high-quality data may be critical to our understanding of how geopolitical tensions may evolve and how companies can manage those tensions.

Second, firms will have to get creative about the types of data they use, especially if they are building their own AI models. For very large AI companies, there is already the concern that the stock of high-quality textual data on the internet will run out.[17] In the near term, tech companies such as OpenAI and Google are looking to secure sources like social media forums and news outlets. In the longer term, even this type of data will not keep pace with the demands of the more sophisticated models.

Such concerns force companies to take a closer look at more sensitive data sources like texts, emails, Word documents, or text messages, or generate "synthetic" data. Why does this matter? Companies relying on sophisticated AI models to generate insight into geopolitical risks would wonder to what extent the output from the models are accurate and informative.

Companies can build their own LLMs training them with their own accurate data from the ground up, but that exercise can be prohibitively expensive. Additionally, given the rapid evolution of the field, one would want to have the ability to swap out one model for another as technology moves forward, and this could be problematic if one wants to train their own model from the ground up.

Complexity of Geopolitical Phenomena

Geopolitics is a complex phenomenon that encompasses a multitude of factors, including historical context, cultural nuances, economic interdependencies, and military capabilities. While computational

---

994–1028. Chen, X., & Nordhaus, W. D. (2011). Using luminosity data as a proxy for economic statistics. *Proceedings of the National Academy of Sciences*, 108(21), 8589–8594.

[17] AI Firms Will Soon Exhaust Most of the Internet's Data. *The Economist*, July 23, 2024. Available at: www.economist.com/schools-brief/2024/07/23/ai-firms-will-soon-exhaust-most-of-the-internets-data

methods are evolving rapidly, there is also the real concern that they may not be capturing the complexity fully or that they obscure contextual information. Translating complex scenarios into quantifiable metrics can lead to oversimplification, which potentially results in misleading inferences.

The Geopolitics of AI

While advances in computing power and algorithms for data analyses underpin the analysis of geopolitics and its impact on companies, managers, and work, this technology itself is at the center of geopolitical tensions. This includes a sort of techno-nationalism, where technological innovations and capabilities are directly linked to a nation's national security, resulting in state intervention to guard against hostile states or gain a relative competitive advantage against them. AI technology is also at the center of geopolitics as there are significant differences in the governance approaches taken by the United States, the European Union, and China, including around the type of data that can be collected or the use cases for large models.[18]

As discussed elsewhere in the book, an important implication of this form of techno-nationalism is which firms have access to the data, computing power, and algorithms will be determined by geopolitical forces. For instance, semiconductor chips – the cornerstone of the modern economy – are in the center of this global negotiation, with "chip wars" being waged along geopolitical lines.[19] Consequently, whether (or which) companies can effectively quantify, estimate, and understand their geopolitical risk as well as evaluate their strategies to navigate a more complex world will itself be determined by geopolitics.

---

[18] Larsen, B. C. (2022). The Geopolitics of AI and the Rise of Digital Sovereignty. Brookings Paper, December 8, 2022. Available at: www.brookings.edu/articles/the-geopolitics-of-ai-and-the-rise-of-digital-sovereignty/

[19] Miller, C. (2022). *Chip war: The fight for the world's most critical technology*. Simon & Schuster.

EMPOWERING INSIGHTS

Computational geopolitics holds significant potential for enhancing our understanding of global political dynamics through data-driven analysis and modeling. However, it is essential to recognize and address the challenges and limitations inherent in this approach. Researchers and analysts working in computational geopolitics should bring a good amount of humility with them. The world in general is not easily tractable into a set of equations to forecast the future. So, a model is just that – a step in understanding complex systems. By improving data quality, addressing algorithmic biases, fostering interdisciplinary collaboration, and integrating qualitative insights, the field can evolve to provide more accurate and nuanced analyses of geopolitical phenomena. As the landscape of global politics continues to change, the ability to adapt and refine computational approaches will be crucial for effectively navigating the complexities of international relations in the twenty-first century.

SOME DATA SOURCES

Here is an incomplete list of data sources that may be useful in studying geopolitics and its influence on companies' investments, strategies, and other outcomes. Some are free to access, while others require a subscription (Tables 7.1–7.4).

Table 7.1 *Data sources for international trade and investment flows*

Topic	Description	Data source
Trade Data Monitor	Bilateral trade flows (global)	Private data provider
UN COMTRADE	Bilateral trade flows (global)	United Nations
fDi Markets	Announcements of new physical projects and expansion of existing investments that create jobs and capital investment	*Financial Times*

Table 7.1 *(cont.)*

Topic	Description	Data source
FDI flows	Annual International Direct Investment Statistics Yearbook for international direct investment into and from OECD countries	OECD
Refinitiv Eikon	Deal-level information on cross-border mergers and acquisitions	Thomson Reuters/ London Stock Exchange Group

Table 7.2 *Data sources for measuring geopolitical tensions*

Topic	Description	Data source
Militarized Interstate Disputes	Conflicts in which one or more states threaten, display, or use force against one or more other states.	Correlates of War MID v5.0[a]
Alliances between countries	Formal alliances among states, including defense pacts, nonaggression treaties, and ententes	Correlates of War Formal Alliances v4.1[b]
Similarity in UN voting patterns	Similarity in two countries' foreign policy orientation as reflected in their voting pattern at the United Nations General Assembly	Bailey et al.[c]
International conflicts	Incidents of armed conflicts across states or internationalized intrastate conflicts	Uppsala Conflict Data Program (UCDP) (ucdp.uu.se/encyclopedia)
Events-based conflict–cooperation score	The extent of conflict or cooperation between a pair of countries based on events captured by the global news media	Global Database of Events, Language, and Tone (GDELT) (www.gdeltproject.org/)

(continued)

Table 7.2 (cont.)

Topic	Description	Data source
Armed conflict	Political violence and protest events around the world	Armed Conflict Location & Event Data Project (ACLED) (acleddata.com/about-acled/)
Geopolitical risk index	Share of news articles covering adverse geopolitical events and associated risks	Caldara & Iacoviello[d]
Geopolitical risk indicator	Relative frequency of brokerage reports and financial news stories associated with specific geopolitical risks	BlackRock Investment Institute
Historical events data	Captures agents, locations, and issues at stake in a wide variety of conflict, cooperation and communicative events over a historical period (1945–2019)	Cline Center Historical Phoenix Event Data

[a] Palmer, G., McManus, R. W., D'Orazio, V., Kenwick, M. R., Karstens, M., Bloch, C., Dietrich, N., Kahn, K., Ritter, K., & Soules, M. J. (2020). The MID5 dataset, 2011–2014: Procedures, coding rules, and description. *Conflict Management and Peace Science, 39*(4), 470–482. https://journals.sagepub.com/doi/full/10.1177/0738894221995743

[b] Gibler, D. M. (2009). *International military alliances, 1648–2008.* CQ Press.

[c] Bailey, M. A., Strezhnev, A., & Voeten, E. (2017). Estimating dynamic state preferences from United Nations voting data. *Journal of Conflict Resolution, 61*(2), 430–456.

[d] Caldara, D., & Iacoviello, M. (2022). Measuring geopolitical risk. *American Economic Review, 112*(4), 1194–1225.

Table 7.3 *Data sources for government policy measures*

Topic	Description	Data source
Trade policy uncertainty	Frequency of joint occurrences of trade policy and uncertainty terms across major newspapers in the United States	Caldara et al.[a]
Trade restrictions	Policies adopted by countries that affect global trade and investment	Global Trade Alert (www.globaltradealert.org)
Capital control measures	Restrictions on international trade and payments, capital controls, and other measures that affect capital flows	IMF Annual Report on Exchange Arrangements and Exchange Restrictions (AREAER)
Sanctions	Sanctions applied by countries, groups of countries, the United Nations, and other international organizations	Global Sanctions Database (www.globalsanctionsdatabase.com)
Foreign aid	Development finance activity records from official aid donors	Aid Data from William and Mary (www.aiddata.org
Foreign investment policies	Country-specific data on foreign investment policies, agreements, and dispute settlement	UNCTAD Investment Policy Hub (investmentpolicy.unctad.org/)

[a] Caldara, D., Iacoviello, M., Molligo, P., Prestipino, A., & Raffo, A. (2020). The economic effects of trade policy uncertainty. *Journal of Monetary Economics*, 109, 38–59.

Table 7.4 *Data sources for international enterprise and public opinion survey data*

Topic	Description	Data source
World Values Survey	Global project capturing people's values and beliefs across countries	WVS Database (www.worldvaluessurvey.org)
Attitudes to US Foreign Policy	American public opinion on US foreign policy	Chicago Council on Global Affairs (globalaffairs.org/)
Americas Barometer	Attitudes, evaluations, experiences, and behavior across 34 countries	Center for Global Democracy, Vanderbilt University (www.vanderbilt.edu/lapop/about-americasbarometer.php)
Enterprise Surveys	Surveys of top managers/owners of companies in 150 countries assessing their business environments across	World Bank (www.enterprisesurveys.org)

8 Geopolitics and E-Commerce

While TikTok's battles around data privacy in the United States received a lot of attention, half-way across the world the company faced a different set of problems in its second largest market.

Indonesia was home to more than 100 TikTok million users. It was here that the company first waded into e-commerce, launching TikTok Shop. In 2021, TikTok users in Indonesia could watch a video about a product – an eyelash serum, a soccer ball, a camera, or millions of other items – and use the shopping cart symbol at the bottom to order it without leaving the platform. Instead of relying on the traditional advertising model where interested users would be redirected to the brand's webpage or its Amazon/Etsy storefront, TikTok's new model allowed them greater control of the flow of money. TikTok Shop was a successful experiment and was eventually rolled out in other markets, including the US. But TikTok was forced to end its stand-alone e-commerce feature in Indonesia in 2023. President Joko Widodo was quoted as saying: "We need to be careful with e-commerce. It can be very good if there are regulations but can turn bad if there aren't any regulations."[1]

Indonesia put in place new rules to separate the social media and e-commerce functions, arguing that "social commerce" practices threatened local and small businesses.[2] To get back into business, TikTok's parent company ByteDance announced a long-

---

[1] TikTok Shop to Reopen after $1.5 Billion Deal. *BBC*, December 11, 2023. Available at: www.bbc.com/news/business-67678703

[2] Indonesia Moves to Ban TikTok Sales, Drawing Mixed Reactions from Shopkeepers. *The Straits Times*, September 26, 2023. Available at: www.straitstimes.com/asia/se-asia/indonesia-s-potential-ban-on-social-media-transactions-including-on-tiktok-draws-mixed-reactions

term investment of $1.5 billion to create a partnership with GoTo, an Indonesian technology company.

The social media company would take a controlling stake in Tokopedia, the e-commerce arm of GoTo, and combine TikTok Shop with it. Indonesian users could once again shop and pay for their purchases without leaving the super-popular video app because the shopping component was owned by a separate entity.[3] One analyst described the deal as "a masterstroke" that turned "a group of Indonesian interests from enemies into allies, greatly reducing the political risks operating in the country."[4] GoTo and TikTok also aimed to promote Indonesian goods on the platform and help the country's small and medium-sized businesses develop their production and sales strategies.

On the other side of the world, the Tijuana two-step highlights another tricky challenge. Trying to make life a little bit easier for (among others) tourists bringing in souvenirs from abroad, the United States Congress introduced a trade rule exemption in the 1930s. Called the de minimis exemption, which means "too small to be trifled with," the rule allowed packages worth less than $200 to enter the country without facing duties. In 2016 the cap was lifted to $800 to save on enforcement. But in 2018–19, the US increased tariffs on many Chinese products. To offset some of these costs, Chinese retailers began to look for workarounds. One was to ship products from China to the US but use "bonded" trucks to carry those goods directly into a Mexican warehouse in a place like Tijuana. Because goods were not offloaded in the US, they were treated as if they have not entered the country. But once they arrived at a Mexican distribution hub, they can be split into smaller packages each worth less

---

[3] TikTok Announces $2billion Deal to Restart Indonesia Online Shopping Business. *The Straits Times*, December 11, 2023. Available at: www.straitstimes.com/business/tiktok-announces-2-billion-deal-to-restart-indonesia-online-shopping-business

[4] Will TikTok's Deal with Indonesian E-Commerce Giant Tokopedia Set Precedent to Make Allies Out of Enemies? *South China Morning Post*, February 5, 2024. Available at: www.scmp.com/week-asia/economics/article/3250697/will-tiktoks-deal-indonesian-e-commerce-giant-tokopedia-set-precedent-make-allies-out-enemies

than $800 and sent back to individual American shoppers. According to *The Economist*, seven in ten de minimis packages arrived from China, with Shein and Temu – two of the largest online retailers with Chinese supply chains – accounting for three in ten.[5]

These incidents are just some examples of a broader trend where geopolitical forces are fundamentally altering the landscape of e-commerce and digital trade. E-commerce was once meant to break down borders. Today, it is increasingly fragmented along geopolitical lines. As supply chains are being reshaped and investment patterns altered, e-commerce companies are forced to reckon with the security implications of their operations.

INDUSTRY FEATURES

What Is E-Commerce?

On August 11, 1994, Phil Brandenberger of Philadelphia bought a CD of Sting's "Ten Summoners' Tales."[6] While his $12.48 (plus shipping) purchase may seem ordinary, his transaction made history as perhaps the first online sale. Mr. Brandenburger used his computer in Philadelphia to log into another one in New Hampshire. Using a data encryption software designed for privacy, he paid for his online purchase using his credit card. Moments later, a team of young tech entrepreneurs at Net Market Company celebrated the first retail transaction on the internet. Led by the twenty-one-year-old Chief Executive Daniel M. Kohn, the new company was seen as creating a shopping mall equivalent in cyberspace.

Since that first transaction, e-commerce has been growing consistently. Since COVID-19 pandemic lockdowns, however, it has accelerated even more. By 2020, e-commerce sales as a percentage of total retail sales ranged between 20% and 27% in the United States,

---

[5] How Chinese Goods Dodge American Tariffs. *The Economist*, June 27, 2024.
[6] Attention Shoppers: The Internet Is Open. *The New York Times*, August 12, 1994. Available at: www.nytimes.com/1994/08/12/business/attention-shoppers-internet-is-open.html

United Kingdom, and China.⁷ Year-on-year growth of e-commerce as a share of total retail sales grew a staggering 4.7 times in Spain, 3.3 times in the United States, and 2.1 times in India. In the United States, e-commerce sales penetration more than doubled in 2020, translating to roughly the equivalent of ten years of growth squished into a three-month period.⁸

Broadly, e-commerce is essentially an online sales channel by which companies promote or sell their products. It builds value for companies by driving efficient sales and creating alternative revenue streams. Sales can be to other businesses (business-to-business or B2B) or directly to consumers (business-to-consumer or B2C). When these products are sold across borders, as opposed to domestic transactions, it is referred to as cross-border e-commerce.

While some companies have invested in their own website or platform to showcase their products and sell online, many choose to list their products on third-party websites that host vendor pages. These pages act as online store fronts and the transactions themselves are processed by the marketplace service provider.

Recent Trends in E-Commerce

Online retailers continue to find new and innovative ways to meet customer demands and expectations.⁹ The digital shopping experience has been transformed since the pandemic. Social media platforms have transformed from entertainment sites to dynamic online marketplaces. TikTok and Instagram have incorporated shopping features into their app, enabling users to explore and buy products without leaving the app.

---

[7] How E-Commerce Share of Retail Soared across the Globe: A Look at 8 Countries. McKinsey & Company, March 5, 2021. Available at: www.mckinsey.com/featured-insights/sustainable-inclusive-growth/chart-of-the-day/how-e-commerce-share-of-retail-soared-across-the-globe-a-look-at-eight-countries

[8] The Quickening. McKinsey Quarterly, Five Fifty. Available at: www.mckinsey.com/capabilities/strategy-and-corporate-finance/our-insights/five-fifty-the-quickening

[9] Summarized from: Global E-Commerce: 12 Key Trends in 2024. HSBC, December 22, 2023. Available at: www.businessgo.hsbc.com/en/article/global-ecommerce-key-trends

At the same time, brands have begun to take advantage of interactive formats such as Instagram reels and TikTok videos to generate immersive and interactive shopping experiences for users. Customers can visualize products as well as interact with influencers and key opinion leaders before making a purchase. Augmented reality and virtual reality developments offer the possibility of allowing users to virtually test drive cars, preview how a new hairstyle would look on them, or explore potential vacation destinations. Chatbots offer 24/7 multilingual, global support to customers' most frequently asked questions. Their shopping habits have been put under the microscope and new AI-driven tools deliver personalized recommendations. When they are ready to complete their purchase, customers have a wider range of payment options, including credit cards, e-wallets, cash on delivery, and buy now pay later schemes. They can buy immediately at the market price or enjoy lower prices by inviting their social network contacts to form a joint purchasing team.

On the back end, machine learning and artificial intelligence have made the sorting process in warehouses more optimized. As a result, there is a more seamless flow of goods and the supply chain is more efficient. Business-to-business e-commerce platforms allow wholesalers, manufacturers, and distributors to connect directly with smaller traders, wherever they may be geographically located.

Cross-Border E-Commerce

Superbowl 2024. There was immense speculation about whether the superstar Taylor Swift would make it to the game in Las Vegas in the middle of her record-breaking world tour. In a tight game, the Kansas City Chiefs narrowly defeated the San Francisco 49ers 25 to 22. But one company hogged the primetime slot for US advertising. Temu, an online discount marketplace and a subsidiary of the Chinese company PDD Holdings, aired five commercials during and shortly after the game.[10]

---

[10] What Is Temu? What We Know about the E-Commerce Company with Multiple Super Bowl Ads. *USA Today*, February 12, 2024. Available at: www.usatoday.com/story/money/2024/02/12/what-is-temu-super-bowl/72573203007/

Each ad highlighted colorful animated characters purchasing goods for as little as ninety-nine cents and promised viewers the chance to "shop like a billionaire." Shoppers, however, could expect longer shipping times since goods were mostly shipped from China and other parts of the world.

Digital revolution has made cross-border e-commerce more accessible and convenient than before. In essence, cross-border e-commerce involves consumers purchasing products online from retailers located outside their home country. The global B2C cross-border e-commerce market is projected to reach a staggering $7.9 trillion by 2030, up from just 785 billion in 2021.[11]

For many companies, cross-border e-commerce allows them to reach a much larger and diverse customer base. It also helps in building a global brand presence. No wonder then that more than half of retail and manufacturing companies indicated that they shipped internationally.[12]

Of all cross-border sales, Chinese companies stand out in a crowded market. In one large survey of consumers across forty-one countries, 40% of respondents said they had bought from China (for comparison, only 12% responded that they bought from the US).[13] The increase of purchases from China was primarily driven by two firms Shein and Temu. Although the most popular product categories for cross-border e-commerce consumers varied by country and region, the leading ones were clothing and footwear (39%), consumer electronics (20%), and personal care and beauty products (17%).

At the same time, cross-border e-commerce thrusts sellers into an unfamiliar world of customs duties and compliance issues. They

---

[11] Cross-Border Business-to-Consumer (B2C) E-Commerce Market Value Worldwide in 2021 and 2030. Statista 2024. Available at: www.statista.com/statistics/1296796/global-cross-border-ecommerce-market-value/

[12] Cross-Border E-Commerce Adoption among Manufacturers and Retailers 2023. Statista 2024. Available at: www.statista.com/statistics/1239767/cross-border-e-commerce-company-adoption/

[13] Cross-Border E-Commerce Shopper Survey 2023. International Post Corporation. Available at: www.avalara.com/dam/avalara/public/documents/pdf/state-of-global-cross-border-ecommerce-report-2023-2024.pdf

face challenges related to language barriers, payment method compatibility, fraud, and unpredictable delivery times – all of which can deter potential customers.

Top E-Commerce Companies

The top e-commerce companies (by market capitalization, in 2024) were based in the US, China, and Argentina.[14]

1. Amazon (US)
   With a market capitalization of $1.9 trillion, Amazon is by far the largest global e-commerce company. It started as an online book retailer and was incorporated in 1994. Since then, it has vastly expanded to become a general retailer offering consumer products, advertising, and subscription service through online and physical stores. It also offers e-readers, cloud services, and home entertainment. Amazon began embracing AI-driven recommendations and social commerce efforts. Additionally, the company expanded globally through the Amazon Global Selling program to simplify cross-border transactions.
2. PDD Holdings Inc. (China)
   The parent company of Pinduoduo and Temu was incorporated in 2015 and has a market capitalization of $200 billion. The multinational e-commerce group owns and operates Pinduoduo, an e-commerce platform offering various products including agricultural produce, apparel, shoes, bags, food and beverage, electronic appliances, furniture and household goods, cosmetics and personal care, sports and fitness items, and auto accessories.[15] Temu is PDD's cross-border e-commerce platform that operates in many markets, including the US, Europe, and the Middle East. It is one of the most downloaded apps in multiple markets. It is based in Dublin, Ireland.
3. Alibaba (China)
   Another Chinese company, Alibaba was incorporated in 1999 and has a market capitalization of $184 billion. The company provides technology infrastructure and marketing reach to enable retailers

[14] Top eCommerce Companies by Market Cap 2024. ECDB, July 1, 2024. Available at: https://ecommercedb.com/insights/the-world-s-most-valuable-ecommerce-companies/3946
[15] https://finance.yahoo.com/quote/PDD/

and other businesses to reach users and consumers in China and internationally.[16] It operates digital retail platforms (Toabao, Tmall, and Freshippo), wholesale market places (1688.com and Alibaba.com), and other e-commerce platforms (Lazada, Trendyol, and Daraz). The company also runs an import e-commerce platform (Tmall Global) and a logistics services platform (Cainiao Network). Other businesses include computing, database, application development, IoT, online video, and live events. The retail giant has focused on enhancing its international commerce and AI capabilities.

4. Meituan (China)

    Founded in 2003 and headquartered in Beijing, Meituan has a market capitalization of $95 billion. It operates as a technology retail company offering food delivery services and helping consumers purchase services provided by local merchants in multiple in-store categories.[17] In recent years, the company has expanded its e-commerce offerings and hopes to leverage content-driven e-commerce trends. Its global shopping channel offers products from other markets such as the US, Japan, and Australia.

5. MercadoLibre (Argentina)

    Incorporated in 1999, MercadoLibre is a leading e-commerce and financial services company with a market capitalization of $80 billion. It is an Argentinian company that is headquartered in Montevideo, Uruguay, and incorporated in Delaware in the United States. The company has operations is Latin America's most popular e-commerce site with operations in multiple countries including Argentina, Brazil, Chile, Colombia, Ecuador, Mexico, Panama, and Venezuela. It also operates online commerce platforms in the United States, where it opened a distribution center in 2024.

Other e-commerce companies with global operations include JD.com (China), SEA's Shopee (Singapore), Shein (China), eBay (US), and Coupang (South Korea).

Social media companies are also becoming an important e-commerce platform. Globally, one in two online shoppers have made a purchase on social media, but in Thailand this jumps to nine

---

[16] https://finance.yahoo.com/quote/BABA/profile/
[17] https://finance.yahoo.com/quote/3690.HK/profile/

out of ten shoppers.[18] The most popular social media platforms are Facebook (where 37% of online shoppers have made a purchase), Instagram (28%), and TikTok (18%).

There are other players in the global e-commerce market too, though we see them in slightly different light. Traditional retailers who offer online sales of their products are also in the e-commerce business. Consumer electronics companies such as Apple, Dell, and Xiaomi sell devices through their websites. Prices and hardware customizations may be localized to suit tastes by market, but the product often ships from distant locations. The e-commerce sector expects to witness global growth, but it has also faced rising competition. Emerging players and business models challenge established incumbents. To keep ahead, companies are focused on four key areas[19]:

1. Greater investment in digital technologies and e-commerce
2. More mature technology stacks, including digital and data platforms, and employing third-party platforms
3. Ambitious e-commerce initiatives, including promos, assortment, pricing, and disruptive technologies
4. A strong organizational structure with teams that work in an agile, cross-functional, and autonomous way.

GEOPOLITICS AND THE GLOBAL E-COMMERCE MARKET

For many consumers, purchasing a cheap t-shirt online from a foreign seller might seem like an benign act. Indeed, the rise of cross-border e-commerce has made it easier for consumers to access products from around the world. However, simple transactions like these can also lead to significant backlash, with far-reaching implications in the context rising geopolitical tensions.

---

[18] 2024 Online Shopper Trends, DHL e-commerce Trends Report. DHL ecommerce. Available at: www.dhl.com/content/dam/dhl/local/global/dhl-ecommerce/documents/pdf/g0-dhl-e-commerce-trends-report-2024.pdf

[19] Winning Formulas for E-Commerce Growth. *BCG*, October 31, 2023. Available at: www.bcg.com/publications/2023/winning-formulas-for-e-commerce-growth

Traditionally, geopolitical considerations were the domain of companies in "strategic sectors" such as defense, infrastructure, energy, and oil. So, why would fast fashion or cosmetics matter for national security?

For an increasing number of governments, there are two main considerations. First, as my coauthors and I highlighted in other research,[20] geopolitical considerations often coalesce around data security and sovereignty in the digital economy. And since many e-commerce companies are data giants, they are heavily scrutinized. E-commerce companies owe much of their success to harvesting and monetizing vast amounts of data. Exhibit A is Shein, the rapidly growing fast fashion company. According to media reports, the company's secret sauce is big data, and it "operates less like a traditional clothing company and more like a tech startup, with powerful internal management software, and a nimble advertising and social media apparatus layered on top."[21] At the same time, data ownership and governance have emerged as critical issues for governments. They have intensified efforts to regulate data management practices and secure the data of a country's citizens locally. When foreign firms collect extensive data on the behavior of the country's consumers, they can generate political leverage for the foreign government. Firms can potentially act on behalf of their government and leverage these data to shape behavior or spread information in the country. This is especially worrying if the foreign firm is from an adversarial country with incentives to leverage data negatively.

A second reason for governments' concern about foreign e-commerce companies stems from the rapid growth of these foreign e-commerce companies. When a foreign firm plays an important role in the domestic economy, local governments have limited means to

---

[20] Blake, D., Jandhyala, S., Beazer, Q., & Cunha, R. (2024). Managing Geopolitics in the Digital Age. Working Paper.

[21] How Fast Fashion Giant Shein Used Big Tech to Change the Way We Shop. Vice, January 20, 2023. Available at: www.vice.com/en/article/93bq7z/how-fast-fashion-giant-shein-used-big-tech-to-change-the-way-we-shop

encourage those firms to act in the "national interest" or broader societal and economic goals beyond maximizing profits. At the same time, a foreign government could influence the firm to act in ways that support their own interests – which may be at odds with the domestic ones. Furthermore, governments worry about competition and negative spillover effects on domestic firms. As the example of TikTok Shop in Indonesia highlights, the country put in place new rules to limit e-commerce practices because this threatened local and small businesses.[22]

Given these concerns, the geopolitical risks facing e-commerce companies are broadly around market access, level playing field, investment security, and institutional alignment.

Market Access

For cross-border e-commerce firms, market access refers to their ability to enter a foreign market and sell their goods and services there. However, many governments have imposed specific conditions or requirements for firms to access their domestic markets.

Take the case of Temu, a firm that connected manufacturers directly to consumers. Since its 2022 launch in the US, it expanded rapidly with operations in seventy markets within two years. However, it attracted controversy even before the company officially entered Indonesia. Lawmakers there were worried about how the firm would disrupt local micro, small, and medium-sized enterprises and disrupt domestic supply chains. As one Trade Ministry official pointed out, the platform's business model was incompatible with the country's domestic regulations.[23] The firm would not be allowed

---

[22] Indonesia Moves to Ban TikTok Sales, Drawing Mixed Reactions from Shopkeepers. *The Straits Times*, September 26, 2023. Available at: www.straitstimes.com/asia/se-asia/indonesia-s-potential-ban-on-social-media-transactions-including-on-tiktok-draws-mixed-reactions

[23] Chinese-Owned Temu to Face Compliance Issues in Indonesia, Local Officials Warn. *South China Morning Post*, June 24, 2024. Available at: www.scmp.com/tech/article/3267847/chinese-owned-temu-face-compliance-issues-indonesia-local-officials-warn

to sell from manufacturers directly to consumers but would require an intermediary or a distributor. The ministry vowed to monitor Temu's operations, even as the firm was yet to obtain an operating license in the country.

Indonesia was not an isolated risk for Temu, and the stock performance of the parent company PDD Holdings Inc. reflected some of the backlash and geopolitical risk the company faced in markets around the world. In mid 2024, the US-listed stock was trading at just thirteen times expected earnings; at roughly half the valuation of the Nasdaq 100 and PDD's steepest discount until that point. Some analysts justified the discount, at least in part, on the harsh trade-war rhetoric between the US and China.[24]

Another example of a firm that has faced significant geopolitical tensions is Shein. The company was among a set of Chinese apps that were banned by India in 2020 following border clashes between the two countries along the Himalayan border. At the time, the Indian government responded by blocking fifty-nine apps that they viewed as "engaged in activities which are prejudicial to sovereignty and integrity of India, defence of India, security of state and public order."[25] But Shein was a popular app in the country: The company worked with about 2,000 Indian influencers before the ban.[26] Since then, the company attempted to reenter the Indian market. In 2023, the Chinese-founded firm received approvals to do so, but only after agreeing to a stringent licensing deal with the domestic giant Reliance Industries. According to the terms of the deal, Reliance would fully own the domestic business, and Shein would

---

[24] Temu's Parent PDD Trades Near Cheapest Level Ever as Geopolitical Risks Bite. Bloomberg.com, May 28, 2024. Available at: www.bloomberg.com/news/articles/2024-05-28/pdd-trades-near-cheapest-level-ever-as-geopolitical-risks-bite

[25] Government Bans 59 Apps Including China-Based TikTok, WeChat. *The Hindu*, June 29, 2020. Available at: www.thehindu.com/news/national/govt-bans-59-apps-including-tiktok-wechat/article31947445.ece

[26] Shein Is the World's Most Popular Fashion Brand – at a Huge Cost to Us All. *Time*, January 17, 2023. Available at: https://time.com/6247732/shein-climate-change-labor-fashion/

be paid a licensing fee only from the profits of the Indian entity. Further, all data generated by Shein's app and from its operations in the country would be stored in India and be inaccessible to the company. At the same time, the Singapore-headquartered e-commerce company would offer production support and training to over 25,000 small and medium-sized suppliers in India to enable them to produce for Shein-branded products around the world.[27] With this, Shein would have to increase the share of made-in-India goods sold on its platform. Ultimately, Shein could tap into the world's most populus country but would only take a cut from sales while training suppliers there.

In the US and EU, Chinese e-commerce firms that have specialized in the manufacturer-to-customer model faced the threat of raised tariffs. These firms were able to charge low prices in part because of the "de minimis" rule that allowed imported items below a certain threshold to avoid customs duties. However, by 2024, the European Commission began exploring ways to scrap its € 150 threshold, while American politicians investigated lowering or removing the generous $800 ceiling.[28]

For Amazon, the American e-commerce giant, operating in China was hard from the very beginning. Amazon entered the Chinese e-commerce space in 2004 but found itself competing against domestic competitors who offered lower prices. The company struggled for many years and by 2019 called it quits, closing its e-commerce platform in China.[29] Amazon continued offering accessibility to third-party sellers in China aiming to reach global buyers but did not sell directly to Chinese customers. Heightened geopolitical tensions

---

[27] Shein Deal to Re-enter India Comes with Strict Licensing Rules. Bloomberg.com, June 21, 2023. Available at: www.bloomberg.com/news/articles/2023-06-21/shein-deal-to-re-enter-india-comes-with-strict-licensing-rules

[28] Shein, Temu and the Parcel Wars. *Financial Times*, July 5, 2024. Available at: www.ft.com/content/67319cc8-1f0e-4155-8f5e-664fe8603d2d

[29] Amazon Admits Defeat against Chinese E-Commerce Rivals Like Alibaba and JD.com. *The Verge*, April 19, 2019. Available at: www.theverge.com/2019/4/18/18485578/amazon-china-marketplace-alibaba-jd-e-commerce-compete

shaped Amazon in other ways as well, as tariff risk impacted product pricing. By one estimate, when the US imposed 15% tariffs on $112 billion of goods from China in 2019, Amazon would have had to increase prices by an average of 2.1% to 2.6% to offset the cost of the new tariffs.[30]

Level Playing Field

As countries reevaluate their de minimis rules, there is some indication that new rules may favor some firms from some foreign countries over those from other countries. Take the case of the United States. In 2023, two bipartisan bills were introduced in the US Congress aimed at collecting more information on all shipments under the $800 threshold. But importantly, the bill also targeted "nonmarket economies"[31] including China and Russia.[32] This means that European or Indian firms selling goods to American customers may still be exempted, but their Chinese rivals would face higher tariffs; leading to an uneven playing field.

While many of the examples of e-commerce discussed above include the transmission of physical goods following an electronic purchase, a rapidly growing segment of international trade comprises digitally delivered products and services. Think of cloud computing, software sales, data vendors, and streaming services. By 2022, the value of global trade in digitally delivered products reached $3.82 trillion, accounting for a 54 percent share of services trade.[33]

---

[30] How the Trade War Is Impacting Amazon. *Investopedia*, September 6, 2019. Available at: www.investopedia.com/how-the-trade-war-is-impacting-amazon-4769431

[31] Countries designated by Commerce as nonmarket economies include: Armenia, Azerbaijan, Belarus, China, Georgia, Kyrgyz Republic, Moldova, Russia, Tajikistan, Turkmenistan, Uzbekistan, and Vietnam (status under review). See: www.trade.gov/nme-countries-list

[32] Bipartisan Proposals Would Hit E-Commerce Like Fast Fashion. *The New York Times*, June 15, 2023. Available at: www.nytimes.com/2023/06/15/business/ecommerce-shein-us-china-trade.html

[33] Ruta, M., & Jakubik, A. (2023). Why Digital Trade Should Remian Open. IMF Blog, December 13, 2023. Available at: www.imf.org/en/Blogs/Articles/2023/12/13/why-digital-trade-should-remain-open#:~:text=The%20value%20of%20global%20trade,outpaced%20other%20categories%20like%20goods

With an 8.1 percent average annual growth rate over the last two decades, trade in digitally delivered services has outpaced international trade in goods.

While trade in international goods has been governed by a robust set of free trade rules negotiated at the World Trade Organization, the rules around trade in electronic transmission and digitally delivered products and services have been murkier. Since 1998, temporary World Trade Organization agreements prevented members from imposing customs duties on digital e-commerce. The initial agreement was to suspend customs duties for a period of two years, but this had been extended periodically. At the 2024 meeting in Abu Dhabi, member countries clinched a deal to continue to exempt tariffs for another two years. As reported by the *Financial Times*, the World Trade Organization statement from member countries indicated that[34]: "We agree to maintain the current practice of not imposing customs duties on electronic transmissions until the 14th session of the ministerial conference or 31st March, 2026, whichever is earlier. The moratorium ... will expire on that date."

But without permanent agreed-upon principles, the system was beginning to show signs of strain. Some member countries argued that the moratorium should not be extended, raising the possibility of unilateral moves by some governments to tax cross-border digital transmissions.

Negotiating an extension every two years was politically charged and increased policy uncertainty. As one member of a Washington-based lobby group noted, "It's a relief to see the moratorium survive by the skin of its teeth. [...] The endless brinkmanship over the moratorium crowds out the ability to make progress on a broader agenda and undermines the viability of the WTO as a useful forum for trade ministers."[35]

---

[34] WTO Agrees to Extent Ecommerce Tariff Exemption for 2 More Years. *Financial Times*, March 2, 2024. Available at: www.ft.com/content/72ddf2e7-f467-473d-8ec2-07f09a7862d9

[35] Ibid.

One issue was that governments worried about missing out on customs revenue as goods were replaced by services (think: DVDs to streaming, for example). A study by the OECD suggested that lifting the moratorium on applying customs duties on electronic transmissions would disproportionately hurt developing countries and small actors.[36] Countries like India argued that the moratorium favored big tech companies and prevented the growth of competitors from developing nations. South Africa similarly reiterated the right to collect state revenue from such transmissions. Other concerns about privacy, digital vulnerabilities, and national security were also raised.

But negotiations to deliver more permanent rules continued among a group of ninety-one countries – a subset of the World Trade Organization's full membership. While the US joined this group, along with China, Japan, the UK, and major economies of the European Union, it also signaled a reluctance to fully endorse it.[37] Absent from the list were South Africa and India, who had already raised concerns.

Importantly, this approach is a stark departure from how the World Trade Organization functions. If the ninety-one World Trade Organization member countries – roughly half of the organizations' members – successfully negotiate a deal, they favor keeping the benefits exclusively for those who sign it. In other words, those who do not sign the agreement lose both the obligations and privileges of an e-commerce deal. Such an agreement would discard the traditional "most favored nation" terms by which all members are accorded equal treatment and any favorable terms extended to one partner would automatically apply to all other World Trade

---

[36] Understanding the Scope, Definition, and Impact of the WTO E-Commerce Moratorium. OECD Trade Policy Brief, October 2023. Available at: https://issuu.com/oecd.publishing/docs/oecd-policy-bief-ecommerce-moratorium

[37] WTO Members Signal Progress on Draft E-Commerce Deal. *Bloomberg*, July 27, 2024. Available at: www.bloomberg.com/news/articles/2024-07-27/wto-members-signal-progress-on-draft-e-commerce-deal

Organization members.[38] This clause conferring universal equal treatment has been one of the underlying principles of the World Trade Organization and multiple trade agreements around the world. For the most part, if a country belonging to the World Trade Organization reduces or eliminates tariffs on a particular product for one trade partner, the clause requires the country to extend the same treatment to other members of the organization. Traditionally, this conferred a level playing field for all competitors.

The new deal threatens to abandon this basic tenet of the World Trade Organization. If adopted, the playing field for e-commerce will not be level.

Investment Security

To facilitate cross-border e-commerce, firms invest in identifying foreign markets, advertising, developing marketplace platforms that adhere to local regulations, and building an international shipping infrastructure. These investments, however, are challenged by rising geopolitical tensions. Geopolitics shapes investment security through the rules and administrative procedures related to cross-border shipping and data localization demands.

While selling internationally has grown, many companies struggle with operating cross-border e-commerce successfully. Customs procedures and cross-border shipping remain a challenge, with the risk of delays and added costs. If a seller fails to attach the right documentation, there may be delays in customs clearance. This typically adds to the supply chain and delivery costs as the retailer needs to resolve the issue, reschedule delivery, and often address additional customer care. In some cases, incorrectly specified documentation can even generate additional tariffs, increasing the final costs and inviting further scrutiny from regulators. Failing

---

[38] Rockwell, K. (2024). E-Commerce Deal at the WTO Is Suddenly Back in Play. Hinrich Foundation Note, May 7, 2024. Available at: www.hinrichfoundation.com/research/article/wto/e-commerce-deal-at-the-wto-is-back-in-play/

to assign the right code can be devasting for e-commerce where margins are slim and costs of failing to deliver high. As one supply chain professional noted[39]:

> The book to import into the US is about a foot-and-a-half to two feet thick and the language in there is very vague and hard to determine. Then translating that for whichever country you're importing to just adds a whole host of issues to it.
>
> So, what we see a lot is customers who just classified goods for the US and tried to use that same code to ship all around the world. Then they wonder why their goods are getting held up in customs.

Given the central role of customs procedures in e-commerce, geopolitical tensions can incentivize governments to use administrative policies in blunting the competitiveness of products from certain countries. Take the example of tulip bulbs. Japan was once a major producer of the flower. Its production peaked in 1993, when 358 Japanese farmers grew 61 million bulbs over 252 hectares. By 2015, however, there were only 85 farmers growing 17 million bulbs over 77 hectares.[40] A part of the reason for this decline was competition from cheaper Dutch bulbs. But at one point, Netherlands exported tulip bulbs to almost every country in the world except Japan. This was because Japanese customs officials took a particular interest in Dutch tulips. They insisted on checking every single bulb by cutting it vertically down the middle.[41] Even Japanese ingenuity could not stich them back to together and bring them to the market.

A similar example comes from American businesses in China in 2019, when China and the United States both raised tariffs on each other's imports. Among 250 respondents surveyed by the American Chamber of Commerce in China, almost three-quarters

---

[39] Reported in "The State of Global Cross-Border E-Commerce Report 2023–24," Produced by Reuters Events and Alvara. Available at: www.avalara.com/dam/avalara/public/documents/pdf/state-of-global-cross-border-ecommerce-report-2023-2024.pdf

[40] Niisato, Y. (2018). Dynamics of production and trade of flower bulbs in the Netherlands, China and Japan (Doctoral dissertation, University of Toyama).

[41] Quoted in Hill, C. (2009). *Global Business Today*. Mc-Graw-Hill – 6th edition.

said the tariffs were hurting their competitiveness. Particularly, they faced increased obstacles such as government inspections, slower customs clearance, and slower approval for licensing and other applications.[42]

A different concern for global e-commerce companies is related to data. A defining characteristic of cross-border e-commerce is its dependence on big data and the frictionless flow of information. However, as discussed above, this very characteristic of the industry is putting it in the crosshairs of geopolitical tensions. Governments worry about foreign firms collecting extensive data on the behavior of their country's consumers. To buffer against potential leverage by foreign adversaries, and gain greater local control over these data, governments impose data governance and storage restrictions. One argument is that localization will help local agencies access data as and when needed. At the same time, this would also protect domestic consumers from foreign attacks and surveillance. It was for this reason that the Reserve Bank of India issued guidelines in 2018 mandating the storage of all financial and e-commerce data of Indian users, including by multinational companies, on servers in India.[43] While domestic companies pushed for these rules, their foreign competitors including Google, MasterCard, Visa, and Amazon lobbied against these regulations. They raised concerns about increased operational costs as they would have to set up fresh infrastructure in the country. They also argued that data localization would keep new innovations out of the Indian market; if foreign companies had to exclude Indian data from their operations and analysis, it could potentially limit the functionality of services offered in the country. But India was hardly alone in demanding data localization. The number of countries that

---

[42] U.S. Business Group Says Retaliation Rising in China amid Trade War. *Reuters*, May 22, 2019. Available at: www.reuters.com/article/business/us-business-group-says-retaliation-rising-in-china-amid-trade-war-idUSKCN1SS00T/

[43] RBI to Examine Concerns over Data Localization Rule: Government. *The Economic Times*, June 18, 2019. Available at: https://economictimes.indiatimes.com/news/economy/policy/rbi-to-review-data-storage-rules-for-payment-firms-government/articleshow/69838249.cms

have enacted similar requirements nearly doubled from 35 in 2017 to 62 in 2021, as have the number of data localization policies (from 67 in 2017 to 144 in 2021).[44]

As restrictions on the territorial mobility of data exploded, a number of potentially conflicting regulations with extraterritorial scope have made it even more difficult for companies to operate across borders. The examples of the US CLOUD Act and the European Union's General Data Protection Regulation (GDPR) demonstrate the potential for such incompatibility. The US CLOUD Act allows federal law enforcement to require US companies to hand over requested data stored on servers regardless of whether those data are in the United States or on foreign soil. Such an action could potentially violate the European Union's GDPR, which governs the transfer of personal data of Europeans outside the European Union. Given the difficulties, it is possible that the free flow of private data would be restricted to likeminded countries with similar or equivalent privacy regulations, which would likely greatly reduce the scope for e-commerce.[45]

Institutional Alignment

Southeast Asia witnessed a historic e-commerce boom, with growth rates of 24 percent year-on-year in 2020–23.[46] By 2022, the Philippines, Indonesia, and Vietnam were among the fastest growing e-commerce markets in the world. But the prolific markets still face the problem of payment system interoperability as different national systems still don't work with each other. According to one study, about a third of

---

[44] Cory, N., & Dascoli, L. (2021). How Barriers to Cross-Border Data Flows Are Spreading Globally, What They Cost, and How to Address Them. Information Technology & Innovation Foundation Report, July 2021.

[45] Geopolitical Aspects of Digital Trade. Policy Department, Directorate-General for External Policies, European Parliament (November 2020). Available at: www.europarl.europa.eu/RegData/etudes/IDAN/2020/653616/EXPO_IDA(2020)653616_EN.pdf

[46] Suominen, K. (2023). Integration, Interoperability, Inclusion: Igniting the E-Commerce Boom in Asia. Asian Hub by IMD (October 2, 2023). Available at: www.imd.org/ibyimd/asian-hub/integration-interoperability-inclusion-igniting-the-e-commerce-boom-in-asia/

firms in Southeast Asia reported losing online export sales because they were unable to accept payments from foreign customers.[47]

But which payment system should they adopt? There is growing competition with multiple payment systems vying for efficiency and supremacy. And in a world of rising geopolitical tensions, they also aim to dethrone the dollar and western control of cross-border payment systems.

The largest system in use was developed by the Society for Worldwide Interbank Financial Telecommunication (SWIFT) and allowed banks across countries to communicate using standard codes and formats. Headquartered in Belgium, it comprises the vast majority of cross-border deals. It was also a vehicle by which the US government could monitor third-party compliance with sanctions and regulate their access to the US financial system.

While this Western system once dominated the world, other national payment systems – particularly in Russia, China, and India, have also arisen.[48] Since 2014, Russia focused on developing its own financial messaging system for interbank transfers (SPFS) and a card-payment network (Mir) to substitute for Western providers such as Visa. Consequently, when the country was cut off from SWIFT in 2022 following the war in Ukraine, corporate Russia was still able to function even if it was with inconveniences.

China has likewise developed another financial messaging system – CIPS – as an alternative to SWIFT. Launched in 2015, the number of financial institutions on it is growing, although still small in absolute number or in the value of transactions. However, China's retail payment providers have grown dramatically and challenge Western incumbents such as Mastercard and Visa. By 2024,

---

[47] Alliance for eTrade Development: Interoperability of Digital Payments for Inclusive Trade in Southeast Asia. USAID Alliance for eTrade Development II Activity, June 30, 2022. Available at: www.allianceforetradedevelopment.org/_files/ugd/478c1a_46e4a911a04a48d0a46fa99a5a6dd895.pdf

[48] See National Payment Systems Are Proliferating. *The Economist*, May 3, 2024. Available at: www.economist.com/special-report/2024/05/03/national-payment-systems-are-proliferating

UnionPay, a Chinese card network, was the world's largest by transaction volume and was accepted in 183 countries. Alipay, a digital payment service, was accepted by 80m merchants worldwide (compared to Visa's 100 million).

India's Unified Payments Interface (UPI) was launched in 2016. It allows users to make fast, cost-free payments by either scanning a QR code or sending a text. By 2023 processed annual transactions worth about $1.7 trillion or 50 percent of GDP. In an attempt to expand its global reach, the payment system has been linked to those in Sri Lanka, the United Arab Emirates, Singapore, Mauritius, Bhutan, and France. Other markets targeted include Malaysia, Thailand, the Philippines, Vietnam, Cambodia, South Korea, Japan, Taiwan, and Hong Kong. India also allows other countries to access the underlying technology of the digital infrastructure so that they can build their own systems – which would also be more interoperable.

While competition can spur innovation and generate service improvements, it also brings the risk of fragmentation. With growing geopolitical tensions, governments may push their own systems to avoid the scrutiny of their rivals. For e-commerce companies, the lack of institutional alignment can be a real challenge in cross-border sales.

In addition to payment systems, e-commerce standards around software architecture, business-to-business communications, and quality supervision are also evolving. Over the years, there have been multiple efforts to develop these standards, including by the United States, World Customs Organization, the European Union, and the United Nations Center for Trade Facilitation and Electronic Business. The most concentrated efforts have been led by China, where setting e-commerce standards has been a strategic focus as it can shape the global architecture according to its vision and ambition.[49]

---

[49] de La Bruyere, E. (2022). China's Ambitions to Set the Foundations for Global Commerce. Hinrich Foundation Report. March 2022. Available at: www.hinrichfoundation.com/research/wp/digital/china-foundations-for-global-e-commerce/

Primarily, China's efforts have been focused on defining a system for the collection, transmission, and analysis of commercial data, under government oversight. If successful, they will bring commercial advantages for Chinese firms, greater access to and control over information for the Chinese state, and enhanced influence over international trade. To this end, China has been an active participant in the International Standardization Organization – a global body that develops technical, commercial, and industrial standards for worldwide adoption. In 2019, the first technical committee on e-commerce was established with an office in Hangzhou, China. The chair was from China and the committee's work has focused on three areas proposed by China: one targeting information sharing of product quality and the others on terminology and frameworks for transaction assurance.

STRATEGIES FOR MANAGING CORPORATE NATIONALITY AND GEOPOLITICAL TENSIONS

E-commerce firms recognize at least some of their liability (or strength) in international markets arises from their nationality. While they can't change their country of origin, or where they were founded, these firms have experimented with multiple strategies to shape others' perceptions of their nationality.

Masking Country of Origin

Geopolitical risks are highest for Chinese e-commerce companies trying to expand in the US. Although a very lucrative market, it is also in some ways the most difficult one for these companies. They have tried to reshape public perceptions of their companies by creating corporate structures that emphasize their global operations. Temu, for example, is officially incorporated in Delaware and headquartered in Boston. Its parent company PDD Holdings itself has been listed on the NASDAQ in the United States since 2018. Their webpage describes the company as a "multinational commerce group that owns and operates a portfolio of businesses."⁵⁰ In 2023, the parent company shifted its headquarters to Ireland and listed Dublin rather than Shanghai as the "address of principal executive offices" in US exchange filings even as its core operations and the majority of its employees remained in China.⁵¹

Shein similarly describes itself as a company that is "headquartered in Singapore" serving customers in 150+ countries from "key centers of operation around the world, including the U.S., Brazil, Ireland, and Southern China."⁵² The company highlights offices in Los Angeles, São Paulo, Dublin, Guangzhou, Paris, Washington DC, London, and Singapore. The headquarters moved to Singapore and the company deregistered its original company in Nanjing.⁵³ The disjointed messaging about where the company is from was highlighted by the company's executive chair. In a 2024 speech that quickly gained attention around the world, he said that identity was a difficult question.⁵⁴ The company was born in China, with many employees and a significant portion of its supply chain still there, so it could be considered Chinese, but that its headquarters and incorporation also made it Singaporean. Its biggest market was the US and American values had made it successful. "It is about innovation, it is about freedom to express individuality, it is about fair play, fair competition, rule of law, all these things that we stand for is exactly what United States ethos are. So if you look at it that way, we are an American company," reported the company's executive chairman.

---

[50] PDD Holdings | Investor Relations – Who We Are. See https://investor.pddholdings.com/

[51] Pinduoduo Owner Moves Headquarters to Ireland amid US-China Tensions. *Financial Times*, May 4, 2023. Available at: www.ft.com/content/801ac5c4-9863-444e-986a-1e40280ea07f

[52] Shein | Our Global Presence. See www.sheingroup.com/about-us/our-global-presence/

[53] As Ties to China Turn Toxic, Even Chinese Companies Are Breaking Them. *The New York Times*, June 15, 2023. Available at: www.nytimes.com/2023/06/15/business/economy/china-business-tiktok-shein.html

[54] Shein Tries to Suppress Chair's Claim That Fashion Retailer Is "American." *Financial Times*, June 14, 2024. Available at: www.ft.com/content/6ecb58d1-2582-48ae-8503-773b228da57e

In contrast, MercadoLibre has primarily been a company of Latin America, from Latin America, and for Latin America.[55] And while US and Asian competitors have tried expanding into Latin America's growing e-commerce market, the company has held its ground. For instance, Shopee, closed most of its Latin America operations in 2022 despite much-hyped expansion.

Diversifying Supply Chains

A significant factor tying Chinese e-commerce companies to their country of origin is presence of extensive supply chains in the country. Consequently, they are diversifying their suppliers and exploring new production hubs in countries such as Vietnam, Thailand, Brazil, and Mexico to reduce dependence on China.

For example, Shein announced an investment of nearly $150 million in Brazil to establish a network of thousands of textile manufacturers there.[56] By 2026, about 85 percent of Brazilian sales were expected to be sourced from local manufacturers and sellers. A production facility in Mexico was also under consideration,[57] as were others in Europe and the UK. The company also committed to offer production support and training to manufacturers in India.[58]

On the other hand, the American e-commerce company Amazon increased its presence in China to take on the competitors. In a plan to help Chinese merchants sell their products in international markets using the Amazon platform, the company

---

[55] The Founder Who Launched the "Amazon of Latin America" from a Parking Garage Has Transformed Retail in the Region – and Earned Himself $7 Billion. *Fortune*, February 2, 2024. Available at: https://fortune.com/2024/02/01/mercadolibre-ceo-marcos-galperin-interview-ecommerce-payments/

[56] Fast Fashion Giant Shein to Invest Nearly $150 Million in Local Production in Brazil. *Inside Retail*, April 21, 2023. Available at: https://insideretail.asia/2023/04/21/fast-fashion-giant-shein-to-invest-nearly-150-million-in-local-production-in-brazil/

[57] Fast Fashion Giant Shein Plans Mexico Factory – Sources. *Reuters*, May 25, 2023. Available at: www.reuters.com/business/retail-consumer/fast-fashion-giant-shein-plans-mexico-factory-sources-2023-05-24/

[58] Shein Deal to Re-enter India Comes with Strict Licensing Rules. Bloomberg.com, June 21, 2023. Available at: www.bloomberg.com/news/articles/2023-06-21/shein-deal-to-re-enter-india-comes-with-strict-licensing-rules

announced an innovation center in Shenzhen and increased the number of items sold from China via Amazon.[59]

Relocating Control Rights

For most firms, control rights refer to their ability to shape the systems, methods, and decisions that drive the company toward specific outcomes. When control rights are located in a given jurisdiction, they are subject to influence of the country's government. And firms cannot make credible commitments to other stakeholders about the actions of their home country governments. Thus, one strategy to delink a firm from its country of origin is to move control rights and decision-making to another country. This will signal that the company's managers are less beholden to their country of origin's geopolitical interests. It is partly for this reason that Shein moved its headquarters and top management from China to Singapore and PDD relocated its headquarters to Dublin, Ireland. Alternately, companies can transfer equity control of local operations to domestic partners in countries where geopolitical tensions are high. This is what some American lawmakers demanded of TikTok, for it to continue operating in America. In Shein's case, it planned to reenter India via a partnership with the local company Reliance, where the latter would hold full equity control.

Focus on Alternate Markets

Although TikTok Shop was available in many countries, including the US, it was Southeast Asia where it all started. When TikTok's Chief Executive Officer Shou Zi Chew landed in Jakarta in June 2023, he received a warm welcome – a striking contrast to the grilling by angry lawmakers in Washington, DC.[60] To create alternate revenue

---

[59] Amazon Doubles Down on China E-Commerce Strategy as Rivals Shein, Temu Gain Traction. *South China Morning Post*, December 13, 2023. Available at: www.scmp.com/tech/big-tech/article/3244976/amazon-doubles-down-china-e-commerce-strategy-rivals-shein-temu-gain-traction

[60] TikTok Is Wading into South-East Asia's E-Commerce Wars. *The Economist*, September 7, 2023. Available at: www.economist.com/business/2023/09/07/tiktok-is-wading-into-south-east-asias-e-commerce-wars

streams in markets outside the US and India, where it faced significant threats, the company expected to invest billions of dollars in the region to attract Southeast Asia's nearly 700 million customers. TikTok Shop was available in Singapore, Malaysia, Indonesia, Philippines, Vietnam and Thailand. And the company was betting on growth in these markets.

This is an alternate way for firms to compete when geopolitical tensions are rising. If they don't wish to, or are unable to, delink from their home countries, they can focus their international operations on countries where their company's nationality is not a liability. With many countries in Asia and other parts of the world staking a more neutral stand in the rivalry between the US and China, firms from both countries can compete effectively there.

CORPORATE DIPLOMACY

As in other sectors, geopolitical risk increases the demand on managers to invest in nonmarket strategies. To ensure that firms gain access to foreign markets, face a level playing field, can compete with security for their foreign investments, and push for institutional alignment, they will need to invest in managing governments. More of the top management's time and attention has to be devoted to dealing with global politics, its impact, and its consequences.

E-commerce is no different. Shein spent nearly $2 million over a nine-month period in 2023 lobbying Washington officials during its push for an initial public offering.[61] It hired Washington lobbyists and focused its messaging on its status as a Singapore-based company.[62] TikTok, in an attempt to save its short-video entertainment and e-commerce operations, deployed Washington power brokers and high-priced lawyers. They pushed along at least

---

[61] Shein Profits Double to over $2bn Ahead of Planned Listing. *Financial Times*, March 31, 2024. Available at: www.ft.com/content/702223df-2e52-4e62-8f7c-93695a100d9b

[62] Shein's New DC Lobbying Campaign. *Politico*, June 5, 2023. Available at: www.politico.com/newsletters/weekly-trade/2023/06/05/sheins-new-d-c-lobbying-campaign-00100168

three fronts.⁶³ On the legal side, it has hired $1,500-an-hour attorneys to challenge the US government's new law barring the app unless it divested. Additionally, waging a battle for public opinion, the firm forked out roughly $4.8 million for ads promoting how the app improved users' lives. Before the law was signed, TikTok lobbyists blanketed Capitol Hill. With over forty-five outside lobbyists, including former lawmakers, and an in-house team of fifteen, the company's representatives argued that a ban would be unconstitutional and only benefit the US competitor Meta.

Ultimately, these efforts also come with additional, and unintended, costs. When companies are unable to have confidence in government policies or determine what form they will eventually take, they will withhold or underinvest in technology, operations, and workforce.

---

[63] TikTok's Survival Is at Stake in All-Out Fight against US Ban. *Bloomberg*, July 26, 2024. Available at: www.bloomberg.com/news/articles/2024-07-26/tiktok-goes-all-out-in-washington-with-its-us-survival-at-stake

9 Geopolitics and Green Energy

> You'll see change everywhere ... In 15 years' time, the world energy scene will look nothing like what it does now. Any country which does not take green energy very seriously, but clings to polluting energy, will eventually get left behind.
>
> —Andrew Forrest, Chairman of Fortescue Metals Group[1]

In the cold, remote areas of the Arctic, a flotilla of ships from competing nations creep mile by frozen mile. There seems to be an undercurrent of an impending confrontation. American, Chinese, and Russian missions are scouring the frozen ocean for treasures, scrambling to access the rich deposits of precious resources such as oil, gold, nickel, and rare earth metals. Reminiscent of a nineteenth-century gold rush, this scene underscores a twenty-first-century reality: The race for critical minerals essential for green technologies is intensifying.

Rare earth elements include the "lanthanide series" – the fifteen elements with atomic numbers 57 to 71 near the bottom of the periodic table – as well as two chemically similar elements.[2] They are "rare" not because of the quantity available but rather to their wide dispersion – it is difficult to find an economically meaningful quantity in a single location. Coveted for their magnetic and conductive properties, they make technologies faster, stronger, lighter, and more efficient. When extracted, elements such as praseodymium, gadolin-

---

[1] How the Race for Renewable Energy Is Reshaping Global Politics., *Financial Times*, February 4, 2021. Available at: www.ft.com/content/a37d0ddf-8fb1-4b47-9fba-7ebde29fc510

[2] Fatunde, M. (2024). The Race to Produce Rare Earth Elements. *MIT Technology Review*, January 5, 2024. Available at: www.technologyreview.com/2024/01/05/1084791/rare-earth-materials-clean-energy/

ium, neodymium, yttrium, and thulium find applications in aircraft engines, MRI imaging, and computer hard drives. And increasingly, along with other elements like lithium and cobalt, they are imperative for batteries, wind turbines, and solar panels.

The transition to renewable energy, once seen primarily as an environmental imperative, has morphed into a geopolitical chess game. The concentration of critical mineral production in a few countries, notably China, exacerbates vulnerabilities for western nations. Looking to reduce their dependence on strategic rivals, the US and its allies are exploring ways to diversify their supply chains. While these efforts are complex and time consuming, the geopolitical landscape remains volatile even as the demand for renewable energy technologies grows. The clean energy transition is essential for combating climate change but is reshaping global power dynamics in ways that are both profound and unpredictable. For companies in this sector, the interplay between resource security, environmental sustainability, and geopolitical strategy will define the contours of this new era.

INDUSTRY FEATURES

What Is Green Energy?

Green energy (sometimes also referred to as renewable energy or clean energy) tends to top the list of changes the world needs to implement in order to minimize the worst effects of rising temperatures. Broadly, it refers to energy that is derived from renewable sources. Since they don't emit greenhouse gases, they tend to have a relatively low adverse impact on the environment.

The sources of green energy are varied. It includes solar power that is generated through solar panels converting sunlight into electricity. Wind turbines can transform the kinetic energy of wind into electric power. Hydropower harnesses the movement of water to generate electricity. Heat stored beneath the earth's surface can be used for direct heating applications or in generating electricity. Organic materials like plant and animal waste can be converted to biomass or biofuels.

For many countries, investing in green energy is compelling and the shift to solar, wind, hydropower, or other renewable sources is framed as a necessary transition for a sustainable future. For one thing, it allows countries to combat the worst effects of climate change. To meet their international climate commitments, such as the Paris Agreement, they have to find a way to reduce carbon emissions and carbon-intensive energy sources. Investing in green energy can sometimes also present substantial economic opportunities as jobs in manufacturing, installation, maintenance, and research and development in renewable technologies provide chances for growth and employment. Additionally, with technological advancements in recent years, the cost of green energy has decreased dramatically and increasingly becoming competitive with conventional fossil fuel generation.[3] Innovations in energy storage, smart grids, and energy efficiency have made it easier to integrate renewable energy into existing energy systems. For instance, better battery technologies facilitate improved storage of solar and wind energy, thereby addressing the intermittency challenges often associated with these sources. Finally, a diversified energy supply that can harness locally available resources reduces dependence on imported fuels. As governments look to provide affordable electricity to their citizens, green energy may play an important role.

Recent Trends in Green Energy

Globally, there have been big changes in green energy production and use. Investment in clean energy technologies is expected to significantly outpace spending on fossil fuels. In 2023, for instance, investment in different forms of clean technologies – including solar, wind, electric vehicles, and batteries – was expected to be more than $1.7 trillion globally; roughly 70 percent more than the $1 trillion in

---

[3] Projected Costs of Generating Electricity. Report Generated by the International Energy Agency and the Nuclear Energy Agency. 2020 Edition. Available at: www.iea.org/reports/projected-costs-of-generating-electricity-2020

fossil fuels.[4] Investment in solar power alone was expected to overtake the amount going into oil drilling. Faith Birol, the executive director of the International Energy Agency, was quoted as saying[5]:

> We look at energy data on a daily basis, and it's astonishing what's happening. Clean energy is moving faster than many people think, and it's becoming turbocharged lately.

China is leading the turbocharge. The country was on track to double its solar and wind capacity five years ahead of the ambitious target set by its central government.[6] Additional growth in solar and wind projects was also underway in the US, the EU, India, and Brazil.

At the same time, businesses and consumers also increasingly put green energy at the center of their own transitions. Several automakers have prioritized electric vehicles, making them central to their business strategies. Industrial and consumer heating, cooling, and cooking became increasingly electric. Rapid electrification of manufacturing has followed. Industrial companies have turned to electrifying equipment and industrial fleets, transitioning to electric equipment ranging from tugs to forklifts.[7]

A parallel technology evolution has supported electrification and investment in green energy. Renewable energy sources, especially solar and wind, generally face a critical challenge: They are vulnerable to environmental conditions and are difficult to provide

---

[4] Clean Energy Investment Is Extending Its Lead over Fossil Fuels, Boosted by Security Strengths. International Energy Agency, May 25, 2023. Available at: www.iea.org/news/clean-energy-investment-is-extending-its-lead-over-fossil-fuels-boosted-by-energy-security-strengths

[5] The Clean Energy Future Is Arriving Faster than You Think. *The New York Times*, August 18, 2023. Available at: www.nytimes.com/interactive/2023/08/12/climate/clean-energy-us-fossil-fuels.html

[6] China Poised to Double Wind and Solar Capacity Five Years Ahead of 2030 Target. Global Energy Monitor, June 28, 2023. Available at: https://globalenergymonitor.org/press-release/china-poised-to-double-wind-and-solar-capacity-five-years-ahead-of-2030-target/

[7] Electrification in Industrials. *Deloitte Insights*. August 12, 2020. Available at: www2.deloitte.com/us/en/insights/industry/power-and-utilities/electrification-in-industrials.html

in a stable and resilient manner. Technological advances in storage and transportation are hence important to build more resilient systems using these sources of energy. For example, with advances in battery technologies, utility companies can better manage load during periods of low- or non-production.[8] Similarly, improved storage has given rise to a global electric vehicle industry.

Spurring at least some of this growth and technological development has been government policy. In the United States, for example, initiatives such as the infrastructure law, the CHIPS and Science Act, and the Inflation Reduction Act channeled funding toward enhancing power grids, electrifying transportation fleets, secured semiconductors necessary for manufacturing electric vehicles, and subsidized the construction of a national network of electric vehicle chargers. They also provided tax breaks for solar panel and wind turbine manufacturing, and clean hydrogen production. China has done more than any country in the world to support clean energy. In 2022 alone, the country invested more than $500 billion in the sector – nearly half of the world's low carbon spending.[9] This has produced integrated and efficient value chains for components such as solar panels and battery cells, which make up a substantial portion of the county's export revenues.

Green Energy Companies

Unlike many other industries, it is difficult to identify a core set of firms that constitute the green energy sector. Companies in this sector are varied, reflecting the expansive nature of the industry and the different technologies used. Among the largest companies, there are those involved in the development of renewable energy technologies (e.g., inverters, silicon wafers, and battery solutions), energy and utility

---

[8] Renewable Energy Trends and Developments Powering a Cleaner Future. IBM, March 8, 2024. Available at: https://globalenergymonitor.org/press-release/china-poised-to-double-wind-and-solar-capacity-five-years-ahead-of-2030-target/

[9] China Invests $546 Billion in Clean Energy, Far Surpassing the U.S. Scientific American, January 30, 2023. Available at: www.scientificamerican.com/article/china-invests-546-billion-in-clean-energy-far-surpassing-the-u-s/

companies that invest in green energy generation, as well as traditional fossil fuel giants that are reorienting toward renewable energy. The top companies (by market capitalization) are spread around the world.[10]

Renewable Energy Technology Companies

1. LONGi Green Energy Technology (China)
   Commonly known as LONGi Solar, this is the world's leading solar technology solutions provider (market capitalization of $53.3 billion). The company produces monocrystalline silicon wafers and modules, with fifteen manufacturing bases and more than thirty branches around the world.
2. Enphase Energy (US)
   This California-based company is the world's largest supplier of microinverter-based solar and battery systems. These products allow users to have back up power during outages and facilitate switching on and off the grid seamlessly. The company also offers battery solutions as well as software to manage the generation and utilization of energy. With a market capitalization of $39.5 billion, the company has deployed its systems across 145 countries.
3. Orsted AS (Denmark)
   With a market capitalization of $34.4 billion, Orsted AS was created from the divestment of its upstream oil and gas business. The company focuses on the development, construction, and operation of wind farms, solar farms, energy storage facilities, renewable hydrogen and green fuels facilities, and bioenergy plants.

Energy and Utility Companies

1. NextEra Energy Inc. (US)
   This Florida-based company (market capitalization of $151 billion) provides electric power and energy infrastructure in the US and Canada.

---

[10] For an expanded list, see: 15 Largest Renewable Energy Companies by Market Cap, Yahoo! Finance, November 7, 2022. Available at: https://finance.yahoo.com/news/15-largest-renewable-energy-companies-145142806.html and 5 Largest Renewable Energy Companies by Market Cap, Insider Monkey, November 7, 2022. Available at: www.insidermonkey.com/blog/5-largest-renewable-energy-companies-by-market-cap-1084512/

Its renewable energy portfolio of ~40 GW of operational and planned power generation is spread across onshore wind and solar power projects.

2. Enbridge, Inc. (Canada)
   Much of this company's $79 billion market capitalization is driven by its core business in crude oil and natural gas pipelines, and gas distribution and storage. However, its renewable energy portfolio has increased, with wind farms and solar energy operations, among others.

3. Duke Energy Corporation (US)
   Duke Energy is a US-based energy and utility company that provides electricity and natural gas to nearly 10 million customers (market capitalization of $71.8 billion). Its focus on renewable energy generation has increased, with plans to add 30 GW of solar and wind power by 2035.

4. The Southern Company (US)
   Another traditional energy and utility company, The Southern Company (market capitalization of $68.9 billion) is one of the largest producers of electricity in the US. Its renewable energy comes primarily from wind and solar projects.

5. Iberdrola (Spain)
   With a market capitalization of $62.2 billion, this multinational electric utility company supplies energy to close to 100 million people across Europe, the United States, Brazil, Mexico, and Australia. Its renewable energy generation has focused on wind, hydro, and solar power – which the company plans to increase as a share of its total power generation.

6. Adani Green Energy Limited (India)
   Part of the Indian conglomerate Adani Group, Adani Green Energy Limited is a company that develops, builds, owns, operates, and maintains utility-scale grid connected solar and wind farms. With a market capitalization of $40.9 billion, it is one of the largest renewable power companies with significant expansion plans.

Traditional Fossil Fuel Companies

1. Shell Plc (UK)
   This company's approximately $198.1 billion market capitalization is primarily driven by its traditional petrochemical and energy operations. While Shell has committed to increasing its renewable power generation like other oil companies, it has only about 8 GW of operational or planned renewable energy capacity.

2. TotalEnergies SE (France)
   Known formerly as Total, this leading multi-energy company produces and markets fuels, natural gas, and electricity across 130 countries around the world (market capitalization of $145.7 billion). Its renewable energy portfolio comprises 16 GW of solar and wind power, with plans to increase their share.
3. Equinor ASA (Norway)
   Formerly known as Statoil, this international energy company – with a market capitalization of $118.1 billion – was known for its exploration, development, and production of oil and gas. In recent years, it has grown its renewable energy portfolio with a focus on offshore wind and solar power.
4. BP (UK)
   This leading multinational oil and gas company (market capitalization of $101 billion) plans to transform itself into an integrated energy company with net-zero carbon emissions in the future. To this end, it plans to develop over 50 GW of renewable power by 2030.
5. Eni S.p.A (Italy)
   One of the traditional large oil majors (market capitalization of $47.2 billion), this Italian company increased its commitment to green energy. It plans to scale up the share of green energy in its installed capacity to 15 GW by 2030. This includes acquiring other solar and wind project companies across Europe and other locations.

Other Companies

Apart from these three categories of companies, there are specialized battery storage companies, electric vehicle manufacturers, solar panel and wind turbine manufacturers, and others. For instance, Tesla (USA) and BYD (China) design, develop, manufacture, and sell electric vehicles. Contemporary Amperex Technology Company (CATL – China) is the world's leading manufacturer of lithium-ion batteries for electric vehicles and energy storage systems. Chemical companies such as Albemarle (US) contribute to technology advancements in lithium production, while mining companies such as China Northern Rare Earth High-Tech Co. (China) focus on rare earth extraction.

While these companies do not directly generate green energy, they are nonetheless important players in the industry. They offer scale, technologies, components, and raw materials that are needed by other companies producing green energy. Because of their ability to shape downstream applications and markets, these alternate companies face greater geopolitical risk. Government policies have coalesced around the raw materials needed for the production of green energy. They have also focused on electric vehicles, which is central to global efforts in reducing greenhouse gas emissions and combat climate change. Consequently, much of the discussion below is focused on these alternate companies.

GEOPOLITICS OF GREEN ENERGY

Energy has long been at the center of geopolitics. Securing reliable supplies at affordable prices has been a driver of global security. In the age of coal, the British Empire's wealth and naval power grew to cement it as the world's preeminent power. The country's dominance of coal supply and coal-powered technology contributed to wealth and naval power.[11] British exporters sold coal and the related technology to other countries, generating their dependence on Britain. The resulting foreign earnings contributed to the national wealth and allowed the British to import goods and increase their military strength. But by the beginning of the twentieth century, British research suggested oil was a more efficient fuel. Oil vessels could carry more weapons, provide greater range, and were easier to refuel. So, British demand for oil grew, with the Americans, Germans, and Russians following suit. As greater oil exploration and global supply drove down prices, the fuel began to be used more widely. But while Britain had been a world-leading source of coal, it had to import its oil from elsewhere. And the need to secure oil supplies shaped the British, and subsequently the American, foreign policy for decades.

---

[11] The Geopolitics of Oil and Gas. KPMG, 2023. Available at: https://assets.kpmg.com/content/dam/kpmg/au/pdf/2023/geopolitics-of-oil-and-gas.pdf

Energy security, or the reliable access to fuel supplies, is an important part of the geopolitical calculation for any country. Since transportation and industrial sectors in the United States were largely reliant on oil, a disruption of oil markets could potentially paralyze a major power. To protect against this, US interests were in maintaining an open global market, even forcefully.[12] According to one study, between one-quarter to one-half of all interstate wars since 1973 have been connected to one or more oil-related causal mechanisms.[13] Some of these were resource wars, where states tried to acquire oil reserves by force. Other conflicts were driven by risky foreign policy stances of leaders insulated by oil reserves. Some others were instigated by the need to control (or limit control domination) of oil or oil transit routes.

While efforts to increase green energy production and consumption are underway, there is little agreement on whether and how it will reshape geopolitical tensions.[14] On the one hand, some see green energy as the key to reducing conflict and lowering the temperature on geopolitical tensions. This group emphasizes the fact that sources of green energy are more widespread, which means it is more difficult to control, cut the supply, or manipulate the price of renewable energy than of traditional fossil fuels. In other words, it shifts the focus from external to internal supply. As the Chief Executive of Shell, the oil major, noted, "in oil and gas you need an asset base. It is about having the best rocks, the lowest cost of production."[15] But electricity from one solar farm is as good as the next. Thus, some expect the expansion of green energy to lead to greater energy self-sufficiency and less conflict among states.

---

[12] For an Overview of How Oil Dependence Drove US Foreign Policy, see: Oil Dependence and US Foreign Policy, 1850–2023. Council on Foreign Relations. Available at: www.cfr.org/timeline/oil-dependence-and-us-foreign-policy

[13] Oil, Conflict, and U.S. National Interests. Belfer Center for Science and International Affairs at Harvard Kennedy School. Policy Brief: October 2013. Available at: www.belfercenter.org/sites/default/files/pantheon_files/files/publication/colgan-final-policy-brief-2013.pdf

[14] Vakulchuk, R., Overland, I., & Scholten, D. (2020). Renewable energy and geopolitics: A review. *Renewable and Sustainable Energy Reviews*, 122, 109547.

[15] How the Race for Renewable Energy Is Reshaping Global Politics. *Financial Times*, February 4, 2021. Available at: www.ft.com/content/a37d0ddf-8fb1-4b47-9fba-7ebde29fc510

Others, however, raise the opposite possibility – of renewed conflict. In other words, a world that derives most of its energy from renewable sources may see similar types of conflicts as those caused by fossil fuels or new but just as severe types of conflicts. This is because while solar or wind energy may be more widely spread around the globe than fossil fuels, the critical materials and technologies needed to convert them to useable electricity continue to be concentrated. Access to critical materials required for renewable energy generation, distribution, or storage technology could pose a new but similar dependence on countries that have them. China is a key player, controlling more than 70% of all solar photovoltaic panels and 50% of electric vehicles. It is also the biggest battery producer and controls several raw materials needed in green energy production, including cobalt, rare earth minerals, and polysilicon for solar panels.[16] The Chinese government used this advantage toward geopolitical ends. For instance, the country blocked exports of rare earth elements to Japan following a dispute with that country in 2010.[17] China similarly announced export controls on gallium and germanium products to the US following American restrictions on sale of advanced computing and semiconductor products to the country.[18] This has raised alarm bells in the West, with the European Union highlighting its dependency problem.[19] The US Department of Energy similarly noted that "U.S. decarbonization goals are reliant on both Chinese firms and the Chinese government."[20]

---

[16] How the Race for Renewable Energy Is Reshaping Global Politics. *Financial Times*, February 4, 2021. Available at: www.ft.com/content/a37d0ddf-8fb1-4b47-9fba-7ebde29fc510

[17] Amid Tensions, China Blocks Vital Exports to Japan. *The New York Times*, September 22, 2010. Available at: www.nytimes.com/2010/09/23/business/global/23rare.html

[18] Beijing Jabs in US-China Tech Fight with Chip Material Export Curbs. *Reuters*, July 5, 2023. Available at: www.reuters.com/technology/us-firm-axt-applying-permits-after-china-restricts-chipmaking-exports-2023-07-04/

[19] EU Sounds Alarm on Critical Raw Materials Shortages. *Financial Times*, August 31, 2020. Available at: www.ft.com/content/8f153358-810e-42b3-a529-a5a6d0f2077f

[20] Rare Earth Permanent Magnets – Supply Chain Deep Dive Assessment. US Department of Energy Response to Executive Order 14017, "America's Supply Chains." February 24, 2022. Available at: www.energy.gov/sites/default/files/2022-02/Neodymium%20Magnets%20Supply%20Chain%20Report%20-%20Final.pdf

One study compared the net import reliance of China and the United States to assess their foreign supply risk.[21] The researchers found that out of forty-two non-fuel minerals, China relied on imports (covering over half its consumption) for nineteen, compared with twenty-four for the US. Importantly, both countries relied on imports for eleven common minerals. It is for these minerals that competition between the two countries may be most contentious. Take, for example, Cobalt. China Molybdenum, a Chinese mining company, controls one-tenth of the world's cobalt supplies, a key ingredient in electric vehicle batteries. The company's dominance of the market stems in part from their ownership of a mine in the southern tip of the Democratic Republic of Congo (DRC) with rich deposits of copper and cobalt. Importantly, this mine was acquired by China Molybdenum from the US copper giant Freeport-McMoRan.[22] By the time of the sale, the US government had already identified cobalt as a critical mineral based on supply risk, production growth, and market dynamics.[23] The US government had spent decades providing aid to the DRC and building diplomatic ties with the country. Freeport-McMoRan had also invested billions in the mine and in corporate social responsibility efforts to support the regions near the mine. Yet, when the company was looking to raise cash when some of its other market bets went south, Freeport-McMoRan's financial interests took precedence over the country's national interest. The Chinese company

---

[21] Gulley, A. L., Nassar, N. T., & Xun, S. (2018). China, the United States, and competition for resources that enable emerging technologies. *Proceedings of the National Academy of Sciences, 115*(16), 4111–4115.

[22] Freeport Sells Key Copper Mine for $2.7 Billion to China Molybdenum. *Financial Times*, May 10, 2016. Available at: www.ft.com/content/f222487c-15d3-11e6-b197-a4af20d5575e

[23] Assessment of Critical Materials: Screening Methodology and Initial Application. National Science and Technology Council: Report by the Subcommittee on Critical and Strategic Mineral Supply Chains of the Committee on Environment, Natural Resources, and Sustainability. March 2016. Available at: https://int.nyt.com/data/documenttools/2016-03-obama-critical-and-strategic-minerals-supply-chains-ssessment-of-critical-minerals-report-2016-03-16-final/eaa128fa7a5e8616/full.pdf

was ready with cash and in 2016 Freeport-McMoRan sold its assets in the DRC. With China controlling most of the cobalt supply, US companies were forced to examine other technologies, including older ones, to reduce dependence on hard-to-source materials.[24] As one US diplomat reportedly observed ruefully[25]:

> We don't currently have a mechanism to handle that discrepancy when it comes up ... this gap between corporate interest and national interest.

Fast forward a few years. The US government, along with European allies, set up several initiatives to secure cobalt and copper supplies from Congo. The US Development Finance Corporation began scaling up financing for mining projects there. They invested in a rail corridor project to ease shipments minerals to ports. But there was a sense of missed opportunity. As a top official at the US Development Finance Corporation noted,[26]

> Do I wish we had gotten in the game earlier? Of course.

Yet, the efforts spurred some US companies to go back to Congo's cobalt deposits. KoBold Metals, a California-based startup began to explore for new cobalt reserves in the Congo using artificial intelligence. According to their CEO,[27] "[o]ur plan is to develop the mines ourselves and ultimately in the next 10 to maybe 15 years from now, we want to be the largest supplier of critical metals."

---

[24] The US Inches towards Building EV Batteries at Home. *Wired*, January 18, 2022. Available at: www.wired.com/story/the-us-inches-toward-building-ev-batteries-at-home/

[25] How the U.S. Lost Ground to China in the Contest for Clean Energy. *New York Times*, November 21, 2021. Available at: www.nytimes.com/2021/11/21/world/us-china-energy.html

[26] US DFC Boosts Congo Funding, Bids to De-Risk World's Top Cobalt Supplier. *Mining Weekly*, February 6, 2024. Available at: www.miningweekly.com/article/us-dfc-boosts-congo-funding-bids-to-de-risk-worlds-top-cobalt-supplier-2024-02-06

[27] Billionaire-Backed KoBold Metals Widens Lithium Hunt across Four Continents. Reuters, December 14, 2023. Available at: www.reuters.com/markets/commodities/billionaire-backed-kobold-metals-widens-lithium-hunt-across-four-continents-2023-12-14/

Market Access

For companies in the green energy sector, market access refers to their ability to enter and compete in a foreign market, either to source raw materials or sell their products. However, many governments have imposed stringent conditions or requirements for firms to access their domestic markets.

One type of market access issue arises when governments aim to assert control over a country's natural resources. Take the case of nickel in Indonesia. Nickel is a key ingredient in lithium-ion batteries used in electric vehicles. In 2018, Indonesia had proven nickel reserves of about 698 million tons and produced about 560,000 tons of nickel.[28] This was more than a third of global nickel production. However, through successive government policies between 2009 and 2020, the Indonesian government banned the export of raw nickel ore. The goal was to transform the country from an exporter of nickel to a central player in the global value chain by incentivizing nickel customers to invest locally in refining of the ore and battery manufacturing.

It was a plan that resonated with the EV industry's growing demand for nickel. In a 2020 earnings call, Tesla CEO Elon Musk called on miners to ramp up nickel production.[29] "Any mining companies out there, please mine more nickel. Tesla will give you a giant contract for a long period of time if you mine nickel efficiently and in an environmentally sensitive way. Hoping this message goes out to all mining companies, please get nickel."

Chinese mining companies saw an opportunity on the Indonesian islands of Sulawesi and Halmahera, where they built refineries, smelters, and a new metallurgy school.[30] Companies like

---

[28] Indonesia to Ban Nickel Exports from January 2020. *The Jakarta Post*, September 2, 2019. Available at: www.thejakartapost.com/news/2019/09/02/indonesia-to-ban-nickel-exports-from-january-2020.html

[29] Quoted in: How the EV Boom Led Chinese Companies to Take over Indonesia's Nickel Industry. *CNBC*, July 27, 2024. Available at: www.cnbc.com/2024/07/27/chinese-dominance-in-indonesias-nickel-industry-during-ev-boom.html

[30] For an overview, see Chinese Companies Are Flocking to Indonesia for Its Nickel. Bloomberg.com, December 16, 2022. Available at: www.bloomberg.com/news/articles/2022-12-15/chinese-companies-are-flocking-to-indonesia-for-its-nickel

GEM Co., a supplier to Samsung Electronics and Contemporary Amperex Technology Co. (CATL), started a production line. Tsingshan Holding Group, the world's biggest producer of nickel and stainless steel, began supplying semifinished products to its Chinese customers from the Indonesian plant. The value of Indonesian nickel exports surged from $3 billion to $30 billion in two years. And the country had bigger ambitions. As President Jokowi was quoted,

> We want to benefit from added-value exports so that there's income for the state in the form of taxes and new job opportunities. We don't just want to build batteries. This is just half of it. We want to build electric cars in Indonesia.

Another type of market access issue is protectionism when governments adopt nationalistic policies to limit foreign firms' presence in domestic markets. India was long dependent on China for solar module imports. But to ensure self-sufficiency in solar manufacturing, cut imports, and boost domestic manufacturing, India imposed tariffs of 40% on solar modules and 25% on solar cells in 2022.[31] Further, the country created an approved list of Indian manufacturers to provide domestic firms a preferential opportunity to participate in government-backed projects.[32] On the other hand, when countries offer policy support for green energy, they draw foreign investors. One study examining new foreign investment by European firms in the solar industry focused on where they choose to locate their investments within the EU.[33] Following the firms from 2004 to 2013, the researchers found that companies in the solar power industry

---

[31] India Slashes Solar Imports from China as Domestic Manufacturing Thrives. *Business Today*, September 14, 2023. Available at: www.businesstoday.in/latest/economy/story/india-slashes-solar-imports-from-china-as-domestic-manufacturing-thrives-398373-2023-09-14

[32] India Creates Non-Tariff Barrier for Chinese Solar Products. April 30, 2024. Available at: www.pv-magazine.com/2024/04/30/india-creates-non-tariff-barrier-for-chinese-solar-products/

[33] Georgallis, P., Albino-Pimentel, J., & Kondratenko, N. (2021). Jurisdiction shopping and foreign location choice: The role of market and nonmarket experience in the European solar energy industry. *Journal of International Business Studies*, 52(5), 853–877.

were actively engaged in jurisdiction shopping. They scouted for the best policy deals and eventually invested in countries that offered the most generous feed-in-tariffs. The was especially true for companies that had previously relied on state guaranteed feed-in-tariffs. A different form of market access is the export ban. This tool is used to not just protect domestic industry but also restrict the opportunity for foreign firms in other countries and their national security. China was the world's leading producer of antimony, generating 48 percent of global production. In 2024, China initiated restrictions on antimony-related products; to export these products, firms will need to apply for a special license from China's Commerce Ministry. Since the US imports 63 percent of its antimony from China, its defense industry was significantly concerned. Antimony is used in armor-piercing ammunition, night vision googles, infrared sensors, bullets, and precision optics. It is also a critical element in semiconductors, cables, and batteries. Combined with a series of previous export controls announced by China on graphite, germanium, gallium, and rare earth processing technologies, American electric vehicle firms faced a significant challenge in sourcing and securing alternate supplies.

Level Playing Field

One of the biggest flashpoints in the quest for green energy is whether companies from different countries are on a level playing field. A particularly contentious issue has been whether companies benefited from subsidies provided by the state. In solar power, for example, state subsidies and policy support were viewed as crucial in allowing Chinese firms to control up to 80 percent of the market for solar panel manufacturing.[34] Manufacturers, customers, and users in other countries worry that such dominant players could undercut domestic and local rivals before hiking up prices without fear of competition.

---

[34] Solar PV Global Supply Chains. An IEA Special Report, July 2022. Available at: www.iea.org/reports/solar-pv-global-supply-chains

Additionally, firms that did not receive subsidies or similar state support may not be competitive in the market. Take the example of Meyer Berger, a Swiss company that announced plans to open a solar panel assembly facility in the US. Within a year, those plans were suspended as it was "no longer financially viable for the company."[35] The CEO of First Solar, an American solar manufacturer, explained in testimony to the US Congress[36]:

> The relentlessness of the Chinese subsidization and dumping strategy has caused a significant collapse in cell and module pricing and threatens the viability of many manufacturers who may never be.

These concerns have led other countries to similarly offer subsidies to "their" companies. In the US, the Inflation Reduction Act provided up to $369 billion in subsidies and tax credits for clean energy technologies. To remain competitive, the EU got into the race to provide large scale public funding for green projects.[37] The Indian government rolled out measures to finance and support domestic solar module manufacturing.[38] In other countries as well, government subsidies to support green technologies grew.

From a market perspective, this means the most competitive companies may be the ones that have access to the biggest subsidies. SolarPower, the American solar power company whose

---

[35] Meyer Berger Pulls Plan for Silicon Cell Manufacturing in US. *Solar Power World*, August 26, 2024. Available at: www.solarpowerworldonline.com/2024/08/meyer-burger-pulls-plans-for-silicon-cell-manufacturing-in-us/

[36] Testimony of Mark R. Widmar, Chief Executive Officer First Solar, Inc. before the Senate Finance Committee Hearing on *American Made: Growing U.S. Manufacturing Through the Tax Code*. March 12, 2024. Available at: www.finance.senate.gov/imo/media/doc/03122024_widmar_testimony.pdf

[37] EU Opens Subsidy Race with US to Fight Exodus of Green Projects. *Financial Times*, March 10, 2023. Available at: www.ft.com/content/a7438c5a-41da-42ab-845f-25176205a5c7

[38] Government Implementing PLI Scheme for Boosting Domestic Production of Solar Modules: Union Power & NRE Minister. Ministry of New and Renewable Energy Press Release, March 23, 2023. Available at: https://pib.gov.in/PressReleaseIframePage.aspx?PRID=1909958

CEO highlighted the competitiveness of Chinese companies due to their favorable subsidies, benefitted from US government support, estimated to be as much as $10 billion over a decade.[39] Will this translate to market power? That is the question policymakers are waiting to find out.

The playing field has also been shaped by the use of tariffs. As with subsidies, the goal is to protect domestic manufacturers and limit dependence on foreign suppliers. Electric vehicles are a case in point. Since the late 2010s, China emerged as a dominant player in both the sales of electric vehicles as well as the manufacturing of these automobiles. Chinese electric vehicles were also one of the cheapest available. For comparison, Tesla's cheapest model in China sold for about $34,000 while BYD – a Chinese competitor – had a model priced at about $9,700.[40] The lower cost comes, in part, from long standing subsidies that Chinese firms had access to. At the same time, the availability of lower cost of Chinese electric vehicles boded well for governments that prioritized decarbonization. For instance, the EU set a goal of having at least 30 million zero-emission vehicles on its roads by 2030. The US similarly planned to have electric vehicles comprise half the number of cars sold by 2030.

Western governments were also worried about reliance on Chinese automakers and the implications it would have for their domestic car manufacturers. By 2024, the US slapped a 100% tariff on Chinese electric vehicles and the Europeans followed with up to 37.6% tariffs.[41] These policies put Chinese manufacturers at a relative disadvantage than domestic ones. But they also have other

---

[39] A Signature Biden Law Aimed to Boost Renewable Energy. It Also Helped a Solar Company Reap Billions. AP, June 26, 2024. Available at: https://apnews.com/article/biden-solar-inflation-reduction-act-dca914675cd0855004214d82aab5b10c

[40] How Tesla and Its Chinese Competitor Compare, in 4 Charts. *CNN*, April 3, 2024. Available at: https://edition.cnn.com/2024/04/03/cars/china-tesla-byd-competition-hnk-intl-dg/index.html

[41] The EV Trade War between China and the West Heats Up. *The Economist*, July 10, 2024. Available at: www.economist.com/business/2024/07/10/the-ev-trade-war-between-china-and-the-west-heats-up

consequences. For one thing, limiting the number of cheaper vehicles will slow down the adoption of electric vehicles. US manufacturers such as Ford and GM, for instance, prioritized larger and higher-priced electric sports utility vehicles and pick-up trucks that had smaller markets. European manufacturers could also struggle to meet the demand for millions of new electric vehicles from their domestic plants. Second, it is not even clear that the tariffs will work as intended. Chinese manufacturers, scouting for alternate production locations, focused on Mexico. BYD planned to build a plant in Mexico, turning it into an export hub.[42] Since Mexico has a free trade agreement with the US, Chinese firms that produce in Mexico and use enough locally made parts could bypass US tariffs entirely. Finally, it may even hurt domestic companies. Leading western automakers such as Tesla, BMW, and Volvo produce a number of electric vehicle models in China. If those cars face greater tariffs – as they are manufactured in China – they will have a hard time selling in their home markets. And in a perceived tit-for-tat measure, China launched an anti-dumping investigation into imported European dairy products.[43] Tariffs may have been designed to keep "their" companies out, but may end up hurting "our" companies as well.

The ownership of a company was also a factor in the uneven playing field. Like in other sectors, state-owned companies in the green energy sector were more sensitive to geopolitical relations. One study found that while private multinational corporations were at the forefront of investment in renewable energy, state-owned companies tended to adopt less-risky strategies and were more responsive to host country incentives.[44]

---

[42] BYD Nears Huge Mexico EV Plant Deal with 50,000 Sales in Sight This Year. *Electrek*, June 21, 2024. Available at: https://electrek.co/2024/06/21/byd-huge-mexico-ev-plant-deal-50000-sales/

[43] China Hits Back at EV Tariffs with European Dairy Probe. *Financial Times*, August 21, 2024. Available at: www.ft.com/content/6848d459-2d70-4519-a4b8-3c0262b514db

[44] Patala, S., Juntunen, J. K., Lundan, S., & Ritvala, T. (2021). Multinational energy utilities in the energy transition: A configurational study of the drivers of FDI in renewables. *Journal of International Business Studies*, 52, 930–950.

Investment Security

When firms invest in a mine, manufacturing facility, or commercial development in a country, they expect to be able to recover the initial investment and make a market profit. Under heightened geopolitical tensions, however, a company's objectives may be secondary to a country's geopolitical position. In the green energy sector as well, governments policies and/or objectives influence firms' investments in a country.

Let's revisit Indonesian nickel. As discussed above, the country has one of the largest nickel reserves in the world – a crucial mineral in batteries and electric vehicles. Indonesia banned the export of raw ore and drew in foreign investment, particularly Chinese, to develop local refining and battery manufacturing. Exports of refined nickel – rather than unprocessed ore – grew, suggesting the policy had some effect. However, Indonesia simultaneously also wanted to limit Chinese ownership. While having greater control of the domestic economy may have been one of the criteria, a big push also came from geopolitical forces.

Halfway across the world, the US passed the Inflation Reduction Act that provided generous tax breaks for electric vehicles, batteries, and critical minerals. South Korean battery makers, including LG Energy Solution, SK On, and Samsung SDI, received billions of dollars in support under the Inflation Reduction Act to invest in battery facilities in the US. They were expected to dominate the North American market, accounting for about 44 percent of the total battery capacity by 2030.[45]

But South Korean battery manufacturers faced a significant hurdle in using Indonesian nickel. This is because US rules would exclude any products or minerals sourced from "foreign entities of concern," including from companies with more than 25 percent

---

[45] China's EV Supply Chain Dominance Risks "Collapse" of US Subsidies, Warn South Korea. *Financial Times*, April 26, 2024. Available at: www.ft.com/content/7a7ba474-7068-46fc-89da-19d87e83f9d3

Chinese ownership. The problem – more than three-quarters of Indonesia's battery grade nickel output came from majority Chinese-owned producers such as Tsingshan Holding Group, Zhejiang Huayou Cobalt, and Lygend Resources and Technology.

To remain in the game, Indonesian policymakers began looking to restructure investment deals with Chinese companies in the country. The goal was to reduce Chinese ownership to less than the 25 percent threshold. For example, a Chinese company was expected to have a minority stake in a new $700 million project while Indonesian and South Korean partners held a majority. But for some Chinese companies, taking minority stakes was not a good deal. As a manager at a nickel producer reportedly noted[46]:

> We have the technology, we have the market and we only get a small percentage of the profit? It does not make sense for us.

Institutional Alignment

A company or country that sets global standards for equipment specifications or norms of engagement stands to gain significantly in market competition. Who shapes the rules matters. In different parts of the clean energy industry, the contest to set standards is heating up.

As green hydrogen gained in importance as a potential factor in the transition to a net-zero global economy, there is a need for standards in the area of distribution, storage, and transfer.[47] One area of relevance is the international trade in hydrogen. Countries such as Australia, Chine, Japan, and Saudi Arabia emerged as early adopters of cross-border low-carbon hydrogen trading, with the ability to set

---

[46] Indonesia Moves to Reduce Chinese Ownership of Nickel Project. *Financial Times*, July 26, 2024. Available at: www.ft.com/content/0f8e2fe8-c7cb-4d6a-9436-1cb1806af4e0

[47] See International Trade and Green Hydrogen: Supporting the Global Transition to a Low Carbon Economy. A Report by the International Renewable Energy Agency, December 2023. Available at: www.irena.org/Publications/2023/Dec/International-trade-and-green-hydrogen-Supporting-the-global-transition-to-a-low-carbon-economy

infrastructure standards and certification norms for this fuel. Their favored technologies and equipment will then have an edge in global competition.[48] Similarly, companies and/or countries that define the standards for digital tools that optimize electric grids or manage consumer demand will be able to export compatible domestic systems as well as mine data across them more efficiently.

Standard setting is also relevant in nuclear energy. As the International Energy Agency noted, nuclear energy generation is a critical component of global decarbonization efforts. This means new plants may need to be constructed across several countries. But western companies lost market leadership in this sector. Twenty-seven out of thirty-one reactors that began construction since 2017 have Russian or Chinese designs.[49] These countries will therefore influence norms regarding nuclear safety and operational standards, and their companies will have a competitive advantage in a sector that can play a major role in the world's evolution in meeting decarbonization goals.

STRATEGIES FOR MANAGING CORPORATE NATIONALITY AND GEOPOLITICAL TENSIONS

As countries around the world shape policies to influence the geopolitical balance in the crucial green energy sector, companies face a complex landscape that shapes investments, supply chains, and regulatory frameworks. Corporate strategies to adapt constitute a diverse set. A few are discussed here.

Reshaping Country of Origin

Geopolitical risks are highest for Chinese green energy companies trying to expand in the US. But it is also a market the Chinese firms

---

[48] Bordoff, J., & O'Sullivan Meghan, L. (2022). Green upheaval: The new geopolitics of energy. *Foreign Affairs, 101,* 68.

[49] Nuclear Power Can Play a Major Role in Enabling Secure Transitions to Low Emissions Energy Systems. IEA Press Release, June 30, 2022. Available at: www.iea.org/news/nuclear-power-can-play-a-major-role-in-enabling-secure-transitions-to-low-emissions-energy-systems

STRATEGIES FOR MANAGING GEOPOLITICS 247

don't want to or can't afford to lose. They have tried to reshape perceptions of their companies by changing how they are structured and where they locate their manufacturing activities.

Consider Trina Solar, a company that is based northwest of Shanghai and the biggest maker of solar panels in the world.[50] Like other solar firms, the company watched as US tariffs went up, and up again. At first, Trina considered US manufacturing as a way to avoid tariffs on panels made in China but ruled it out as the cost of production would be too high. Instead, the company followed other big Chinese manufacturers to Southeast Asia and adjusted supply chains to keep selling panels to the US.

But a new US law in 2022 effectively halted imports of solar panels that used high-grade silicon from the Xinjiang region in western China. Faced again with being shut out of the US market, Trina made another big switch. They started sourcing high-grade silicon from US and European suppliers for their US modules. And when the Commerce department tightened standards for country-of-origin, Trina moved the production of silicon wafers, another important component, to Vietnam.[51]

When the Inflation Reduction Act was passed, Trina finally bit the bullet and announced a $200 million factory in Texas to produce five gigawatts of solar panels a year. Even with generous production subsidies, the cost of production was still higher in the US. But Trina didn't want to lose its footing in an important market. The company worked hard to establish its good intentions and demonstrate its commitment. The subsidiary was a US-registered company. They employed US citizens to work in the American unit, including the President of the US unit. Staffers joined local officials in Texas in a

---

[50] For this example, see broadly: American Wanted a Homegrown Solar Industry. China Is Building a Lot of It. *The Wall Street Journal*, February 6, 2024. Available at: www.wsj.com/business/america-wanted-a-homegrown-solar-industry-china-is-building-a-lot-of-it-a782f959

[51] Trina Solar Begins Producing 210 nm Wafers at 6.5 GW Vietnam Facility. *PV Magazine*, September 1, 2023. Available at: www.pv-magazine.com/2023/09/01/trina-solar-begins-producing-210-mm-wafers-at-6-5-gw-vietnam-facility/

Christmas tree lighting ceremony featuring a real reindeer and two plastic snowmen blasting fake snow. The company announced plans to reinvest US earnings locally, rather than send it back to China. It also tried to bring its suppliers to the US and considered building upstream products like solar cells in the country. As one company executive explained[52]: "We are committed to be here and we are spending a lot of time and money to make that a reality."

The US needs companies like Trina to provide cost-effective products in the fight against climate change. But tensions arise as the US is also trying to simultaneously expand domestic manufacturing and recapture leadership in solar technology.

Turning Geopolitical Rivalry into Opportunity

For some companies (and countries), growing geopolitical tensions between the US and China in green energy offers market opportunities. One example is Indian solar manufacturers. India's focus on solar manufacturing intensified following the COVID-19 pandemic. As the government put in place a series of policy measures to encourage domestic manufacturing, including financial incentives for producers and domestic content requirements in procurement, the country's solar module production capacity more than doubled between 2020 and 2023.[53] A notable feature of this growth is the dramatic increase in India's exports to the US. Over a twelve-month period between 2022 and 2023, solar cell and module exports to the US increased more than 1000 percent (yes, not a typo). As the US kept (cheaper) Chinese products away from its market, Indian manufacturers had a windfall year. The Chairman of Waree, a leading Indian solar module manufacturer,

---

[52] Many US Solar Factories Are Lagging. Except Those China Owns. *Reuters*, July 18, 2024. Available at: www.reuters.com/business/energy/many-us-solar-factories-are-lagging-except-those-china-owns-2024-07-17/

[53] India Could Become the World's Second-Largest Solar Photovoltaic Manufacturer by 2026. Institute for Energy Economics and Financial Analysis, April 4, 2023. Available at: https://ieefa.org/articles/india-could-become-worlds-second-largest-solar-photovoltaic-manufacturer-2026

observed that "certain trade barriers brought into place by other nations have given non-Chinese manufacturers an opportunity to export."[54] This was echoed by an analyst at Wood Mackenzie, an energy consulting firm, who explained[55]:

> Indian module manufacturers flourish through US exports, capitalising on the US-China trade tensions and government incentives.

Diversification of Supply Chains

One strategy common to companies in different parts of the green energy sector is diversifying supply chains to minimize their exposure to (and fallout from) geopolitical tensions.

For Chinese solar firms looking to avoid trade frictions with the West, Southeast Asia became a major offshoring destination. Chinese investments in Malaysia and Vietnam have made those countries major exporters of photovoltaic products while sidestepping hefty tariffs on Chinese products.[56]

At the same time, Western firms looked to reduce their dependence of China for critical parts of their supply chain. Siemens Gamesa, a wind turbine maker, was dependent on China for nearly 100 percent of its critical materials such as rare earths and permanent magnets. To diversify, the company signed a deal with an Australian company to procure materials needed for permanent magnets.[57]

---

[54] Solar Module Exports up 1000% as US Keeps China Out. *The Hindu Business Line*, October 12, 2023. Available at: www.thehindubusinessline.com/economy/solar-module-exports-up-1000-pc-as-us-keeps-china-out/article67408232.ece

[55] India Wants Its Own Solar Industry but Has to Break Reliance on China First. *Climate Home News*, January 30, 2024. Available at: https://cleanenergyfrontier.climatechangenews.com/india-wants-own-solar-industry-break-reliance-china/

[56] Chinese Solar Firms Ramping Up Investments in Southeast Asia to Evade US, European Trade Tensions. *South China Morning Post*, July 29, 2022. Available at: www.scmp.com/economy/china-economy/article/3186923/chinese-solar-firms-ramping-investment-southeast-asia-evade

[57] Siemens Garema to Cut Reliance on China for Rare Earths, Permanent Magnets. *Reuters*, May 26, 2023. Available at: www.reuters.com/business/energy/siemens-gamesa-cut-reliance-china-rare-earths-permanent-magnets-2023-05-25/

A more diversified supply chain was also more expensive but lowering Chinese exposure was deemed necessary.

Similarly, KoBold, the California-based startup looking for new cobalt reserves in the DRC, was also concerned about the lack of alternatives to Congolese cobalt. In an attempt to diversify supply chains, the company began exploring in Disko, an island off the remote west coast of Greenland. Here is the CEO, Kurt House, making a case for his approach[58]:

> If we diversify supply, if we find a major cobalt discovery in Greenland, we can guarantee that cobalt is going to be produced under extremely high labor standards, and extremely high environmental standards, and then you have a choice. [...] Apple can then buy its cobalt from us, where it'll have a really reliable chain of custody, and no corruption issues, and no child labor issues, and minimal environmental impact.

Random Shocks and Entry

As indicated above, the green energy sector comprises a variety of companies from different traditional industries. One reason for this is random shocks that drive companies to expand into this space. In one study, researchers examined when traditional automakers expanded into plug-in hybrid products and battery electric vehicles.[59] They found, perhaps unsurprisingly, that demand shocks drove firms to do so. In other words, when there was a greater market demand for these types of vehicles, traditional automakers were more likely to expand to electric vehicles. But what drove demand shocks? This study highlighted the role of extreme-weather related events. Extreme heat-related events such as heat waves, wildfires,

---

[58] Forget Gas Prices. The Billionaire Club's Run on Cobalt Says Everything about Our Battery-Powered Future. *Vanity Fair*, April 21, 2022.

[59] Dutta, S., & Vasudeva, G. (2025). How Demand Shocks "Jumpstart" Technological Ecosystems and Commercialization: Evidence from the Global Electric Vehicle Industry. *Strategy Science*, 10:1, 1–31.

and drought drove up demand for electric vehicles when those events were abnormal or deviant from typical patterns of seasonality, temperature, and precipitation. Similarly, abnormal cold weather events such as cold waves, extreme unseasonal wintery conditions, and winter storms drove demand.

CORPORATE DIPLOMACY

Geopolitical risk increases demand on managers to invest in nonmarket activities. Top executives need to act as diplomats and manage government relations in order to gain access to foreign markets, face a level playing field, compete with security for their foreign investments, and push for institutional alignment. In the green energy sector, as well, more of the top management's time and attention has to be devoted to dealing with global politics, its impact, and consequences.

First Solar benefited from US subsidies and its share price nearly doubled after the Inflation Reduction Act was passed. To compete with Chinese producers in the US, First Solar along with other domestic producers turned to their government and demanded new tariffs on components and equipment from countries where their Chinese rivals had built factories to supply the US.[60] As one analyst noted,[61] "First Solar's strength really is its lawyers. It's purely about the trade wars."

Similarly, US electric car industry including companies such as Tesla, Uber, Rivian, Lucid Motors, and others joined forces to create a new lobbying group for electric vehicles.[62] Mineral and battery

---

[60] Many US Solar Factories Are Lagging. Except Those China Owns. *Reuters*, July 18, 2024. Available at: www.reuters.com/business/energy/many-us-solar-factories-are-lagging-except-those-china-owns-2024-07-17/

[61] First Solar Searches for Breakthrough to Cut China's Clean Energy Lead. *Financial Times*, July 29, 2024. Available at: www.ft.com/content/cda2ba95-5c55-461c-b886-5dffaf241563

[62] The Electric Car Industry Now Has Its Own Lobbying Group. *The Verge*, November 18, 2020. Available at: www.theverge.com/2020/11/17/21571747/zero-emissions-transportation-association-tesla-uber-rivian-lobby

companies seeking a share of the billions in government incentives hired lobbyists for the first time to influence lawmakers and agencies.[63]

Ultimately, these efforts also come with additional, and unintended, costs. When companies are unsure about government policies or what incentives they will get, it will result in underinvestment in technology, operations, and workforce. And the world's climate may be worse off.

---

[63] Lobbying "Frenzy" Follows Biden's Electric Car Push. *Politico*, April 17, 2023. Available at: www.politico.com/news/2023/04/17/biden-electric-car-lobbying-companies-00091779

10 Looking Ahead

When the World Trade Organization was launched in 1994, the average tariff rate – or taxes that countries imposed on goods coming from foreign locations – was nearly 16 percent. This meant foreign goods were more expensive, and international trade was costly. In the years since, the average tariff rate fell, reaching about 5 percent in 2017. In some developing countries, the decline was more dramatic. India's average tariff on manufactured goods fell from a whopping 70% in 1990 to roughly 6% in 2017. Governments stopped relying on tariffs as a source of revenue, and incentivized companies to invest in foreign markets.

But the long-term trend of declining tariffs reversed as governments revisited other motivations for imposing them. In the US, for example, the Trump administration began to raise tariffs on Chinese products in 2018 and China responded with retaliatory ones. Within two years, US tariffs on Chinese products had increased from under 5% to over 20%.[1] One reason was to protect domestic industries, especially those deemed vital to national security. Another was to incentivize foreign companies and countries to change their practices. These motivations fundamentally transformed economic policymaking and reshaped the practice of international business.

NATIONAL SECURITY AND ECONOMIC POLICY

With the rise of strategic rivalry and geopolitical competition, countries (or groups of nations) began to vie for influence, power, and resources in the global arena. Dominant countries wanted to retain

---

[1] Asdourian, E., & Wessel, D. (2024). What Are Tariffs, and Why Are They Rising? Brookings Commentary, July 1, 2024. Available at: www.brookings.edu/articles/what-are-tariffs-and-why-are-they-rising/

their premier status while rising powers like China challenged it. To influence the global order and remain competitive, governments turned to economic policy. The defining feature became the pursuit of national interest, or the goals and objectives that ensure a country's survival, security, and leadership in the international arena. In the economic realm, this meant strengthening "our" companies, while weakening "their" companies. In other words, because foreign control of the domestic economy was considered a threat to the survival and security of the country, governments had to intervene in market competition to support "our" companies and shutting out "their" companies. As the US National Security Advisor noted[2]:

> The role of national security in trade and investment policy and strategy is rising everywhere. [...] There are changes in the way that people are approaching the question of trade policy, international economic policy and that's true in market economies the world over.

The national security justification was invoked to introduce investment screening policies, increase tariffs, prevent cross-border M&A deals, expropriate assets, restrict technology transfer, provide preferential subsidies, and create national champions.

When the US introduced tariffs on imports of steel and aluminum, other countries complained to the World Trade Organization. They argued that US actions were inconsistent with their international obligations, which capped maximum tariff rates and barred discrimination between trading partners. In defense, the US cited the "national security exception," which allowed countries to violate trade rules in times of war or other emergencies in international relations. The tariffs were necessary – the US argued – to ensure the survival and viability of domestic steel and aluminum industries, which

---

[2] How National Security Has Transformed Economic Policy. *Financial Times*, September 4, 2024. Available at: www.ft.com/content/6068310d-4e01-42df-8b10-ef6952804604

were vital to US national security.[3] The World Trade Organization disagreed, ruling that these tariffs violated global trade rules.[4] But the die was cast. The self-restraint in invoking the national security exception that countries demonstrated for decades came apart.

Soon governments around the world began to use national security as the rationale for any number of measures. Several products and technologies were called out as having dual use, with applications in the military sphere or as espionage tools. Foreign companies – especially from rival countries – were treated with suspicion. And the fundamental institutional framework to support cross-border commercial interactions began to fray.

GOVERNMENT CONTROL OF THE COMMANDING HEIGHTS

Writing about globalization, Kevin O'Rourke and Jeffrey Williamson reflected in their book that[5]:

> ... there was hardly a village or town anywhere on the globe whose prices were not influenced by distant foreign markets, whose infrastructure was not financed by foreign capital, whose engineering, manufacturing, and even business skills were not imported from abroad, or whose labor markets were not influenced by the absence of those who had emigrated or by the presence of strangers who had immigrated.

Their book was published in 1999, and you might easily assume they were describing the world of the previous decade. But they weren't. They were writing about the world in 1914 and the first era of globalization.

---

[3] The "National Security Exception" and the World Trade Organization. Congressional Research Service Legal Sidebar, LSB10223, November 28, 2018. Available at: https://crsreports.congress.gov/product/pdf/LSB/LSB10223

[4] WTO Says Trump's Steel Tariffs Violated Global Trade Rules. *Politico*, December 9, 2022. Available at: www.politico.com/news/2022/12/09/wto-ruling-trump-tariffs-violate-rules-00073282

[5] O'Rourke, K. H., & Williamson, J. G. (1999). *Globalization and history: The evolution of a nineteenth-century Atlantic economy*. MIT Press.

That era didn't last forever. After World War I and the Great Depression, protectionism rose. After World War II, there was a reversal of globalization. Trade and global investment declined. Growth of multinational companies virtually ceased. Government regulation of the economy increased. In particular, the commanding heights of the economy – strategically important economic sectors – were often owned or highly regulated by the state.

While the 1960s and 1970s began to show some signs of revival, the transition back to a global market economy was slow. It wasn't until the early 1990s that worldwide foreign direct investment as a share of world output reached the same levels as in 1914.[6] But what started as a trickle became a flood. The free-market system began to make a comeback around the world. Privatization and liberalization were back in fashion and the global economy was once again becoming connected.

Daneil Yergin and Joseph Stanislav traced the rise of the free market system around the world in their bestseller *The Commanding Heights*. The transition was not smooth, and many countries faced difficult choices. By the end of the 1990s, however, there was a general sense of greater integration around the world. Commenting on the emergence of market forces, they wrote[7]:

> Boundaries of every sort are coming down. Political, economic, and ideological borders among nations continue to erode, promoting the flow of investment and trade. Regulatory systems and national monopolies that provided protection against competition are being altered. Restrictions on the movement of information and knowledge are disappearing in the face of advances in communications technology and computers (and declining costs thereof) and in the freer flow of ideas.

---

[6] Jones, G. G. (2017). International business and emerging markets: A long-run perspective. *Harvard Business School General Management Unit Working Paper* (18-020).

[7] Yergin, D. & Stanislaw, J. (1998). *The commanding heights: The battle between government and the marketplace that is remaking the modern world.* New York: Simon & Schuster.

But some of the barriers remained, with long-lasting consequences. For years, Ford, the American auto manufacturer, built its Transit Connect vans in Turkey and shipped them to the United States. As soon as they landed in the country, Ford would rip out the windows and seats and convert the vehicles into cargo vans. Why strip out perfectly good seats and windows? American chicken. Stay with me.

In the 1960s, some European countries slapped tariffs on American poultry exports. In retaliation, the US imposed tariffs on foreign made brandy, dextrin, potato starch, and vehicles – specifically, light trucks such as pickups.[8] Over time, the tariff on US chicken disappeared but America's 25 percent tax on foreign-made light trucks stayed in place.

But the tariff on passenger vehicles imported from Europe was only 2.5 percent. So, Ford imported passenger vehicles, paying the lower tariff, and converted them to light trucks once they were in the country.[9]

More than the stubborn legacies of an earlier era, rising geopolitical tensions are again fundamentally reshaping the global economy. As we saw in multiple contexts in this book, the openness of globalization is being replaced by the prioritization of national security interests. Government policy is again prioritizing control over strategically important sectors of the economy. At the same time, both governments and businesses are constantly asking themselves and updating their assessment of what a strategically important sector is, and the tools to best protect it. This means companies will face greater complexity, uncertainty, and barriers when competing in global markets.

---

[8] Why Trump Is Talking about a Chicken Tax. *CNN*, November 28, 2018. Available at: https://edition.cnn.com/2018/11/28/politics/donald-trump-general-motors-gm-chicken-tax/index.html

[9] In 2013, the US Customs and Border Protection changed its ruling, arguing that Ford should have paid the higher tariff all along. This led to legal battles between the automaker and the state. See Ford Could Get Hit with $1.3 Billion Penalty for Importing Vans from Europe. *CNN*, June 3. 2021. Available at: https://edition.cnn.com/2021/06/03/business/ford-transit-connect-penalty/index.html

NAVIGATING THE CHOPPY WATERS OF GEOPOLITICAL TENSIONS

As we reflect on the intricate interdependence of geopolitics and business, it becomes clear that understanding this relationship is not just an academic exercise; it is a vital skill for companies, managers, and employees in every sector.

A multipolar world has fundamentally altered the rules of engagement. Nations that once held unassailable dominance are facing challenges from emerging powers, each vying for influence and economic supremacy.

What is the future of geopolitical competition? Which new crisis will emerge? When will tariffs go up in a given industry? Where will new restrictions emerge? How long will governments emphasize decoupling or derisking?

These are complicated questions. Whatever the answers to these questions are, global companies will be well placed to respond if they recognize the systemic changes underway and develop capabilities to address them.

First, it is important to acknowledge that when national security becomes central to government policymaking, global companies will come to be defined by their nationality. Because foreign firms cannot credibly commit to not acting in the interests of their home governments, corporate nationality will be one of the most significant factors defining a company's geopolitical risk. As I have argued in this book, corporate nationality will determine whether a company benefits from opportunities or faces challenges in a given context. It will be more important than the company's technical proficiency, its market adaptability, and managerial capabilities in determining where the firm will be successful. It will shape the type of government resources the company will have access to – at home and abroad. Firms with a favorable corporate nationality in a particular country or context will be able to leverage it as a key advantage in some situations.

Second, with national security considerations overshadowing policymaking, governments focus on specific policies aimed to contain the influence of foreign firms from adversarial countries. While they have many tools at their disposal, they will choose policies that cluster around four levers to reshape the basic market structure for global companies. This includes policy choices about where a company could compete (market access), the advantage or disadvantage vis-à-vis competitors (level playing field), security of a company's assets (investment security), and the ease of cross-border transactions due to aligned standards (institutional alignment). Companies trying to assess how geopolitical tensions will impact their business will do well to understand the relevance of each of these policy issues to their businesses. How will market access, level playing field, investment security, and institutional alignment impact your company's ability to reach customers in different markets, provide goods and services, make and receive payments, compete for market share, transact with other companies, and employ people?

Third, innovation is one of the most important battlefields of geopolitical competition. This means national security concerns will fundamentally alter the landscape for global innovation. Corporate innovation flourished when knowledge, information, and talent could cross borders. But with techno-nationalism, some companies will be limited in their ability to exploit foreign R&D, constrained in their quest to collaborate with researchers in different locations, and struggle to navigate competing technical standards. At the same time, others will become more innovative as greater restrictions force them to innovate further. Managing corporate innovation in the shadow of geopolitics will entail strategic tradeoffs between accessing diverse knowledge and building fences around innovations.

Fourth, companies cannot afford to take a whack-a-mole approach to addressing geopolitical events when and where they appear. To actively manage geopolitical tensions, companies need to critically assess how geopolitics will shape their resources (who gets what), competitive advantage (how to win), and firm organization (who does what).

Fifth, to manage geopolitics, companies need to invest in skills to **s**can the global landscape, **p**ersonalize the information for your company, **p**lan the most relevant possible responses for your business, and **p**ivot if your firm faces serious headwinds (S-PPP). This falls on many individuals, both within and outside the company. External advisors and experts can provide greatest assistance with scanning, while the company's board of directors, top managers, line managers, government affairs teams, and cross-functional teams are critical in personalizing, planning, and pivoting.

Next, geopolitical tensions will have an impact on a company's employees in significant ways. It will influence who works, how work is performed, and where it takes place. There is a shift to more local talent pools and the physical location of work is reevaluated. Remote work, cybersecurity, and new protocols are fundamentally affected by geopolitics.

Advances in data availability and access, computational sophistication, and methodological approaches provide a range of tools for a company to identify and measure geopolitical risks, quantify its impact, and assess the effectiveness of a company's strategic responses. But managing geopolitical tensions also imagination and intuition as much as skill and data.

In this environment, successful companies will be ones that are able to ensure that preferential government policies work in their favor. Managing policymakers becomes a crucial part of managing a global business, and perhaps more important than market competition in some instances.

The key is to proactively build organizational capabilities to anticipate, assess, and respond to geopolitical shifts. This work is never done.

Employees, managers, companies, and nations that can nimbly navigate this new geopolitical reality will thrive, while those that cling to outdated models will struggle.

Index

AB InBev, 126
AbbVie, 81
Abu Dhabi, 145
Adani Green Energy, 231
Afghanistan, 41
AI, 2, 112, 187, 191
Albemarle, 232
Alibaba, 56, 106, 108, 203
Alipay, 218
alliance, 178
    military, 13
    security, 177
Alphabet, 89
Amazon, 89, 170, 203, 209, 215, 221
American Airlines, 28
Anglo American, 125
anti-dumping, 89, 119, 243
Anzu Robotics, 65
Apple, 84, 89, 103, 154, 185, 205
architectural innovations, 137–138
Argentina, 204
Arnold & Porter, 146
Arrival, 98
ASML, 9, 157
Astellas, 23
Astra Zeneca, 110, 154
Australia, 41
    Industry Growth Program, 47

BAE Systems, 148
Baidu, 2
Bain & Co., 22
Banga, Ajay, 133
Bawa, Aparna, 60
Beiersdorf, 58
Big data, 85, 171–172, 206, 215
Birol, Faith, 228
BlackRock, 13, 62, 92, 133, 194
BMW, 98
BOE Technology, 185
BP, 232

Brazil, 52, 204, 221
BYD, 52, 232, 242–243
ByteDance, 17, 42–43, 55, 197

Canada, 16, 41, 113
Carbon Sequestration Leadership Forum, 73
Carney, Mark, 5
CATL, 185, 232, 239
CFIUS, 62, 79
ChatGPT, 2, 145
Chew, Shou, 42, 222
Chile, 204
China
    AI, 112
    airlines, 29
    Belt and Road Initiative, 9, 19, 98
    CIPS, 217
    economy, 5
    electric vehicles, 50, 143, 235, 242
    export ban, 235, 240
    export controls, 80
    foreign direct investment, 82, 102
    Hualong One reactor, 165
    intellectual property, 87
    Made in China 2025, 46, 98
    military, 7, 145
    National Space Administration, 85–86
    nonmarket economy, 210
    pharmaceutical industry, 54
    R&D, 75, 86, 112, 151
    rare earth, 146
    sanctions, 22
    Science and Technology Agreement, 81
    smart city projects, 85
    solar power, 235, 240
    standards, 26, 85, 218
    subsidies, 8, 19, 46
    tariffs, 16
    titanium dioxide, 119
    World Trade Organization, 18
China Molybdenum, 236

China+1, 102
Clegg, Nick, 37
cobalt, 236, 250
Cohen, Stephen, 37
Colombia, 52, 204
Congo, 236
COONC, 10
Coupang, 204
customs procedures, 17, 35, 213–215

Da Jiang Innovations (DJI), 64
data localization, 152, 215
decoupling, 81, 178
Deloitte, 22, 164
Delta, 28
Deutsche Bank, 23
digital e-commerce, 211
Dimon, Jamie, 133
Dubai Ports World, 10, 12
Duke Energy, 231

eBay, 204
Ecuador, 204
electric vehicles, 228, 242, 250–251
Enbridge, 231
Eni S.p.A, 232
Enphase Energy, 230
Equinor, 232
Ericsson, 88
European Union (EU), 50, 119
    GDPR, 216
    Green Deal Industrial Plan, 46–47
    tariffs, 119, 242
exit ban, 23
experiments, 180
externalities, 7

Fairchild Semiconductor Corporation, 10
Fink, Larry, 92, 133
Finnair, 1
First Solar, 241, 251
foreign direct investment, 5, 15, 153, 177, 256
foreign R&D, 86, 111, 259
Fouquet, Christophe, 157
Foxconn, 159
France, 17, 41
Fraport, 23
free trade agreement, 243
Freeport-McMoRan, 236
Friedman, Thomas, 4

Fujitsu Ltd, 10
Fukuyama, Francis, 3

Gates, Bill, 112
GDELT, 173
GE, 70
GEM Co., 239
Germany, 19, 35
global common volatility, 177
GlobalFoundries, 142
Glyscend Therapeutics, 54
Goldman Sachs, 131
Goldstein scale, 173
Google, 84, 170, 190
Google Trends, 174
GoTo, 198
Greenland, 250

Heineken, 23
Hesai, 39
heuristics, 96
Hollywood, 117
Huawei, 88–89, 142

Iberdrola, 231
IBM, 87
import licensing, 29
India, 41
    border clashes, 17, 43, 53, 105, 208
    BYD, 52
    Digital Public Infrastructure, 85
    electric vehicles, 52
    foreign direct investment, 53
    global capability centers, 150
    import licensing, 29
    India Stack, 85
    Indian Meteorological
        Department, 68
    Production Linked Incentive
        Scheme, 47
    Reserve Bank of India, 215
    solar module manufacturing, 248
    tariffs, 239
    telecoms license cancellation, 31
    toys, 116
    Unified Payments Interface, 218
Indonesia, 19
    e-commerce, 216
    nickel, 238, 244
    President Jokowi, 239
    social commerce, 197, 207

INDEX

Inflation Reduction Act, 19
institutional alignment, 14, 24, 93, 129, 245, 259
Intel, 98, 142, 187
International Energy Agency, 246
investment security, 14, 21, 93, 129, 213, 244, 259
Ireland, 59

Janssen Biotech, 80
Japan, 214
JD.com, 204
JP Morgan Chase, 133

Kaspersky Labs, 44
KoBold Metals, 237, 250
Kobrin, Stephen, 127
Kokorich, Mikhail, 143
Korea, 19
    K-Chips Act, 47
    Kyungpook National University Chilgok Hospital, 70
KPMG, 164

Lam Research, 147
Latham & Watkins, 153
Lazard, 131
level playing field, 14, 18, 93, 129, 240, 259
LG, 185
Li, William, 51
liability of foreignness, 103
LLMs, 183
loan guarantee, 45
local-for-local, 109
localization, 60–61, 104, 106
Lockheed Martin, 22, 141
LONGi Solar, 230

machine learning, 171, 175
Macron, Emmanuel, 8
Madan, Sunil, 60
Man Wah, 103
market access, 14–15, 93, 129, 207, 238, 259
Matsushita, 25
Mayer, Kevin, 55
McKinsey, 131, 164
Megha Engineering, 52
Meituan, 204
MercadoLibre, 204, 221
Merck, 110

Meta, 35–36
    Instagram, 205
    social commerce, 200
Mexico, 103, 204, 221
    e-commerce, 198
    electric vehicles, 243
Meyer Berger, 241
MG Motor, 105
Micron, 16, 98, 185–186
Microsoft, 25, 89, 112, 134, 145, 162
military conflict, 178
Miller, Chris, 76
Mintz, 22
Mitsubishi, 133
Mollenkopf, Steve, 43
Momentus, 143
Musk, Elon, 53, 238

national security, 9–10, 16, 115, 206, 253, 258
Nepal, 41
Net Market, 199
Netherlands, 9, 41, 56, 214
    export controls, 157
Netscape, 25
New Zealand, 41
NextEra Energy, 230
Nio, 51
Nokia, 88
Northern Rare Earth High-Tech Co, 232
Northrop Grumman, 148
Norway, 32
Nvidia, 7
NXP Semiconductors, 43

Océinde, 119
OpenAI, 2, 145, 190
Orsted AS, 230

P&O Steam Navigation Company, 12
Pakistan, 41
Panama, 204
Panasonic, 100
Paytm, 56
PDD, 59, 106, 203
Pelosi, Nancy, 60
Penn World Tables, 189
personalizing, 124
Philippines, 41
    e-commerce, 216
pivoting, 130
planning, 126

Pragmatic Semiconductor, 101
Pratt & Whitney, 150
Price, Richard, 125
PwC, 131

Qualcomm, 43, 142, 185

Raimondo, Gina, 24
Rajan, Raghuram, 97
Raytheon Technologies, 22, 148
Reich, Robert, 36
Reliance, 63, 208
remote workers, 153
Resource Dependence Theory, 100
risk assessment, 184
Russia, 1, 23, 28
    Mir, 217
    nonmarket economy, 210
    payment system, 217
    SPFS, 217

Samsung, 185
Samsung Electronics, 20, 52
sanctions, 23
Sankarlingam, Velchamy, 60
Saudi Arabia, 145
scanning, 121
scenario building, 184
Schlumberger, 11
Schmidt, Eric, 76
Schoemaker, Paul, 127
Seafile, 66
semiconductors, 7, 76, 186
sentiment analysis, 183
Sequoia Capital, 108
Shein, 29, 63, 204, 208, 220
Shell, 231
Shopee, 204
Shunwei Capital, 107
Siemens, 25
Siemens Gamesa, 249
Singapore washing, 107
SK Hynix, 185
Slaughter, Anne-Marie, 166
smartphone industry, 184
SolarPower, 241
Solyndra, 45
Sony, 25, 185
South Korea, 20
The Southern Company, 231
spotting trends, 183

structural perspective, 13
Subramanian, Arvind, 97
Subsidies, 8, 19, 46, 241
SWIFT, 217

Taiwan, 20, 41, 83
Taiwan Semiconductor Manufacturing
    Company, 20, 52, 185
tariffs, 51, 119, 210, 213, 215, 239, 242, 253
tax break, 19
techno-nationalism, 259
Teknos, 119
Telenor, 31–32
Temu, 59, 106, 201, 203, 207, 219
Teneo, 131
Tesla, 50, 53, 155, 232, 242
Thailand, 52, 204, 221
TikTok, 17, 22, 29, 41, 43, 55, 87, 197,
    205, 222
titanium dioxide, 119
Toshiba, 25
TotalEnergies, 232
toys, 116
trade war, 16–17
Trina Solar, 247
Tsingshan Holding Group, 239

UK, 41
    Members of Parliament, 183
    Merchandise Marks Act, 35
Ukraine, 76
UNESCO, 25
UnionPay, 218
United, 28
Unocal, 10
US, 41
    airlines, 28
    anti-dumping, 89
    Biden Administration, 7
    CHIPS Act, 19–20, 46, 52, 79, 82, 98,
        187, 229
    CLOUD Act, 216
    de minimis, 198, 209–210
    Department of Defense, 76
    de-risking, 102
    Development Finance Corporation, 237
    drones, 83
    economy, 6
    electric vehicles, 51, 244
    export ban, 7
    export controls, 109, 146, 165

export restrictions, 79
foreign entity of concern, 51, 55, 57, 244
Inflation Reduction Act, 46, 98, 229, 241, 244
investment screening, 79
military, 117
national security, 254
Open Skies Agreements, 27
R&D, 79, 111
Science and Technology Agreement, 81
standards, 25
subsidies, 48, 79
tariffs, 16, 242
tax, 79
Trump administration, 16, 18, 253

Venezuela, 204
Vietnam, 221
   e-commerce, 216

Waree, 248
Warnas, Randall, 65
White, Scott, 101
World Bank, 133
World Customs Organization, 218
World Meteorological Organization, 69
world order, 5
World Trade Organization, 18, 73, 211, 253–254
   most favored nation, 212
WuXi AppTec, 80

Xerox, 137
Xiaomi, 205

Yuan, Eric, 60

Zoom, 60
ZTE, 43

For EU product safety concerns, contact us at Calle de José Abascal, 56–1°,
28003 Madrid, Spain or eugpsr@cambridge.org.

www.ingramcontent.com/pod-product-compliance
Lightning Source LLC
Chambersburg PA
CBHW060322220825
31514CB00004B/113